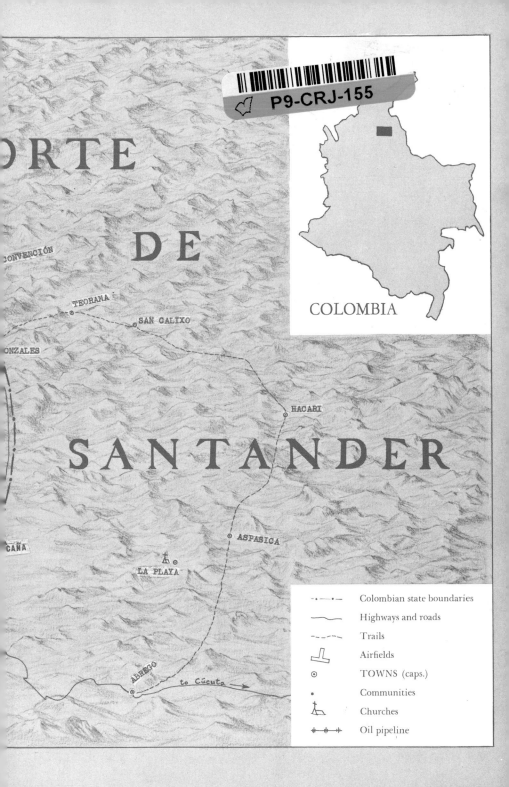

ORTE

DE

CONVENCIÓN

TEORAMA

SAN CALIXO

ONZALES

HACARI

SANTANDER

CAÑA

ASPASICA

LA PLAYA

ABREGO

to Cúcuta

P9-CRJ-155

COLOMBIA

—·—·— Colombian state boundaries

——— Highways and roads

- - - - - Trails

⌐ Airfields

⊙ TOWNS (caps.)

· Communities

⛪ Churches

+—+—+ Oil pipeline

AS A
ROARING
LION

MARTHA WALL

AS A ROARING LION

Foreword by Dr. Donald McGavran

MOODY PRESS • Chicago

Contents

Be sober, be vigilant; because your adversary the devil, as a roaring lion, walketh about, seeking whom he may devour.

I Peter 5:8

Foreword

BOOKS ON CHRISTIAN MISSION should inform readers concerning ways in which men are won to Christ and churches are multiplied. Mission is more than heroism: it is planting self-propagating congregations. It is so proclaiming Christ and so persuading men to become His disciples and responsible members of His church that cells of baptized believers proliferate throughout a city, countryside, or other segment of society. The supreme purpose of the Christian mission to the world is to give every person everywhere the chance to say "yes" to Jesus Christ. Since most persons have a real option to accept or reject the Lord only when they hear the gospel from the lips and see it incarnated in the lives of their own kith and kin, it is clear that a vast increase of Christian churches is demanded. Churches and believers are God's means of spreading the gospel. They are His broadcasting system.

The great merit of Miss Wall's book is that the reader sees how the gospel spreads. As if he were present in person, he observes the struggles, doubts, inner conflicts, persecutions, tentative beginnings and triumphant endings of many a Christian church. The story based on interviews and tape recordings is a history of the rise of a small cluster of congregations. Readers say to themselves, "This is the way Christian belief captures the hearts of men and ramifies throughout a society." Miss Wall lived in the area long enough, and talked to enough men and women that she became a part of the movement to Christ. She writes from the inside. Her portrayal has an authentic ring to it.

The reader is spared the mechanics of missions. He sees not the machinery but the way in which the Holy Spirit, operating in the lives of men and women, gathers believers into congregations.

7

I commend the book. Reading it will revive faith, deepen dedication, and reveal the web of relationship along which the gospel
always travels. The reader will have a deeper appreciation of
how churches grow and of the brotherhood which binds together
all those who truly believe on Jesus Christ.

DONALD MCGAVRAN

Preface

WHEN COLOMBIAN CHRISTIANS related to me what God had done in their midst and in their own lives, they were merely repeating the exuberant testimony for which many of them had been hated by the closest members of their families, beaten with clubs, lashed with whips, imprisoned, stoned, spat upon. I have written it all down just as it came from their lips. It has been like writing a twentieth century edition of the book of the Acts of the Apostles—the Andean Apostles.

I rode, just once, the mountain trails that threaded along the crumbling edges of nothing—trails on which the enemy *as a roaring lion* had stalked them, "seeking to devour." To meet the people who lived this story, to partake of their warm hospitality, to sing with them their choruses of trust and triumph has been a never-to-be-forgotten adventure.

As a Roaring Lion is a narrative, with a wild, colorful setting, of heroic faith and total commitment to Christ and His cause. It is more. For every missionary in every land here is the blueprint for the indigenous church which, when placed upon the Scriptures, is congruent in almost every line. Here is spontaneous church growth untrammeled by the constricting limitations of foreign funds or personnel that so often stifle the progress of Christian missions. Chapels gleaming on many an Andean sum-

9

mit are concrete proof that the original pattern works in our day as it did in the days of the early church.

I make no apology for putting words into the mouths of some of these people, but in no case have I invented any incidents except those used merely to bring true historical situations or local color into focus. The truly pungent statements are those transcribed right from scores of taped interviews. If this were fiction, I would not have dared to fabricate accounts of such daring and tenacity of purpose, nor would my imagination have stretched to the scope of the real situations that continued to thrill me throughout the plodding labor of weaving the individual stories into the warp and woof of the historical and geographical background.

Though I had to learn a language to capture this story, though I panted and perspired in the steaming heat of the Magdalena River Valley and had to ride on mountain trails so rugged that I held my breath lest I upset the mule's precarious balance, my greatest difficulty was the diffidence of some of those who played major roles in the story. For instance, when I asked Don Manuel Contreras to tell me about the attitude of his neighbors on Palmira, he said mildly, "They were antagonistic." Then, thinking he might have said *too much*, he added, "Better said, they were against us." The force of this superb understatement will only become clear when you read of this gentle man's courage in the face of persistent harassments and great physical sufferings.

So succinctly did Don Vicente Gómez sketch the entire movement from start to finish, including his own personal testimony from birth to that date, that it did not fill two pages of double-spaced notes. His reticence has robbed us of participating in any of these adventures from the viewpoint of his monumental vision and faith. Though I have managed to learn of the events themselves, the deep spiritual stirrings that produced the story are hidden in the heart of this man who was able to inspire such sublime faith and selfless consecration.

Since this burgeoning upcropping of new churches that swept thousands into glowing commitment is truly a "people movement," the missionaries have asked not to be named. This has resulted in some awkwardness in the telling of a few of the stories.

I acknowledge my indebtedness for the material to each person who told me his story, but especially to Armenio Pabón, José Pinzón, Ramón Nieto, Inocensio Trillos, Emalina Franco de Sánchez, Ana and Arcenio Sumalave, Lucila and Gratiniano Pino, Santos Millán and Manuel Velásquez. Much of the warm detail would have been lost without Carmen Pabón's assistance in transcribing the material from the taped Spanish interviews, and Angel Pabón's technical help with my transistor tape recorder.

To Cora Soderquist, who has not only a knowledge of the Spanish language but of the history of the church in Colombia, I owe a great debt of gratitude for invaluable help with the manuscript and for providing several photographs taken while the story was unfolding. I owe similar acknowledgment to Elof Anderson who helped me to grasp the political and religious background, provided me with additional information and, most important, the dates.

Finally, I gratefully acknowledge the encouragement and suggestions of Dr. Donald Anderson McGavran, director of The Institute of Church Growth at Fuller Theological Seminary, author of *The Bridges of God,* a book that outlines the principles of which *As a Roaring Lion* is an illustration.

MARTHA WALL

1

Design for Destiny

RUMPLED AND PERSPIRING, but beaming trustfully, a young man with an intense bronze face under a shock of curly black hair entered the principal's office at the Bible Institute of San Cristóbal, Venezuela. In the frayed pocket of his shiny, ill-fitting suit was one lone *bolivar*.[1] But José Vicente Gómez intended to keep that fact a carefully guarded secret. Neither did he plan to mention the advice given him by the missionary at Cúcuta, where he had been church janitor, when he had confided his glowing ambition to go to the Bible institute.

Minutes later, the distraught Bible institute principal scrawled a letter to the missionary at Cúcuta:

". . . pretty crude material you're trying to palm off on us!"

But Vicente had not been "palmed off" on the indignant principal. The missionary to whom the principal was writing had kindly but firmly discouraged the rather ludicrous idea. The struggling mission school, with limited facilities, could accept only young men of promise. Vicente Gómez did not fit that category.

A minister--*Vicente*? Why this inept young mestizo lacked both polish and background. Son of a common-law marriage, he had grown up on Bogotá streets. After his father abandoned the family, Vicente worked at whatever menial jobs he could find

[1] Less than thirty cents.

13

to help his mother support her children. He was practically illiterate. He spoke as though his mouth were full of marbles.

Though cheerful and willing, Vicente even bungled his janitorial duties. He had acquired the nickname of Elijah, a dubious distinction earned by his tendency of seldom being where anyone would expect to find him. No, by the longest stretch of Christian charity, Vicente was not a suitable candidate for the clergy.

Before the harried school official had stamped his envelope, Vicente had found his way to the barnlike dormitory where other hopefuls were unpacking their belongings and getting acquainted. Vicente, who had carried from his interview a much clearer impression of the exasperated principal's opinion than the latter had intended to convey, introduced himself diffidently to the nearest of the students, who was crouching over a cardboard carton from which he had loosened the knotted twine.

Skillfully avoiding the frame of the upper berth, the latter swung his head out into the open aisle.

"Juan Gonzales, *para servirle.*[2] I'm from Maracaibo." He waved an arm toward the double-deck bunks ranged closely along each side of the room. "First come, first served."

He resumed his crouched rummaging through the heterogeneous tangle of his belongings. As Vicente continued to stand there, still not sure of himself in the strange surroundings, Juan held up a gray sock by a carefully mended toe. "Looks like Mamá never got the other one in." He shrugged. "Who wears socks, anyway?"

Vicente relaxed somewhat in this atmosphere of casual acceptance; a grin replaced the strained disappointment on his dusky face. "If you wouldn't mind," he muttered humbly, "I'd like to take the empty one above you."

"Help yourself," returned Juan. "We usually leave the uppers for latecomers. Or for—" He hesitated, bringing his head out again in another careful arc.

"Or for first year students!" A twinkle that rose readily out from Vicente's innate good humor, met Juan's reevaluating glance.

[2]At your service.

"In that case, I'll be where I belong." He paused. "Unless there's a certain section—"

"On the contrary, why don't you take the lower bunk here, opposite me?" Juan rolled over to a stooped sitting position on his own bunk, craning his neck to meet Vicente's grin with genuine approval. "I like to look at the fellow I'm going to be talking to. Where's the rest of your stuff?"

Vicente colored. "This is all—" He fumbled self-consciously at the knot holding his scant roll together. "It's all I brought."

"Didn't you get their list?"

"List?"

"Who's responsible for you? Didn't they give you the list the school sends out for new students?"

The rumble of talk that had accompanied the process of hanging out clothes on nails in the wall, or on ropes strung between bunks, ceased suddenly. In the taut silence, the numbing comprehension flashed upon Vicente that his direct approach toward an education was somehow highly irregular. It might even make him unacceptable. He sensed, rather than saw, that the other students were silently gravitating toward them. One of the students threw a heavy comforter onto Vicente's bunk somewhat apologetically.

"Here's a quilt to sleep on. Mamá's a worrier. I've got more bedding than I need."

Surprise and gratitude lighted Vicente's dejected features. "Thanks. Thank you so much, but your Mamá—she might not like my having it." He dropped his glance, once more shuffling his feet awkwardly. "I've slept on bare boards—many times. Don't worry."

"What worries me," said Juan, "is your finances. Don't you have anyone backing you—with money?"

"The church at Cúcuta said they'd send a peso a month," said Vicente uncertainly. His suggestion elicited groans, in various pitches of male maturity. A peso, one of Colombia's smallest coins, would not cover the price of one full meal.

"But we've got to pay in advance," somebody said. "At least for a semester."

Vicente turned toward the speaker. "What's a semester? That's what the man in the office said. I thought it was—I thought he didn't know Spanish."

"He knows Spanish. Anything that's in the books, he knows."

"Well, he sure didn't seem to understand me," said Vicente. His face grew even more serious as he recalled the brief but trying interview. "He kept asking me to say things over. I didn't know what he was talking about either."

"That's his gringo accent. You'll get used to it. You've got to slow down for them too. We all have to."

"Let's get back to your fees. Is your father paying them, then?"

At the latter suggestion, Vicente's eyes twinkled again, and he chuckled. "That's what the principal asked me. He pretended to have understood my answer but he couldn't have."

"Understood *what?*"

"I said, yes, that my Father in heaven would take care of the expenses."

A gasp of amazement and shock followed his response. Vicente looked around with surprise, noting that genuine anxiety had settled on the whole ring of his new and sympathetic friends.

"What did he say?"

"He looked at me for a minute, and stopped writing. He opened his mouth, as if he wanted to ask me to repeat what I said, but he didn't. He just said, 'Can you get in touch with him?' I said, 'Yes, of course,' and he said, 'How soon? We always ask for this money in advance.' I said, 'I'll tell Him so at once.' 'But is he here—in Venezuela?' he said. That's when I knew he hadn't understood what I was saying."

"No wonder," said one of the boys whose faces projected over the edge of the upper berth opposite Vicente's. "You talk as if you had mush in your mouth. You'll have to—"

"That's not it. He couldn't believe he was hearing right! What are you going to do? He thinks you're going to talk to your father."

"I'm going to do just exactly that. I'm going to talk to my heavenly Father, and—"

"But what good will that do?" snapped Juan. "What you need is good hard cash."

Vicente whirled around to face Juan, but he spoke only after he had seen Juan's acute concern, and his voice was gentle.

"You have been asking me," he said, looking about from face to face, "who sent me—who's backing me. I don't have a good answer for you, except that God has not allowed me to sleep or to rest unless I would come here to learn how—how to be His servant. *He* has asked me to come. He's backing me."

He looked about again, searching the faces that had grown quiet, thoughtful. "Do you think that He didn't know that the school had these semester fees?"

Vicente sat down on the edge of the bunk, drawing a tattered Bible from his roll of clothing. "We've come here to be taught from the Word of God. Surely you believe it is reliable?"

The young men met his searching eyes without responding, though a few exchanged startled or incredulous glances as Vicente turned quickly to promises that he apparently believed without reservation.

"Faithful is he that calleth you, who also will do it," Vicente read. Then flipping back a few pages, he read again, "My God shall supply all your need according to his riches in glory by Christ Jesus." "And this is the confidence that we have in him, that, if we ask any thing according to his will, he heareth us. And if we know that he hear us, whatsoever we ask, we know that we have the petitions that we desired of him."[3]

"Look, Vicente," said Juan earnestly, beads of perspiration on his forehead. "We all know about these Scriptures. But what if the principal asks some of us about your father? He didn't understand you, but we can't beat around the bush like—I mean, what shall we tell him?"

"Tell him that my Father will take care of my expenses." The twinkle of quick humor was back in Vicente's eyes. He spoke

[3] I Thessalonians 5:24; Philippians 4:19; I John 5:14-15.

again firmly, but with a grin. "And if you really think that the principal might have more confidence in my earthly father, then you needn't tell him that that isn't the one I'm counting on."

Before many days had passed, the other young men knew that Vicente's faith had not been misplaced. Vicente had also introduced them to a dimension of spiritual reality such as they had never supposed attainable. His implicit trust in God's provision, his unquestioning confidence in God's personal involvement in mundane matters, communicated itself and spread through the school like an epidemic. Youths, whose faith had been in a kindly but nebulous God, entered into a new and vitally powerful personal relationship.

A month after school opened, the missionary in Cúcuta received another letter concerning the former church janitor, but this one carried a different note.

> Vicente Gómez has transformed this institute. His prayer life is changing the attitudes and lives of students; it is bringing greater reality into our own faith!

Vicente virtually prayed his way through the classwork, the assignments, and the term examinations. Lacking a formal education, Vicente had learned to read by stumblingly following the words in hymnals and could now spell his way through a passage in his well-thumbed Bible. He found studies offered at the institute overwhelmingly difficult. To aggravate his formidable problems, his eyesight was extremely poor.

Vicente knew, with unshakable conviction, that his heavenly Father had placed in his heart this urge for training. So he took his perplexities and impossibilities confidently to the throne room of heaven for solution, and one by one they were overcome.

God, who had sent him to school, carried the strain of Vicente's financial obligations. When opportunities quickly opened for Vicente to serve in various churches, Vicente welcomed them as added blessings from God. He graduated early in 1948 with all bills paid and a few pesos in his pocket.

"Why don't you stay with us?" urged one of the elders of the

San Cristóbal church, after Vicente had been told that the mission
leaders had assigned him a church in El Páramo de la Paz, a Colombian mountain community not far from the Venezuelan border. "It's only two years ago that they shot José. They're rough
up there, Vicente!"

Vicente nodded. He knew that in January of 1946, José de la
Cruz Bolívar had been ascending the steep trail from Sardinata to
El Páramo. Though he had known Christ for only eighteen
months, Bolívar had been the evangelical group's oldest believer
and, as such, was the focus of antagonism. He had been ambushed
and shot to death. Missionaries, on their way to minister to the
isolated believers of El Páramo, had been attacked on three occasions. Now they were asking Vicente to climb that trail.

"Because it's hard, that's why they need a pastor," said Vicente
simply.

"But Colombia's not safe these days. You know how many are
coming here to Venezuela to live. They say over a hundred people are dead. They're looting and burning houses. They talk
about rape and brutality—"

"Gaitán will change all that. They've already set him up as
the Liberal candidate. This time he'll win the election."

"Many things can happen before the 1950 election. I tell you
Colombia isn't the peaceful country it used to be!"

Vicente's decision had been made on his knees on the basis of
where God needed him most. The fact that the bleak mountain
would offer no personal advancement posed no problem whatever for Vicente. Survival might. Any qualms about his fate in
this hostile area Vicente turned over to God as he would any
other problem.

To reach El Páramo de la Paz, seven thousand feet above the
city of Cúcuta, Vicente traveled by truck to the foot of the mountain range. From there he had to follow a mule trail for five hours
until he reached the chill barrenness of the summit.

Vicente discovered a delightful kinship with the evangelicals
of El Páramo. They had a rugged faith and were fearless in proclaiming it. They had laid the cornerstone of their church build-

ing on the first anniversary of Cruz Bolívar's martyrdom, and every man involved in the daring gesture knew that he might well be the next victim. In sharing the danger and the exhausting labor of building a church in such a location, Vicente came to know his flock. More important, they quickly shared the humble simplicity of his relationship with God.

El Páramo de la Paz, so isolated from the rest of the world, soon became aware of a turbulence boiling out from the nation's capital like molten lava spreading from the mouth of a volcano. Colombia, from its beginning, had indulged in less political strife than most of its Latin neighbors and, since 1930, had been steadily advancing as a South American power under the leadership of the Liberal party. But for a split in the Liberal platform during the 1946 elections, Jorge Eliécer Gaitán, idol of the Colombian masses, would have been the country's president instead of the weak Mariano Ospina Pérez, who represented the Conservative party which was supported by the landowning class and the Roman Catholic hierarchy.

Early in 1948 the Liberals had already chosen Gaitán as their candidate for the 1950 elections. Ospina, pliable tool of Laureano Gómez, ruthless reactionary leader of the Conservative party, was using every means, fair or foul, to remain in power. Since he could not hope to win over Gaitán through a legal election, he was pushing political and personal hatreds so far that in the strongly Conservative provinces the government-controlled police had begun a campaign of terror, with looting, rape, arson and brutal murder. Most often their victims were those of isolated communities and unprotected haciendas. When they understood that they were marked for death, many Liberals fled to Venezuela for safety. Gómez was determined to terrorize the Liberals until they would be afraid to vote.

Not long after noon on April 9, a man rushed by the evangelicals at work on their church, yelling, "Gaitán has been shot! They've murdered Gaitán!"

Stunned and frightened, the evangelicals joined men already clustered about the only radio on El Páramo. They were just in time to hear President Ospina denounce Gaitán's assassination as a Communist plot. He also blamed the Communists for the ensuing disturbance.

"I wonder what he means—ensuing disturbance," muttered one of the men, turning a worried face toward the others. "What's going on in Bogotá?"

"Shot in the back," said another bitterly. "He wasn't doing anything—just going out to lunch!"

"How did they know the assassin was hiding behind a door?"

"Maybe they caught him."

"Well, it wouldn't be the Communists that President Ospina should blame then for the disturbance! If I'd been there—" The speaker clenched his fists in impotent rage, his reaction reflecting something of what happened in front of the Nieto Building, where Gaitán had his office.

When spectators fully realized what had happened, a cry of horror swept down Bogotá's crowded streets. As word of the tragedy spread, the character of the clotting throng changed to that of a raging mob. Discovering the assassin, they ripped the man's shirt from his body. They tore at his clothes. Someone snatched a shoeshine box from a frightened bootblack who was staring at adults gone mad, and swung it on the gunman's head. Men were kicking at the face and at the now limp body of the assassin; others pounded the head and face into an unidentifiable bloody pulp.

The lifeless body, stripped naked, was dragged by a necktie six blocks along Bogotá's main street and left in front of the palace of the president. By this act the crowd was placing final responsibility for the shooting squarely on the Conservative chiefs. However, as the crowd surged past the crumpled corpse, they bypassed the palace and stormed the capitol, screaming, "Death to Laureano Gómez!'"

Rioters entered the capitol building, and for twenty minutes smashed furniture and typewriters, shouting, "Down with the government. Down with the Conservatives. They killed our leader!" Federal troops intervened, but muttering throngs still hov-

ered in solemn knots along the streets, and moved slowly in the
direction of the hospital to which the mortally wounded Gaitán
had been taken. When Gaitán died that afternoon, the populace
went berserk.

Men broke into hardware stores to get knives and machetes.
They set fire to the presidential palace and other governmental
buildings. They wrecked and burned *El Siglo,* Laureano's paper.
They attacked the municipal transportation lines, overturning
streetcars and setting them on fire. They wrecked cars and taxis.
Police fired sporadically at the mobs, but the hysteria spread.

By six o'clock that evening, flames reached the skies. As night
fell, rioters were surging through Bogotá's streets unchecked, and
had begun looting, not for weapons, but just for the sake of looting. Here and there gun battles between police and plunderers
left other corpses over which the pillaging mobsters stumbled in
the dark. Men staggered by with machetes, clubs, knives or guns
in one hand and with bottles of liquor in the other. Some were
wearing new suits, hats and shoes, and carrying bundles of mer-
chandise.

Throughout the night the sky over downtown Bogotá glowed
red with the reflection of the burning city. At least thirty-five
buildings had been set afire. It took three days for the fires to
burn themselves out. By Saturday night the morgue reported
three hundred dead.

By the rapidity with which the disorders spread through Bogotá
and then to other areas in Colombia, it appeared that the Communists were not allowing such a providential uproar to go un-
exploited. In later events, however, skilled direction came from
a carefully chosen list of officials who held, and intended to main-
tain, control of the government. The network of power followed
well-laid plans of political victory through intimidation and liqui-
dation.

At first the people of El Páramo heard news of other murders
similar to that of Liberal leader, Gaitán. An influential man
with Liberal sympathies was shot at point-blank range in a res-
taurant. A youth from a Liberal family was felled by a charge

from a shotgun as he left a plane. An entire family was massacred, then thrown into their own burning hacienda.

Liberals, frightened and enraged at the unscrupulous political actions, struck back almost blindly, hardly knowing where to look for their enemies. Soon a violence beyond wildest nightmares was sweeping across Colombia and would be almost sure to continue until after the election in 1950.

From the height of El Páramo the people watched with fascinated horror as the signs of violence crept toward them. A fire in the valley, on the opposite mountain range, or on their own, meant a home destroyed. Survivors who were fortunate enough to escape told of rapings and brutal massacres that usually preceded arson. Several times the people of El Páramo formed caravans and went up higher into the mountains when guerrilla bands scoured the neighborhood with systematic deadliness.

Dawn would pinpoint for the mountaineers where the terror had struck during the night, for they had a clear view of the valley. Sometimes they found their clue in the sky, where a slow-wheeling spiral of vultures was gathering to fall upon a horrible banquet. Then the men would saddle their mules and silently file down the trails, carrying spades to take care of their friends, guns and machetes to take care of their enemies.

A rumor that military police and guerrillas were coming up from Sardinata to kill the Liberals on the paramo brought a week of panic. Drawn together by fear in the scant shelter of the harsh crags, they huddled miserably behind a gigantic boulder and shivered in the stinging wind. The church leaders were warned, more than once, that almost any crime could now be committed under the guise of political violence, and that there were people right on the mountain who were not in favor of a Protestant church on El Páramo.

By day the people would creep back to their homes for food. No one dared venture to the farms clinging so precariously to the slopes of the mountain. Angry, frightened men stood in tight knots watching the trails, and the women hovered over their children, keeping them always within reach.

Under duress of recent events and persistent threats, Vicente called on his elders to help him decide on a principle of Christian action in case of attack or of personal danger. They thumbed earnestly through their Bibles, unwaveringly accepting Jesus Christ's policies as their own. Once committed to their course, their resolution was never altered or shaken in ten years of political violence, the lurid background against which Vicente's ministry would cast a living and radiant silhouette.

Men, who had gone to work on the church building whenever they could spare time from their farms, now waited until several could go together, lest a lone man working would be surprised and killed. Women cooked for the men and labored with them from dawn to dark, then often fled again to the bare mountain for the night. Vicente, never very strong, suffered greatly from exposure on these nightly excursions, and became seriously ill.

Besides the delays brought on by their very real danger, heavy rains had twice threatened the walls of the church. At last, however, the roof was up, and the evangelicals dared to invite everyone to the dedication service. They were delighted when many came.

During the singing of a hymn, Vicente was drawn from the center of the platform. "There, near the window—" The hand on Vicente's shoulder was trembling violently. "That's the man who killed José de la Cruz Bolívar!"

But Vicente's Father was also at the meeting, and Vicente was more conscious of His presence than of the danger. Like other visitors who had never before attended a Protestant church, the assassin sat through the entire service in respectful attention.

With the chapel completed, an even more strenuous service opened for Vicente. Though city bred, Vicente had soon adapted himself to mountain life. As itinerant evangelist, he faced continual hardship and personal peril. Weighted down with two burlap bags full of Bibles and other literature, he trudged to the source of every footpath and mule trail, knowing that every path led to people. Before long, the congregation in the new chapel reached twenty. Then thirty.

The political situation worsened in 1949, and the predominately Liberal congress advanced the date for the election from June, 1950, to November, 1949. Needless to say, party tensions, already at the point of national bloodletting, broke all bounds of reason.

Although the army owed a constitutional loyalty to its Conservative president, it had taken a stand against the illegal slaughter of Colombian citizens by the military police, a special contingent of police agents recruited, as some newspapers observed, from among the blackest criminals in the federal prisons. They were men with a natural aptitude for Ospina's regime of politics by violence. Thus there were actual skirmishes between the Colombian army and Colombia's "military" police. Liberals in search of vengeance began roaming the hills in guerrilla bands, determined to hunt down the military police to the last man.

One of the members of Vicente's congregation brought news of trouble in Salazar. The teachers' training school of Salazar had sent their students back to their homes before completion of the term and just before the Conservatives had taken the town.

"The military has forced the missionary to leave Ocaña," he continued. "And he's the lucky one. So are the missionaries from Salazar. They're safe in Cúcuta. One of the elders from Salazar didn't make it. They're still praying that somehow he did escape, but nobody has heard of him or seen him anywhere. The missionary from El Carmen didn't make it either, as far as anyone can tell."

"Has El Carmen been attacked too?"

"By all the rumors, the town's been burned."

The man related what he had heard of the missionary and her companion who had been trapped in El Carmen, as far as anyone could learn, when the city was burned. Communications with the town had been cut off on November 11, and so all anyone knew was what could be gleaned from rumors. "This is sure going to hit Don Marco real hard," he added.

"Don Marco?"

"Yes, Don Vicente. It was Marco Franco's girl that was up there in El Carmen with the missionary."

After a long silence, Vicente placed an affectionate hand on the shoulder of the young believer. "God is still Master of every situation. For that Franco family. For us."

The other shook his head dubiously. "This time it looks as if it's getting out of hand—even for God. When they come into Cúcuta, then where will we run to?"

"God will find a way." Vicente spoke with conviction. "He has promised not to leave us nor forsake us."

As the national violence progressed, Vicente found that many people, shaken by its uncertainty and fears, could be persuaded to occupy themselves with eternal values and the unshakable reality of salvation through Jesus Christ. His small group of believers was growing as more and more turned to God for the way out of their bitterness and terror.

Then, in the last week of January, 1950, a messenger came to tell Vicente that he was wanted in Cúcuta by mission authorities.

"They're sending you to Ocaña to take that church."

"They want me to go to Ocaña?" Vicente exclaimed incredulously.

The order that he might have considered news of advancement staggered Vicente like an unexpected blow. These people up here on the barren paramo were his flock. He loved them. Many of them were very immature in the faith and they depended on him. His dismay was apparent.

"I know things are pretty rough down in Ocaña," commiserated the messenger. "But things are liable to get more dangerous here too."

Vicente glanced at the man's uncomprehending face. "That wasn't what I meant," he said lamely. "Why do they want me in Ocaña?"

The man shrugged. "You know how things are here in Colombia. Maybe they'll let the missionaries get back into Ocaña, maybe not."

Vicente's scant personal belongings were not hard to pack, but leaving his frankly tearful congregation so abruptly tore at his heart. Several men accompanied him on the five-hour descent to the road. The subject of the violence kept coming into the conversation.

"The Conservatives go for the Liberal leaders first," said the Cúcuta man who had described the horrors of attacks on villages and towns. "After that, it's the *evangélicos.*"[4]

In Cúcuta, all through the long night in which he lay tossing sleeplessly in the unaccustomed heat, Vicente's mind was with his flock on the paramo. Even the next morning, when the mission superintendent of the district was briefing him regarding the church in Ocaña, he fought a sense of unreality.

"You will be going by air taxi," he heard the missionary say. "We can't risk your being caught in one of the numerous roadblocks."

It was only after he had checked his battered suitcase at the airport that his move to a new parish began to take on reality. He confirmed the time of his plane's departure and then sat down in the crowded lobby, nervously watching the clock.

After the clean air of the cool mountaintop and the silence of the wide paramo, he seemed to be strangled by smoke and the valley heat, and walled in by the confusion of milling passengers, the drone of dozens of conversations, the shouted orders or farewells.

He could not understand the loud but mechanically distorted directions a woman was announcing over the public address facility, and was unable to assume even a semblance of the relaxed assurance with which accustomed travelers ignored the continual arrival and departure of planes. From time to time he fingered the ticket that bristled in his pocket.

Suddenly Vicente sat erect, then sprang to his feet. The missionary they had supposed dead in El Carmen had just stepped from a plane. She looked drawn and haggard, and walked with difficulty. Vicente rushed out to help her with her baggage.

[4]Evangelicals.

The story of El Carmen,[5] like that of many villages, was one of pillage and subjection and brutal massacres. The missionary and her companion had been drawn into the vortex of violence and slaughter, forced to cook for and serve the invading military police and the guerrillas who had drifted in from the mountains to take part in the arson and rapine. After over a week of terror the two women had fled over cobblestone streets made slippery by the blood of cadavers still sprawled grotesquely where they had fallen. Then they had escaped into the mountains over trails hardly less dangerous because of lurking outlaw bands of blood-inflamed killers.

As the señorita left the station with other missionaries, Vicente bowed his heart in gratitude to God. He had dreaded meeting Marco Franco, a man who had suffered valiantly for the cause of Christ. Now they would be able to rejoice together that God had spared him his daughter.

At last the Ocaña flight was called, and he did understand the thickly blared announcement after all. He picked up a small bag and hurried to the small plane that had darted onto the runway.

Five passengers had taken their places when Vicente arrived at the air taxi. Two men and a woman were sitting in the narrow back seat; one place was left open in the middle row of three seats. He had a choice of sitting in that seat or up front with the pilot. He wanted to sit with the pilot, but his retiring modesty dictated his choice of the seat most easily accessible. He slipped into it quietly.

"You have to fasten the belt," said the man next to him.

"Oh, yes," said Vicente. He fumbled at the strange buckle on the wide band with which he was to strap himself in. This precaution, he thought, proved that air travel was dangerous. What would it be like flying above the mountains? He would be in Ocaña in forty-five minutes. It took over five hours to reach El Páramo de la Paz, just outside Cúcuta.

"Like this," said his neighbor, somewhat condescendingly, show-

[5]*Vanguardia Liberal,* a local newspaper, fell into the hands of the Conservatives a few days before the sacking of El Carmen, so not a word of that bloody surprise attack and the ensuing atrocities appeared in the paper.

ing Vicente how to fasten his belt. Then as the motor started, and the small craft vibrated with the power of the motor, the man shouted above the roar of the engines.

"This your first trip?"

Vicente nodded.

"Scared?"

Vicente thought about this. He shook his head.

"No, Señor," he shouted back, smiling. He was in the hands of God. Underneath him would be the almighty, everlasting arms. His officious seatmate was not so fortunate. He crossed himself nervously as the small craft began its furious race down the strip.

Vicente was quietly elated with his position at a window. He watched the ground flash by, then noted in surprise that they had left it and were climbing steeply into the sky. They circled so that he could look down on the city. They would not fly in the direction of El Páramo de la Paz, but Vicente craned his neck to get a glimpse of it from the air. How small it looked! How much like any other mountain. How far, even now, it seemed in the past.

As they gained altitude, Vicente gazed at the western range of the Andes sprawled out below him in massive splendor. Rivers and mountain streams wove a design of silver strands through the green Astrakhan rug that had been tucked in deep, puckered folds right around the edges of the world. Clumps of flowering trees spread violet or yellow or sparkling white patches of contrast into the purple shadows of the forest greens.

Vicente could identify the various crops by the color of the tiny patches plastered to the slopes of towering mountains. Then he pressed his nose against the glass to look more carefully. Yes! Those fine, zigzag lines were mule trails! From his altitude he could not discern the angle of the slopes, but he knew that mountaineers never weave circuitous trails unless it is impossible to climb directly. And paths, Vicente knew, always lead to people.

Then another pattern began to impress him. Here and there, where white dots showed him that there was a painted home, four or even five paths would converge. These suggested haci-

endas or plantations of prosperous landowners. Yes, there was
another. He could tell by the size of the clearing that it was a
large hacienda. Another! And to these haciendas the tracks led
from surrounding valleys, along ridges, and from within the
green of coffee plantings.

Vicente felt an inner tumult of excitement. God had taken
him up into the sky to show him His map for evangelical strategy.
At the point where trails meet, a person should go first to sell his
Bibles. One must win the owner of such a hacienda, and then the
peons, too, would be drawn to the truth by the change in their
master. Because trails are the focus of travel and therefore of
communication, here lived the man who would talk most of what
he heard, because he would see more people. Characteristically,
Vicente's heart turned toward God in prayer and thanksgiving.

How many of those homes had been evangelized? He could see
scores at one glance. What a field in which to minister! As Vicente prayed for the people whose homes he had glimpsed below, he
forgot that this plane was bearing him from the comparative
safety of the Venezuelan border and was headed into the heat of
a political revolution. His heart had lodged amid the tracery of
mountain mule trails.

Far too soon the mountains grew larger, trees took on individual outlines, then cars and trucks became visible as animated beetles
scurrying along threads of road. Almost at once, Vicente could
see a small cluster of diminutive people waiting for the plane at
the edge of a single, weed-grown landing strip. Finally, he heard
a dull thump and felt the slight jarring as the wheels came down
in what was to be his new parish.

"For ten pesos you can get a seat on the taxi that takes us to
town."

Vicente looked up, startled, at the man who spoke to him. He
still felt as though he were part of a vision. He had been given
enough money to pay for this transportation, and knew it was a
long way to Ocaña from the airport. He picked up his bag and
walked automatically toward the car as a man in a dream.

2

Though He Slay Me

ONE MORNING, very shortly after Vicente arrived in Ocaña, on opening his street door, he found a paper locally known as a *pasquín*. A large drawing of a skull covered the page. Vicente stepped into the sunlight to see the scrawled threat.

You have one week to leave town.

Vicente knew the note was no mere lampoonery. Ocaña was now in the heart of a creeping horror with no end in view; murder was now the way of government. Once a truckload of headless bodies had been paraded around and around the Parque de Santander, a plaza built around the statue of General Francisco de Paula Santander, who had fought for the establishment of honor and justice in the Colombian government and in 1821 had been its first vice-president.

Danger might lurk next door or behind any door he had to pass as he did his pastoral work. Still, in Vicente's opinion, only the craven cowered in dark corners of their homes. Necessity drove most people out to face whatever fate held for the next day. Brutal death had become so commonplace that it aroused no emotion unless its cadaverous hand reached very near to clutch another victim.

Vicente visited faithfully in his new parish. He had left some thirty believers on the paramo. In Ocaña he had less than a dozen. Never a great platform figure, Vicente sensed disappointment in the pews. His informal expositions were being compared, he knew, with the far more polished sermons of the missionary who had returned to Ocaña without his family.

The Ocaña congregation sang hymns more tunefully than the one on the paramo, but with less heart. These people seemed to resist his admonitions to seek for deeper realities, to abandon themselves to God in fuller commitment. Few comprehended the power of their pastor's simple prayers.

The home of Francisco Velásquez at the dead end of a narrow, crooked street, Vicente discovered, was one place where the faithful congregated for spiritual fellowship and mutual encouragement. Evangelicals sometimes made a long journey to seek counsel or even refuge with this rugged cobbler who slipped gospel tracts into the shoes he sold. Some of his patrons had reacted violently, and the heavy door facing the street bore deep scars where it had been gashed savagely with machete blades. Now the door had to be kept closed at all times, and huge double bars gave the family a measure of security.

When on his first visit Vicente had challenged the family to trust God and be at peace in the midst of the terror that lurked in every shadow, Francisco's wife, Emma, had exclaimed, "That sounds like Marco Franco. It sounds just like Marco Franco."

"Did he come to know Christ through your tracts?"

"No, the man is illiterate. He was won to Christ by some of his wife's relatives. They came from Agua de Dios."[1]

"José and Carlos came to help Don Marco on the farm, which really belongs to them," explained Emma.

"Yes, the farm belonged to Doña Rosa's brother-in-law, who has the disease. The Platas heard the gospel at Agua de Dios, and when the boys began to talk about the power of a living, personal Christ, Don Marco couldn't put the boys out very well. Don Marco had a crippled child, just a toddler—"

"Santander. He was born with a clubfoot so twisted that the child was not walking on the sole of the foot at all."

[1]"God's Fountain," a government leprosarium.

"Well, the Plata boys persuaded Doña Rosa to put Christ to a test by believing Him for a miracle. And in a few weeks little Santander was walking on a straight foot. Well, it didn't take long after that until all the Franco children began to listen."

"You should see the boy now. You can't tell he ever had anything wrong with his foot."

"And Don Marco?"

"He wasn't so easily won. He may have been convinced, but he had another woman—"

"Another family, you should say. And now—"

"His cousin, Pedro Castillo, was selling liquor at a fiesta in Aspasica. You know how that is. He got into some kind of brawl, was shot, and they called Don Marco to sit with him while he died. That's when Don Marco began to think of the judgment of God and decided that the life he was leading wasn't worth it. He had been noticing the peace of heart Doña Rosa had in spite of his infidelity and ridicule. He repented and cleared up his life."

"And when Don Marco does something, he goes all the way."

"Don Marco kept coming into town to hear preaching—to ask questions. But every time he came here to Ocaña, they harassed the family. One Sunday evening in December, not long after Don Marco decided for Christ—"

"The fiesta of Santa Catalina is on the twenty-fourth of November."

"The family was having its own *culto*[2] at home. People began throwing rocks at them—right there in their house. Then another time they stole Don Marco's cows."

"Not only that. They killed one, right there in his patio, and divided it up."

"So they built a lean-to stable for all their livestock, right up against the house. And Don Marco didn't come here so often any more. By spring he had to buy up some supplies for the little store he kept up there, and he figured the town had got used to him being an *evangélico*. So he came in for a service and stayed

[2]Worship service.

overnight. That time while he was in town, they burned the barn, which was built of cane stalks. The boy, Toño, woke up in time to untie the cows, but the fire ran up to the thatched roof of the house and burned it off. So the whole family had to sleep in the mountains. You can imagine how Don Marco felt when he got back."

"They'd even burned off their pasture."

"That didn't stop Don Marco from witnessing. But the biggest testimony, I guess, was that he didn't go after them with a shotgun, as he would have done a few weeks earlier. He quietly put up a tile roof and kept right on telling people how the gospel had changed his life. And they knew it had."

"They attacked them again when little Jonas was born."

"That was in March. They hit the gasoline pressure lantern with a rock while the family was having a *culto* again. This time they had a big mob throwing stones at the new tile roof and chopping at the door with machetes. Doña Rosa had to wrap up her new baby and take the children out into the mountains again to wait for Don Marco to come back."

"You see? They just attacked when Don Marco wasn't there."

"While the mob was breaking up that new tile roof with rocks, they kept yelling, 'Kill the infidels!' and 'Chop these *evangélicos* into mincemeat!'—things like that. Don Marco knew they couldn't stay in Aspasica. When he got ready to move, not a man would help him out. He couldn't borrow a donkey to load his stuff. And when it got around town that he was leaving, they decided to kill the family on their way out of town. Don Marco got wind of it, and they had to pick up and leave the house, their crops—"

"During the night, think of it, with those children. In the mountains. They had to leave everything behind. Everything."

"By that time they didn't have much. Their cattle had been stolen and part of their crops destroyed. They went to Agua de Dios, but they couldn't stay there either. That was right after Gaitán was assassinated, and Don Marco is a Conservative."

Vicente nodded. Politics in Colombia was a strange matter involving family loyalty more than a knowledge of platforms or policies. One's political party became almost a matter of heritage. So, though a man might not be in agreement with the activities of his party, or though he divorced himself completely from all participation in politics——as all evengelicals had done since the beginning of the violence—he still wore the label of his political party. The Tolima area, where Marco Franco had gone for refuge from religious persecution, was Liberal.

"So they came here to Ocaña for awhile, until he found a farm at Santa Inés. Everybody's Conservative around there. But that doesn't make it safe for the Francos."

From the day that Francisco Velásquez accompanied him to Santa Inés, Vicente felt a warm spiritual kinship with the peppery Marco Franco, though Marco was illiterate and almost brashly outspoken and Vicente was a mild-mannered seminary graduate.

Marco often came in from Santa Inés to worship on Sundays, but before long Vicente began spending a good deal of time at Santa Inés. This scattered rural community touched the highway leading from Aguachica, in the torrid Magdalena River Valley, to Ocaña, a thriving city on a pleasant mountain plateau. One day as the two Ocaña men jumped from a truck on which they had been passengers, they were waylaid purposefully by Señora Juana Lazzco whose home and general store bordered on the road.

"So you're the preacher Don Marco keeps telling us about!"

"I'm Vicente Gómez—at your service."

"You'd serve me—and everybody around here—if you stayed away from here. That man Franco is stirring up enough trouble for himself without you coming here from Ocaña to help him!"

Juana, an obese woman with bold, heavy features, leaned over a battered wooden railing on fat, folded arms. A white scar cut into the corner of her determined mouth, and her thin lips were set in a hard line. One of her shrewd eyes, slightly out of focus, wandered off to the side, giving her otherwise plain face a rather shifty look.

"Or maybe you can talk sense into him. He's got to stop talking like he has been. You know how the police are acting these days." A glint of anger suddenly came into her eyes. "*I* can tell you about that."

"I guess we all—"

"They came here, twenty-five of them, and the whole lot of them was drunk as hoot owls."

She fixed Vicente with one hard gray eye. "A crumbier bunch of scum you never saw, and I was beginning to wish my man was here. You never know what those beasts will think of next. My man was in Barranca. That was the first of July."

She rambled off on a tangent. "I can't read, but I have good ears. The police are going to wipe out these Liberal towns—all of them. The haciendas, too. That's why they cleaned out San Andrés and Málaga and Molagavita—those small places along that side road out of Bucaramanga—not on the main road—"

"Yes, we know of that, Señora."

"They're not such small towns either. Well, then they went off to the west of the main road—the murderous thieves—and got those other little villages."

"I heard. Barichara and Galán."

"And Cabrera. And Enciso, off to the north. They massacred the unprotected people in the out-of-the-way villages, and then they tackled big towns like San Gil—after they'd got the people scared stiff. When Ospina put his uniforms onto those convicts and set them to killing Colombian citizens, he should have known they couldn't stop with Liberals. Aren't we good Conservatives?"

"You mean—"

"That's what I'm telling you." The señora spat. "I was here all alone with this man we had hired to work on the farm—one of those scrawny little men I could set down in a corner and make him sit." Her gray eyes flashed again. "And maybe you think I couldn't. And you're no bigger. I could—"

Vicente exchanged amused glances with Francisco.

"You were saying—"

"Yes, those policemen were here. And plenty drunk by the time I asked for my money. I wasn't furnishing those bandits with free drinks. Twenty-five of them. You can figure how much that came to. What did they think I was running a store for?"

She grinned as she rubbed her thumb against her first two fingers in the characteristic Latin gesture that suggests the feel of cash in hand. "Sure, I like money. What do you think I—"

"Yes, of course."

"Well, they said they weren't going to pay me, and I said, well then, that was their last drink, and they could get out of here."

It was not hard to visualize this woman glaring twenty-five rough men out of countenance.

"And then the lieutenant—or whatever he was—said they wanted my money, and they began to go through the place. After awhile, I saw I couldn't stop them, so I got into my bedroom. Let them look, I thought. I knew where my money was." Juana tapped her full bosom with a sly chuckle.

"But I hadn't had time to put up the pole. One of the men opened that door so hard he struck me across the right side of the face with it. It nearly knocked me out. So there I was, sitting on the floor with my head spinning while they tore up the house. 'Give us the money,' they were yelling. 'Your money or your life.' And when I could get up, but wouldn't give them the money, one of them hit me. 'Where's the money?' I wasn't going to give those buzzards any money. I showed them a picture of Gaitán. That's a man that stood up for people's rights. But they said Gaitán was dead."

"He has been, since April, last year."

"Well, I let them yell, but that man that worked for me was shaking like a cat in a rain barrel. He came up and whispered— and they could hear him—'Give it to them,' he says. 'Give them the money!' So they knew I had it.

"Well, they hit me again. My neck was out of joint for a month. They might have hurt my hired man, too, if I hadn't given in. So I gave it to them." Juana grew a belligerent red at the very thought. "I gave it to them of my own free will. Twenty-five pesos!"

Possibly the two men were thankful they had not come to negotiate business with this woman who had risked her life for a sum of money worth less than three dollars. And she was making it plain that she did not want to meet these representatives of the law again.

"They've come up here to warn that Marco Franco once. But if they hear about the Gómez boy, they may come back up here and burn us out like we were all *evangélicos!*"

Later, when they were in the Franco home, Vicente questioned Marco.

"Manuel Gómez?" Marco laughed. "You can give Alicia credit for that one. They met him on the trail while they were coming here from El Carmen. He's the first one to accept the Saviour in Santa Inés, but it looks like I'm going to have him in the family as well."

Alicia, a lovely, dark-eyed girl in her late teens, gasped and exclaimed, "Oh, Papá!"

Marco slapped his thigh and broke into a hearty chuckle. "What's this generation coming to? They run for their lives, but they pick out a husband on the run!"

"Oh, Papá!" Though Alicia protested vigorously, the flush on her cheeks suggested that she did not deny the attractiveness of her father's shrewd prophecy which was, in due process of time, to be fulfilled.

"All that boy needed was to have somebody answer a few questions. He'd just heard the gospel once, there on the trail, but he was ready for it. You never know which one is going to listen, so you have to tell them all."

"He doesn't let anybody pass the store without hearing about what God has done to change our lives," said Rosa.

"So your neighbor, Doña Juana, has been telling us. She warns us that you may be getting into trouble."

"Costs me some customers," said Marco. "But I always think that if they get mad enough, they won't be able to forget what I say."

"The Lord Jesus never left anybody neutral," said Vicente, "still—"

"Don't ask for trouble, Marco," interrupted Francisco. "You live in a pretty tough neighborhood."

"Roaring threats just makes them feel like *machos*.[3] No harm in giving them that satisfaction."

Vicente leaned forward in immediate concern. "Did they make threats, Marco?"

"Sure, Vicente. But I'll tell you something else. Remember those Mateus brothers? They've been back. Twice they came together. But then, after a day or two, each of them drifted in casually to ask more questions. Much freer to ask questions and talk when there's nobody else around. Alcario bought a Bible yesterday."

"Alcario, did you say?" Francisco looked puzzled. "Is that the plantation owner that lives on Cerro Bravo?"[4]

"No, the one on Cerro Bravo is Cristóbal. He's a cousin. He's a landholder—has a big coffee plantation. Alcario and Margario both live in La Vega del Gusto.[5] Alcario often comes in with that wily horse trader, Juan Machado. He's a great one to start an argument."

Vicente glanced at Francisco, and both men began to laugh. "I wonder who gets in the last word," said Vicente.

"*I* get in the last word. Who else? And I'll tell you something else. He comes back for more."

"Fine. How's your stock of Bibles holding out?"

"Oh, he's not doing anything so far but argue. Just wait. One of these days he'll have to read it for himself—just like Alcario."

"Well, don't spend all your wind on Alcario. Margario has a big family. And he's got a sister—that young widow with five children. And his father lives there. That's practically a church-ful of people right there."

"Well, you just wait. Since I found that he'll touch a Bible, every time Alcario comes—with Margario or not—I remind him I can't read. I ask him to look me up this verse or that verse and read it to me. Then I ask him to read it again so I can remember

[3]Males.
[4]Fierce Peak.
[5]Delightful Meadow.

it well. And he always folds the corner of the page down. The next time Margario comes, he knows about those verses. They've been talking about them. I can tell by what he asks. Just you wait."

Vicente stood to his feet. "Let's just pray for them right now," he said. A look of humility combined with exaltation had spread over his serious face. Time and again the visits in the Franco home terminated in a session of heartfelt praise or definite, earnest intercession.

Marco had been quite correct about the Mateus brothers' interest, and prayers for them were soon answered. Vicente reported to the church group in Ocaña, his face aglow. "They've got eight to ten people coming to their services down there now. The Mateus brothers have both committed themselves to the gospel of Jesus Christ."

Not much later, Vicente could report, and did so without envy, that the Franco services were now being attended regularly. "They are having a group of around twenty-six people."

Vicente rarely visited Santa Inés without having a service—scheduled or impromptu. Services during the week, often begun on the spur of the moment, depended on who was standing around or could be reached at short notice. They were highly informal, although an unspoken rule dictated that no service was valid without the singing of a hymn. Even for family devotions it was a rule to sing a hymn as well as to read the Bible and to pray all around the family circle.

The Franco children always welcomed Vicente. On those rare occasions when the men had not planned to go to some nearby hacienda or village—or even while Antonio was saddling the horses—the children piled on Vicente's lap or breathed down his neck, while he got out his trail-battered hymnal. They memorized the tunes, but it was Marco, the illiterate, who later remembered the words. Then they sang them together at their neighborhood meetings or, as in the case of the younger children, at serious little meetings held on the kitchen stoop.

One day Vicente noticed that a chubby, gray-eyed girl in her early teens had joined the Franco children on the veranda. Her light brown hair—unusual in Latin America—set her off from the rest of the children in the community. She was Carmen Díaz, he learned, niece of Señora Juana Lazzco. Childless themselves, Juana and her common-law husband, Germán Vanegas, had taken the motherless Carmen and her two half-brothers into their home.

Arturo Quintero, one of the brothers, made his appearance just as Antonio Franco clattered up to the back veranda, riding one horse and leading the horses on which his father and Vicente planned to make an evangelistic excursion in the nearby foothills. Antonio saw Arturo and shouted a greeting as he swung from the saddle.

Arturo strode to his side. Though he lowered his voice, the group on the veranda heard him ask, "Are you going with them on one of their stupid preaching tours?"

"They're not stupid, Arturo. One of these days you'll find out. Then you'll commit *your* life to Christ—"

Arturo did not hear him out but swung on his heel and stalked away, evading "the preacher" by going around the house. His antagonism was obvious by the angry rigidity of his bearing and the furious energy of his stride.

Naturally, on the long miles of trail the Francos' neighbors became a topic of conversation.

"Arturo still comes around," said Marco, "but the older one doesn't have any use for us since Alicia turned him down for a date. He wanted to take her to one of their rowdy parties. Carmen comes whenever she can dodge Doña Juana. That one is a troublemaker!"

"The woman, you mean."

"Yes. Oh, the girl is all right. I talk to her about the gospel, but she keeps coming around. She wouldn't touch a Bible at first. Acted as though it would bite her. So I had Alicia read to her."

"She stayed to listen?"

"Oh, sure. We don't overdo it, of course. But once I sent

Alicia off for some *tinto*[6] for her. I took the Bible—where Alicia was reading—and handed it to Carmen. She nearly let it fall before she finally put her hands out for it. Then I told her to read while Alicia was gone." Marco shook his head sagely. "Just to show her that she wouldn't drop dead if she read from a Bible."

Antonio laughed at the remembrance. "You should have seen her face though. Like a person who's bitten into an *arepa*,[7] and finds he's got a mouthful of ashes. Surprised, and not very happy."

They all laughed, each one able to visualize the girl, startled and vexed, reading glumly from a Bible that she had been taught was the devil's own handbook.

"She was ashamed not to—sort of scared too."

The exhilarating rhythm of hoofs punctuated the men's talk. The trails led past a wild panorama of scenic splendor. But these evangelistic expeditions were not pretexts for social enjoyment.

Nothing took more courage than to offer intensely personal counsel that often caused offense. In presenting the gospel of Christ, these men constantly faced contemptuous rebuff. A threat or blow from a sworn enemy stung far less than scorn or anger in the face of a neighbor or friend.

Visitation—as Vicente and Marco visualized it—compares with most church visitation programs as cuddling a French poodle compares with handling an untamed tiger. These men had no expensive printed brochures announcing spectacular programs with which to lure people into comfortable seats in impressive churches bearing socially acceptable denominational labels. An invitation to one of their meetings was a challenge to face a living God and to allow Him to deal with sin in their lives. By an invitation to accept Christ, these men meant exactly what Jesus meant when He challenged men to follow Him. Jesus also sent His disciples out to fearlessly proclaim a gospel not generally accepted. He defined clearly what they should expect:

[6]The syrupy black coffee is the cup of Colombian hospitality as well as the favorite beverage.

[7]A heavy, unsalted, flat cake made of cornmeal. The Colombian *arepa* is far thicker than the Mexican *tortilla*.

> Behold, I send you forth as sheep in the midst of wolves.
> I have chosen you, and ordained you, that ye should go and
> bring forth fruit, and that your fruit should remain. . . . If the
> world hate you, ye know that it hated me before it hated
> you. If ye were of the world, the world would love his own:
> but because ye are not of the world, . . . therefore the world
> hateth you. Remember the word that I said unto you, The
> servant is not greater than his lord. If they have persecuted
> me, they will also persecute you. . . . But all these things
> will they do unto you for my name's sake, because they know
> not him that sent me (Matt. 10:16*a*; John 15:16, 18-21).

People who became adherents to the unfamiliar but glorious
message of the gospel that was being preached in those hills were
not being drawn by a teaching of "easy believism." The expression
invariably used to signify this faith meant commitment. *Entre-
garse al evangelio* was no light religious gesture. It was, as the
phrase suggested, total commitment to the gospel. They were
committed to Christ and to everything this relationship of faith
would mean in their lives. They were committed to take this
glorious news of Christ and His salvation to everyone who would
listen. Nobody thrust this commitment upon them. Each man
went forward to pick up the cross that he would bear, knowing
that it would be heavy. It was a spontaneous act that demonstrated the reality of their commitment as well as the glory of
their inner release.

Wherever the head of the house would permit him to do so—
however reluctant he appeared—Vicente had a service. Twice the
culto had included only a woman and her children. Some of the
people refused to discuss or hear anything Vicente had to say;
some listened warily and with open suspicion. However, one of
their hosts, who had been in Marco's store the previous day and
knew of their coming, had invited relatives and friends to come
and listen to this strange message of a God of love.

Among the people they were contacting, the common image of
God was one of an angry judge. Jesus Christ was nothing more
in their minds than a helpless babe on the breast of the Virgin
Mary or a lifeless corpse nailed to a rugged cross. Understandably,
with these concepts, they had turned for comfort and help to the

gentle Mother Mary, whom they asked to intercede with an austere and unapproachable deity. Vicente and Marco understood how revolutionary was their presentation of a loving God, a personal relationship with a Christ who is a daily, living Reality, and the evangelical concept of eternal life.

"Come and hear more about this great salvation tonight at the Mateus home," the men announced in each home they visited. "We're going to have a preaching service there."

Cristóbal Mateus of Cerro Bravo openly sympathized with the cause of the evangelicals by this time. He had also been in the saddle all day, inviting everyone in the mountain community to come to hear the preaching.

People began to arrive and chairs were being set in order on the veranda even before the men had finished their meal. Above the murmur of voices, hoofbeats could be heard approaching from the trails leading to the hacienda. Whole families suddenly emerged from the darkness of the wooded hills into the ring of light cast by Cristóbal's pressure lantern. When the chairs were occupied, a trio of young men pulled a log into the edge of light. They had come as much to jeer as to listen, so they preferred to remain in the shadow. Cristóbal brought out a couple of saddles. He placed them on the edge of the veranda and beckoned to women who were standing.

Many of these people had come to satisfy their curiosity; some had come just to enjoy the singing. The evangelicals sang with a note of assurance, and the tunes were militant and joyful, quite different from the melancholy folk tunes they sang in their own homes or the slow chanted music they heard when they attended mass. Many listened alertly, if somewhat fearfully, to the words of the hymns and to the reading of the sacred Scriptures which followed.

When the singing was over, the younger children sprawled on the cement floor and went to sleep. Older children leaned sleepily against their parents or wandered off to the patio beyond the house. As Vicente spoke, the young men gradually stopped their ribald commentary and began to listen in earnest.

After Vicente dismissed the gathering for the night, one of the visitors challenged him to answer a question. A few people had started to move away but came back to listen and to join in the discussion. Although most of these mountaineers would be up at four the next morning, they were too curious to leave. Vicente answered their questions and stilled their prejudices by quoting from the sacred Scriptures.

It was very late when at last Vicente and his two companions saddled their horses. Cristóbal came out to chat.

"There's one more man I've been wanting to invite. Somehow I never see him when we're going to have a *culto*. Armenio Pabón. He's justice of the peace in La Playa. He lives about an hour's ride from here at Las Planadas."

"A government man?" said Vicente.

"Don Armenio won't make trouble," assured Cristóbal, discerning Vicente's unspoken thought. "He's a hard drinker, but he's no assassin."

"You think he might be interested?"

Cristóbal hesitated. "Who can tell? But if we could ever get a meeting in his house, we'd have a ready-made audience. People will come to anything he'd invite them for. Besides, he hires over a dozen peons all year long. He's got a big cattle ranch."

In the dark, with his foot in one stirrup, Vicente recalled the vision of trails criss-crossing in the mountains as he had seen them from the air. He had seen the large hacienda as a center for dissemination of the glorious message of God's grace. If he could get one more man like Marco—

"Some time, when I can get away for a whole day, I want you to take me to see this man."

"And keep coming to the services," said Marco. "Alcario said he and his brother are going to start coming regularly too."

"Sure, Don Marco. I'll come."

"And keep trying to get some of these others from here to ride in with you."

"Don't forget," added Vicente, "that you have to make your own commitment to Christ!"

On the long, dark trail back to Santa Inés, the men planned their next expedition. They had to revisit the homes of all those who had never before showed enough interest to come to a meeting. They had to visit Señor Armenio Pabón, justice of La Playa. More and more, Vicente was becoming involved with the growing congregation that met on Marco's back veranda.

Vicente spent the remainder of the night in the Franco home. Although it was far past midnight when they arrived, sounds of revelry were still proceeding from one of the nearby homes. Later, when they had gone to bed, they heard shouts, then shooting. Often a party ended in violence.

Vicente joined the family for their *culto* just as the sun was coming up. When he appeared, Marco was already seated facing the door. Suddenly he frowned.

"Rosa, look at that door! I can see right through it. Did the children do that?"

Rosa went to the door to examine the damage, then she swung around to her husband. "Come and look at this!"

The urgency in her voice drew the men to the door.

"I heard them shooting last night," said Rosa. "I even heard a thud."

On tracing the course of the bullet to where it was embedded in the wall, they were certain that it had not been an accidental shot gone astray. Whoever had fired the gun had known where Marco customarily slept. The bullet had missed his head by a few centimeters.

"I'll get the brethren in Ocaña to pray for your safety," said Vicente. "The attention you're getting is far too much to be flattering."

Marco was destined to have still more unfavorable attention before much time had passed. Walking along the road toward Ocaña one day, he passed a spot known as La Cuesta. Here Marco was accosted by a former acquaintance who offered him a drink.

"You know that I don't drink now, since I've become an *evangélico*," said Marco. "But many thanks for your hospitality."

"One little drink won't hurt you."

One of the men held a brimming wine glass of whiskey up to Marco's face, confident from his own experience that the pungent aroma would prove a great enough enticement to break down even Marco's stubborn resolve. The latter waved it aside with a smile.

"Friend, you're only proving the power of the gospel! You know what I was like—a soak. Well, God has taken away all my desire for the stuff now."

When Marco continued to refuse, the whole group became loudly abusive. They were determined that Marco would drink, even if they had to force him to do it. In the scuffle that followed, a policeman walked in.

"What's going on here?" he demanded.

All of the men started talking at once, gesturing angrily at Marco. Though none of their shouted accusations seemed to agree, the officer did not bother to investigate. He arrested Marco for causing a disturbance.

Vicente was on hand on another occasion to share in the adverse attention that was directed at Marco. He had just arrived to join Marco on another evangelizing ride through the neighborhood when a group of ruffians appeared at the door. By their coarse, abusive shouts, it was obvious that they had augmented their animosity to the evangelical activities of the two men with a few too many drinks.

Elbowing their way through the house, they ripped the bridles from the horses that stood in the patio ready for the trip. One grabbed Vicente's Bible and struck him a savage blow across the face with it. When Marco barked a sharp reproof, the man turned on him, swinging a leather strap torn from the saddle.

Lashing at Vicente and Marco with whatever they could lay their hands on, the rowdies dragged them from the premises and along the trail. So vicious was the attack that the Franco family felt certain that both of them would be killed. Even as they prayed, Marco broke away from his tormentors and pulled Vicente from the grasp of the man who had been flailing at the evangelist's face.

Marco stumbled into the house, followed by Vicente. As the men painfully peeled off their tattered shirts, they revealed shoulders and backs covered with purple bruises, bleeding where the force of some of the blows had broken the skin.

"My back may look bad," remarked Vicente when Rosa gasped in dismay, "but it doesn't hurt as much as my legs. I kept thinking that if they would break a bone, then there would be no chance to get away. It was the grace of God that kept us on our feet."

Had either of the men fallen, almost inevitably he would have been clubbed to death. As it was, their trip had to be postponed until they could ride a horse again without too much pain. Vicente did not leave until late that afternoon, after he was assured that the men would not fulfill their threat to return and repeat their attack.

During these same difficult days, Francisco Liévano, fiery Colombian evangelist, was fearlessly proclaiming the gospel wherever he could get a hearing. He asked Vicente for permission to have meetings in the Ocaña church. The idea met with instant approval when Vicente spoke to Francisco Velásquez, the cobbler who had not stopped putting gospel tracts into the shoes he made. However, the proposal was not received enthusiastically by the Ocaña congregation, upon whom the spiritual needs of their neighbors weighed less heavily than their own personal risk.

"Revival meetings? We can't invite people. It would be too dangerous."

Vicente shared his disappointment with his friend in Santa Inés.

"Revival meetings?" cried Marco. "Would the man come to a humble shack in the mountains?"

"Why not?" said Vicente, adding with some sadness, "You have a larger congregation right now. But, Don Marco, you know there's much more danger to you here than there would be in Ocaña."

That the *evangélicos* were going to have revival meetings needed no handbill advertising. The news traveled like forked lightning through the local foothills. Señora Lazzco, standing in the doorway of her roadside store with her muscular arms akimbo, her bare feet wide apart, shook a finger at Vicente when he rode by a few days later.

"You're cooking up trouble, young preacher. If you still don't know what trouble is, you'll find out—if you let that fireball *evangélico* come preaching rebellion to the church in these parts. You'd better call him off, if you know what's good for you."

"I know what's good for me, Doña Juana. To know the Lord Jesus Christ as my personal Saviour has been very good for me. He would be very good for you too, if you'd let Him."

The woman held up a rough, obese hand with a deterring gesture. Her thin lips set in scowling incredulity.

"Don't give me that! You and Marco sound just alike, and on me you're both wasting your breath. I'm through with religion. It's never done *me* any good."

"It's not religion that I—"

Juana drowned out the rest of Vicente's sentence. "I was a good Catholic right from childhood, mind you," she said, shaking her work-coarsened finger at him again. "I went to masses, and I burned candles to the virgin in my own house."

"Doña Juana—"

"Now you just listen to me for a change. I had a little altar for the Virgin of Chiquinquirá while we were living in Barranca Bermeja. You want to know what happened? The virgin burned—the Virgin of Chiquinquirá! And the house and all burned right down to the ground. That's all the good she did me." She glowered at Vicente, as though somehow he was responsible for the loss. "So you think I'm an *incrédula?*[8] That's what my in-laws call me. Well, so I am."

"But the Bible—"

"Hah! The virgin. The Bible. All the same. A man in our community had a Bible. You know what happened? He went crazy. That's what happened. I'm afraid of the Bible."

[8]Unbeliever.

Carmen appeared behind her foster mother's elbow. Her gray eyes were merry; her lips parted in a smile.

"I'm not!"

Juana swung around like a barge in a whirlpool, but Carmen slipped past her on bare feet, lightly eluding her menacing gesture.

"Arturo and I are both telling her that what you say is different, Don Vicente. She's just afraid some of her customers will catch her at the Francos, or she'd come to the services too."

While Juana vociferously denied Carmen's charges, Vicente excused himself and turned toward his original destination, the Franco home. He had taken only a few steps when Germán Vanegas, Juana's milder-spoken consort, came out from the shadows of the house.

"I wonder if you should go through with this business of revival," he said. "No, don't get me wrong. I'm not threatening you, but I hear things. In these days—" Germán shook his head. "You ought to warn that cocky rooster, Marco, to crow less."

When Vicente asked his friend about the threats, Marco said, "Well, sure. They've been threatening us ever since we came."

"And more, lately?"

"Why, sure. We've been getting more people to come to our meetings too, haven't we? So if more threats bring more people to listen—let them threaten!"

"Doña Juana—"

"There's a hard one!" Then Marco chuckled. "But she lets the girl come. And one of the boys comes—Arturo. The other one has never had any use for us. Nor has Doña Juana, for that matter."

The next time Vicente came for a service, he was amused to see that Juana's curiosity was stronger than her unbelief. She had come over, ostensibly to borrow some flour, but he noticed that she did not leave after her cup had been filled. She stood with feet apart, a hand on a massive hip, her customary scowl as prominent as ever, but very attentive to the message he was bringing.

As the Liévano meetings which were scheduled for October

drew near, even Marco began to look very serious. Police had paid him several visits at his home during those days, threatening to burn his home. They spoke ominously of doing away with Marco and his son Antonio. More frightening was their manner of leering at Marco's attractive wife and his three beautiful teen-age daughters.

"The women will he herded to Totumal and Aguachica for the pleasure of the police."

As long as Marco could do his own suffering for the cause of Christ, he remained undaunted. Now he feared for his family. He was apprehensive that mob action might be taken against visitors while they would be at the services in his home or even on the trails leading to Santa Inés. He blustered his hearty indifference to personal danger as loudly as ever, but he spent more and more time in prayer.

Crowds of mountain people did come to hear the ringing testimony of young Francisco Liévano. Some loudly avowed they had only come to scoff and cause a disturbance, but no one knew whether the heckling was a screen to disguise unadmitted need. Something was drawing the same people back day after day.

Juan Machado, who had so often come to argue with Marco, made his decision during those days. The Mateus brothers were exultant at the thought of another believer in the La Vega area. Carmen Vanegas and her brother Arturo made public commitments.

Though not many decisions for Christ were made openly during those meetings, large numbers of people heard the gospel for the first time, and many returned to hear more in the months to come. Since many of the local people were attending the services or were secretly wishing they dared, the week went by without undue negative reaction.

Some time later, however, a group of Ocaña police rushed on Marco without any warning. When he complied to their order to halt, they clamped handcuffs on him.

"You're going to jail."

"What for?"

"Because," said an officer, cuffing Marco rudely on the jaw, "you keep talking about this—this *evangelio!*"[9]

He spat out the last word with venomous hatred and emphasized his passion by aiming another blow at Marco's face. When the latter dodged this second blow, the policeman turned livid with rage and, grabbing his club, began beating Marco with insane savagery. Not to be outdone, the other representatives of Colombia's "law and order" joined in their leader's brutality, swinging their clubs at Marco indiscriminately from all sides. A crowd gathered almost at once.

"What are you beating that man for?" demanded a woman who had just joined the cluster of onlookers.

"Because he's a cursed *evangélico!*"

"So that's it. Then give it to him!"

The crowd echoed her insensate words, shouting, "Let him have it! Give it to him!"

Encouraged, the police proceeded to make a public spectacle of their sadism. They thrust Marco to a raised sidewalk so that the crowd could get the full benefit of their performance. One grabbed Marco by the nape of his neck and shoved him, helpless in his handcuffs, viciously to his knees. Then they beat him down to the concrete. Finding this amused the gathered rabble, they further forced Marco to climb a telephone pole, clubbing him all the while. Instead of feeling compassion, the crowd hooted and shouted insults against evangelicals.

Finally, they formed a parade, driving Marco before them, compelling him to climb up to the raised sidewalk, then beating him down to the gutter. They kept repeating their sadistic game until they reached the jail. There, having left the mob in the streets, they tore off Marco's clothes and clubbed his naked body to senselessness.

The Franco family, accustomed to his remaining in Ocaña overnight, knew nothing of Marco's trouble until a day later when one of the evangelicals brought the news that Marco was gravely ill in one of the homes. When they brought him to Santa

[9]Gospel.

Inés, he was vomiting blood from internal injuries and his body was a mass of discolored bruises. Sick at heart, Vicente came to sit with his friend, to bring him comfort and encouragement.

"Our Lord understands the pain you are enduring, Marco. He too was beaten by the officers of the law to provide pleasure for a mocking crowd."

Marco nodded painfully. "I know. And I've asked God to forgive them, but I've been lying here wondering if I'm really sincere. I know it's true—that they don't know what it is they're fighting against. They're against God's truth and love, and His salvation—not me. Pray for me, Vicente. I need more grace of heart. This is teaching me what I'm really like. I am not like Jesus."

Marco turned his head to hide the tears that betrayed the depth of his sense of inner defeat. Finding no words to voice his own thoughts, Vicente gently took Marco's battered hand and read to him from the Word:

> We are handicapped on all sides, but we are never frustrated; we are puzzled, but never in despair. We are persecuted, but we never have to stand it alone: we may be knocked down but we are never knocked out! Every day we experience something of the death of the Lord Jesus, so that we may also know the power of the life of Jesus in these bodies of ours. These little troubles (which are really so transitory) are winning for us a permanent and glorious reward out of all proportion to our pain. For we are looking all the time not at the visible things but at the invisible. The visible things are transitory: it is the invisible things that are really permanent.[10]

Marco held out his hand in a gesture of gratitude. He blinked back the tears that continued to well up in his eyes. Then, as Vicente was about to leave, he revealed the real burden of his heart.

"Don't forget, Vicente, that these people who came to the revival have to have somebody visit them."

Released from the Ocaña pulpit on alternate weekends, Vicente began to take some Sunday services at Santa Inés. While contact-

[10]II Corinthians 4:8-10, 17-18 (Phillips).

ing every family that had been represented in the revival congregations, Vicente did not forget to visit the hacienda of the
justice of the peace, Armenio Pabón of Las Planadas.

A chubby little girl caught sight of Vicente as he was crossing
a clear, gurgling mountain stream just below the Pabón hacienda.
She ran with all her might toward the house, her shining black
curls tossing behind her. She shrilled excitedly as she ran.

"A peddler, Mamá! Mamá! Here comes a peddler."

Even a peddler is welcomed at an isolated mountain home
where the routine of hard work is broken by few diversions.

"Well, we'll see what he has to sell."

"I haven't anything to sell, Señora," said Vicente, grinning at
the charming woman who had come to the door with the child
clinging to her skirts. "What I have is free."

"So much the better. We'll accept your gift gladly." Señora
Carmen de Pabón dusted a chair before she offered it, in the local
manner of hospitality, by whipping at it with her apron. "Have
you come a long way, Señor?"

"From Ocaña. I've come hoping to speak with Señor Pabón."

"He rode to Aguachica today on business." The woman sensed
Vicente's acute disappointment. "I'm sorry. I can't even say that
he'll be back today. He sometimes stays overnight with his
brother."

"Well, I still have something for you that is free, and perhaps
you will share it with your husband."

Vicente was battling a feeling of deep frustration, for he had
allowed himself to build high hopes concerning this visit. He
handed a tract to the señora, explaining its meaning.

"I could make it plainer," he said, "if I could read you something from God's own Word. May I?"

"Why not? We like anything that leads our thoughts to God.
But first let me go to fix you a cup of *tinto.*"

A cup of coffee—when it involves an open wood fire built on a
brick platform and home-roasted coffee beans that are ground
just before using—is not a matter of two or three minutes. While
Vicente waited, he made friends of the children, two girls and a

boy, who stood in a shy cluster at some distance, plainly curious. He gathered the usual data on the number of birthdays and the number of teeth, in and out. Maria, the older girl, even offered to let Vicente wiggle one of hers to see how loose it was.

Since it was near the Christmas season, Vicente taught the children a carol. They were delighted, and by the time the *tinto* was ready, they were no more timid than the Franco children.

"Oh, Mamá!" cried the tiny girl who had so delightedly announced their visitor's arrival. "We've learned a song of the Christ Child. A new one."

When Vicente read the story of Mary and the birth of Jesus, Carmen remarked that it was well known to them all.

"One thing we often forget, Señora, when we read the story, is that the angels told us why God sent His own Son to earth. We needed a Saviour. God knew there was no other way for us to be saved, so He sent Jesus, knowing that Jesus would be crucified for our sins. And so, Christmas is a time to remember that God loves you, Señora. It is a personal love. Jesus is a personal Saviour."

Carmen listened attentively as Vicente talked about what Jesus could mean to her. When he prepared to leave she said, "I want my husband to hear this too."

Vicente returned a few days later with Manuel Gómez, the young convert from Santa Inés. Señor Pabón's reception was many degrees cooler than his wife's had been, and when Vicente asked permission to have a *culto*, he refused curtly.

"But couldn't we even sing the little Christmas one, Papá?" pleaded little Carmen, with tears squeezing out between her long lashes. "You haven't even heard the Christmas one."

"All right," Pabón growled with patent reluctance. "The Christmas one."

While they sang the Christmas carol, Vicente's heart was raised to God in praise. God had foreseen that it would take the little girl to provide this opening. His previous visit, so disappointing to him, had been arranged by God. Now Vicente claimed from God the opportunity to speak of spiritual matters.

Carmen begged Vicente to repeat the Christmas story. The latter looked questioningly at his host.

"What's the harm?" he grumbled. "Go ahead."

"There was nothing new in that," he commented after Vicente had read the story. He ended by relating some stories of Old Testament characters that he had studied in college. From that, they drifted into a discussion of more intimate matters. Before Vicente left, his host had agreed to allow him to come back for another *culto*.

At a later visit, Marco came with Vicente. In his rough eloquence, he told his host how the gospel had revolutionized his whole life, taken care of his drinking problem and bound his family together. Señor Pabón listened without comment, though he nodded occasionally with understanding. He was well aware of the wretchedness that loose living and heavy drinking brought to numerous homes.

"You ought to buy a Bible, Señor Pabón," said Vicente, showing him one of the fine hard-cover books. "They only cost three pesos."

"I don't have the money for one," replied Pabón evasively.

"I'll let you have the Bible on credit."

As they rode off, Marco chuckled. "I went to the patio for a drink before we left. I heard the señora telling him, 'You know you have money for that Bible. What's three pesos?' She was probably thinking about the way he spends money on liquor. So he said, sort of grufflike, 'Well, I've already told him I don't have the money. I'm not going to pay for it.' Did you sell him a Bible?"

Vicente looked chagrined. "That's the kind of thing that keeps getting me in trouble. I sell books on credit, and then when I have to go get more literature, I'm way short. Sometimes I forget who owes me. Sometimes they just won't pay."

He shrugged, and they started on their way. Some minutes later, he spoke again. His thoughts were still on his transaction.

"Somehow I have a feeling that it is very important for this man to have that Bible."

3

Carnival

On December 2, 1951, eighty people had gathered for an evening service in the patio of Marco Franco's home. The woods that encircled the open yard were full of horses and mules tethered there by people who had traveled an hour, two hours, three hours.

Everyone took it for granted that some of those who came to the services were there for no good. Usually a number of young people stood in the shadows beyond the ring of light cast by the one pressure lantern, jeering or even mimicking what was being said. This service was no exception. A rather large group of rowdies kept shuffling between the roadway and the Franco home.

If they had hoped to buy liquor from the blustering Juana, they were disappointed, for her store and all the doors of the Vanegas home were secured with heavy padlocks, and Juana was sitting on one of the Francos' best chairs, right out in front of the meeting. Germán Vanegas was there too, as well as the two young people who had recently made public professions of faith.

Inured to hecklings while he spoke, Vicente did not even pay particular attention to renewed loud and strident talking at the front of the house. Suddenly twelve men, six of them police from nearby Totumal, burst into the yard. The congregation melted into the night and lost itself in the woods.

Having broken up the *evangélico* meeting, the police filled two sacks with what they called arms—the usual machetes, kitchen knives and personal razors one would find in a farm home. These, they said, were the reason for their raid. However, they also con- fiscated any Bibles, hymnals and evangelical literature they could find. Then, forsaking any pretenses of legality, they also helped themselves to whatever cash they found in either the store or the house.

"Where's the preacher?" demanded one of the men gruffly.

Vicente had removed his glasses when he had seen the men, and had not been recognized. Bluntly truthful, as usual, Marco identified him.

"Who owns this place?"

"I do," said Marco.

"Well then, you two will come with us!" A policeman grabbed one of the heavy poles kept on hand for propping against the doors. "Get a move on," he barked.

In a moment the police, habituated to sadism, began to beat the two evangelicals with poles and with the broadsides of ma- chetes they had just stolen from Marco. They drove the two men before them toward the Vanegas store, while the Franco family, frantic with fear that Marco would now surely be killed, fell to their knees in desperate and tearful prayer.

Juana, who had not yet imbibed the evangelical philosophy of love and forbearance, entered the procession at this point and ad- ministered a few well-aimed and purposeful punches at the oppo- sition. Perhaps her energetic diversionary intervention provided just the distraction necessary to allow Vicente and Marco to wrench themselves free from the clutches of their persecutors.

Curiosity is a strange force. The more dangerous it became to entertain evangelicals or to attend services, the more people were consumed by a desire to learn what this illicit religion was all about. Perhaps some offered Vicente their hospitality because a stifled sense of fairness rebelled against the flagrantly unjust treatment to which he and Marco had been subjected. Among these fair-minded people was Armenio Pabón, who became an open sympathizer with the evangelical cause. Vicente was soon making frequent visits to this home, and the Bible—long since paid for—was the focus of every conversation.

"My husband doesn't even sleep these days," reported Carmen. "He reads constantly, now that he has a Bible."

During the days soon to follow, Armenio was to lose sleep even after he had put the now well-thumbed Bible aside.

"What's the matter?" asked Carmen one morning after Armenio had tossed restlessly all night. "I doubt if you slept a wink."

"Let me read you something," said Armenio. "I can't get it out of my mind." He turned quickly to a place he had marked in the Bible. "I found this a couple of days ago. Listen to what it says:"

> Have you forgotten that the kingdom of God will never belong to the wicked? Don't be under any illusion—neither the impure, the idolater or the adulterer; neither the effeminate, the pervert or the thief; neither the swindler, the drunkard, the foul-mouthed or the rapacious shall have any share in the kingdom of God.[1]

Carmen sat silent, reluctant to meet her husband's eyes.

"I'm a drunkard. If this is God's Word—"

A wise woman, Carmen knew when to hold her peace; she knew what her husband was facing. Armenio had always been an honorable and religious man. Never had he had the slightest qualms that his religion or his righteousness might be less than what God would require of him. Was he not better than the average of his neighbors? Still, the Book he was reading was throwing light on areas of his life to which he had never given much thought.

"What shall I do?" he asked. His hand on the Bible trembled visibly, his voice was husky with emotion.

"Repent," his wife said simply. "Receive this gospel. I think I might get in—if you did."

Armenio had been invited to many of the meetings in the Franco home, but he had never gone. He determined to attend the Christmas program.

Though Armenio arrived early, the whole area near the Franco

[1]I Corinthians 6:9-10 (Phillips).

house was teeming with people. Whole families had walked in from every direction.

"What a crowd!" exclaimed Armenio to his host. "I came here today with the purpose of publicly committing myself to Christ. It surely is going to be made public, I can see that."

Marco grinned happily. At no other time had so many people gathered for the services there. It looked as though there would be at least a hundred people present.

"You won't be the only one making a public commitment," he said. "There are a couple of young bucks from the Canónigo family from La Vega where the Mateus brothers and Juan Machado live. And Juan's brother, Sixto Machado from San José, has brought his whole family—five hours of hard riding. They all intend to make their commitment together."

"I should have brought my family too," Armenio said regretfully. "My wife believed, I think, before I did. I had no idea I'd be seeing women here."

"Come on, you have to meet Don Sixto," said Marco, and then bustled away to find Sixto Machado.

Armenio, taller than most Colombians, had the assured bearing of a man of authority. His regular yet striking features suggested a forceful and determined leader who was doing a good deal of his own thinking. As he gave Sixto a hearty handclasp, his face crinkled up in a wide grin of quick liking. His gray eyes looked searchingly into the face of this other landholder who had decided, as he had, to commit himself to a highly unpopular cause.

"So you are going to declare your faith in the *evangelio* today?"

"Yes," responded Sixto.

Sixto Machado was a small, energetic man with a forthright and friendly attitude. Neither his grooming nor his features gave indication of his status in the community of San José. His rumpled coat and casual haircut might have belonged to one of his peons. Now, however, his piercing eyes flashed with quick humor as he added, "That means I'll have to get married." He laughed shortly. "I'm not against matrimony, you understand.

It's having my own grown children at the wedding that makes it a bit embarrassing. But it has taken courage for you to decide to make a public stand as an evangelical, I'm certain—a man in public office."

"I suppose you might say that I've really made a public confession of my faith before the one I plan to make tonight. In Aguachica."

Vicente, who had joined the group, now added his voice to the ejaculations of surprise.

"Aguachica!" barked Marco. "We have to hear about that!"

"Well, I needed five hundred pesos to buy a cow. With a bag of corn worth thirty pesos, I'd have to take a whole lot of corn down to the market. I took two bags, a donkey load, to Aguachica last week Monday. Well, this girl that works there was to pay me my sixty pesos—a fifty and a ten. But she gave me a five-hundred-peso note and a ten. Well, there was the price of my cow. I almost surprised myself when I heard myself saying, 'This bill you gave me is false.'

" 'Rubbish,' she said, 'we don't deal with false money here.'

" 'For me, since I have become an *evangélico*, it is a false note. It may not be for you, but for me it is."

"She was furious. 'You, an *evangélico*! Well, no wonder you cause trouble over a bill.'

" 'Change the bill for me, will you?'

"Well, she snatched the bill out of my hand, and then she nearly fainted. Her mistake might have made it hard for her, you know."

"Let's stop right now," said Vicente, "and thank God for this testimony that has been given in Aguachica. That's one of the hardest places to get anyone to listen to anything about the gospel."

As Vicente bowed his head in prayer, his heart welled with praise. He envisioned once more the pattern he had viewed from the plane—haciendas with many paths converging at their doors. Here, tonight, were two such hacienda owners, Sixto, from about

five hours east of Santa Inés, and Armenio, a bit over two hours
due west. The work in La Vega was growing too.

When Vicente again visited Armenio he found his host eager
to saddle his horse and accompany him. It was not difficult to
have *cultos* in Las Planadas homes. Armenio had already prepared the way.

"God has actually released me to do it."

"What do you mean?"

"You know that I've been justice of the peace at La Playa?"

Vicente nodded, all attention.

"Well, being a civil authority, I have had contact with the
police and with other municipal officials. So, a few days ago I had
to go in to Aguachica to see the mayor. 'I hear those *evangélicos*
are circulating evil and Communistic propaganda in your neighborhood,' he said. 'If you run across any, let me know. I'll burn
them alive.'

"I said, 'Those *evangélicos* aren't Communistic. Nor evil.
They're against violence, thieving, drunkenness and such. I don't
see anything evil in that, do you?'

" 'Nonsense. You sound as though you're taking their part.'
he said. 'Just bring me them—any of them. I'll burn them alive.'

" 'You'd better start on me then!' I said.

" 'You!' he shouted. He was as purple as if he'd swallowed his
tongue. Then he said if I'd become an evangelical, he was re-
lieving me of my post as justice of the peace. So now I'm free
to occupy myself for a higher cause."

As Armenio led Vicente farther and farther toward the towering range just beyond his hacienda to scores of homes already prepared for the gospel message by his own testimony, Sixto Machado
was enthusiastically contacting his acquaintances for Christ on
the shoulder of a mountain facing the Magdalena Valley above
Aguachica. The region of San José in which Sixto lived was par-
ticularly antagonistic to evangelical beliefs, and Sixto was not
received with the same deference that Armenio's neighbors afforded him.

Because the Machados lived five hours of hard riding from Santa Inés, the Machado family began having *cultos* in their home on Sundays. For several weeks, Vicente went to preach at the services, but his host was so seriously studying the Scriptures that soon Vicente was urging Sixto to hold services of his own.

Financially able to occupy himself with his new-found faith, Sixto attended every Bible conference and every mission-sponsored course he heard of, not only in Santa Inés but in Ocaña and often even in the Cúcuta area. Nor was Sixto averse to traveling into Venezuela if, by making the effort, he could learn more about his faith and how to proclaim it.

He traveled fantastic distances too in putting such information into practice. Though the distance to Santa Inés made it difficult for his family to go, he frequently went far beyond Santa Inés with Vicente, Marco or Armenio on evangelization tours.

The group attending the *cultos* in the Machado home was growing, and Sixto's spiritual insight into divine truths was so keen that he was soon in demand as a special speaker in other congregations. In his many hours on the trail with Vicente he had also caught a vision of the power of prayer.

"Why, even Don Sixto's horse prays," said one of his friends.

He had borrowed Sixto's horse to ride down the trail leading from the Machado hacienda, he explained. Coming to a point where a tiny mountain stream added its song to the glorious view, the horse stopped. Moreover, the horse refused to proceed down the trail until the rider dismounted. This was a spot where Sixto invariably dismounted to rest his horse and to spend time in solitary prayer.

"That's where Don Sixto's horse stops to pray."

For Vicente, Santa Inés had become a springboard to the work in every direction. On one Saturday late in February, Vicente arrived at the Franco home for another expedition into one of the outlying areas. As he waited for Marco, little Emalina wriggled up onto his knee.

"Do you sometimes sleep in the mountains, Don Vicente?"

Vicente ran his fingers gently through the little girl's tousled dark hair. He thought of the cruel nights on El Páramo.

"Yes, Nina, I have slept in the *monte*. What makes you ask?"

"Because we all of us have to go there to sleep now. All but Mamá and Papá. They stay so that they won't get all our stuff in the house. Even if they burn it."

"Who are *they?*"

Little Emalina shrugged her thin shoulders. "I guess the priest and the police that came and took Papá away on Sunday. Mamá too."

"They took them away, Nina?"

"Yes. In a big black car. With handcuffs!" The child spoke in a matter-of-fact tone, but as she turned steady eyes up to Vicente, he watched her pupils widen in the recollection of her fear. "We watched them from the mountain."

Vicente turned to Carmen Díaz who had just joined them.

"I was there—up in the woods—with the rest of them," said the older girl. "They sent word that they were taking the whole family off somewhere to say a mass for them. Nobody knew whether there was anything to it, but Don Marco sent us up to the woods to hide. And sure enough, they came with the car, and pretty soon we saw them take Doña Rosa and Don Marco to the car. We all began to cry because we didn't think we'd ever see them again. We prayed too, Don Vicente."

"I'm glad you thought of that, Carmen. God is the one to turn to in case of any trouble."

"They were away a long time, but God made them bring them back."

"And if they burn the house, they won't find our money," piped Emalina. "I know where it's buried too."

"Well, Nina dear," said Vicente absently, his mind on the renewed threat that Marco faced, "you'd better not tell anybody where it is then."

When he and Marco had started down the trail, Vicente asked, "What's this I hear about your family sleeping in the woods?"

"Well, they've been threatening to burn the house down again.

And the woods are safer for the kids than that thatched shack of ours."

Vicente nodded. Marco had been destitute when he had built his low-roofed, adobe house. In case of fire in the rainless season, the dry palm thatch would fairly explode into flames. The Franco house in Santa Inés had no walled patio to protect them on any side.

"However, now that they've taken us to mass, I feel they've vented their spleen. I don't think they'll do anything more."

"What happened, Marco?"

"Why," chuckled Marco, "didn't our little chatterbox tell you? We're good Catholics again."

"Don't be ridiculous. What happened?"

"Well, it scared me, Vicente. They put handcuffs on us and took us off in a car. There was Padre Senel Mirabal from Aguachica, and eight police. But that's all there was to it. They took us to mass."

"They didn't threaten you?"

"Well, sure. They've done that ever since we came here."

Vicente felt weighted with a heavy sense of premonition as they rode toward Las Planadas. As usual, Armenio had their day fully planned when they arrived. The darker the menace that hung over the head of an evangelical, the more desirous people were to know about a faith that made people brave persecution and death. Specific threats against the Francos and the sufferings that they had already endured had been providing the theme of gossip and comment throughout the area. Many people had been weighing the value of their own beliefs against the prospect of violent death.

The gospel caused division. Some it enraged. To some it brought a hope so splendid that the risk of life itself was not too great a price to pay. Yet, only the telling of the gospel could expose a hungry or a resistant heart, so the evangelicals determined to preach the gospel to all. True, when they dropped in on a home not previously prepared for their visit, they never knew whether to expect a cup of *tinto* or a blast of buckshot.

When Vicente left Marco that evening, he thumped his friend's shoulder affectionately.

"I think we'd better stay out of sight, Marco, during the fiesta of the Carnival. Liquor will be flowing; no need to tempt providence."

The day of the Carnival is one last hilarious fling before the beginning of Lent. In Ocaña, as in other Colombian cities or towns, the festivity began early in the day. Masked merrymakers thronged the streets, crowding noisily about open stands where balloons, fireworks and refreshments were being sold. In front of the church, which faced Santander Square, a number of men were setting off thunderous homemade rockets. Anyone still occupied with more serious business became fair target to the handfuls of corn starch aimed at unwary passersby from behind doorways or shrubs, and thus arrived at his destination with his anger or his amusement showing ludicrously through a clownish mask of starch.

A Carnival queen was chosen and, with her coterie of beautiful girls, led a parade through town. Truckloads of wildly painted Indians whooped in the wake of the dark-haired beauties. A band marched in the parade and played for the dancing that followed. The day ended in a great deal of revelry and drinking, and finally the streets were occupied only by the men who—drunk and armed —could become dangerous at the drop of a hat.

In the sprawling valley town of Aguachica, the same kind of hilarity was in progress. Ramón Nieto, on that Monday of the Carnival, February 25, 1952, was congratulating himself for having come to Aguachica when he fled from the terror in the mountains near El Carmen. The Conservative town teemed with national police. A gunmaker by trade, Ramón was doing a lively and lucrative business between the police, whose trade came to him during the day, and Liberal guerrillas, who slipped down from the mountains by night. In Aguachica he was needed by both sides, a fact which created both safety and peril.

A group of police lounged about the large, barnlike room in which Ramón worked but which was also part of his home. He sighted carefully along the gun barrel he had straightened, and from which he had first rubbed a dark stain that had been matted with short black hair. He shuddered as he thought about the bent barrel, recalling the horror-filled nights his own family had spent on the mountains.

Ramón called to a youth at the door. "Here, Pedro. Set this bottle up in that tree." He handed the gun to the waiting police-man. "Try it out. Let's see you take the lip off without breaking the bottle."

The policeman threw him a bill. "Fast work. I may need this gun before tomorrow. Padre Mirabal wants us to do a little er-rand for him tonight. At Santa Inés."

A chill crept along Ramón's spine as he listened to the cold ring of sadistic laughter evoked by the police officer's remark. He tried to shrug off a sickening horror that clutched his entrails even while he made casual conversation. Behind a bantering com-ment that he forced with deliberate effort from his frozen lips, he was resolving desperately to quit reading his Bible. It was bringing him too much disquietude.

Ramón had acquired a Bible—a fact that added even more ten-sion to his already double life. To be discovered with it could be fatal, but he could not leave that Bible alone. He was reading it whenever he could find a free moment and, like a living force—al-most like a personality, he thought—it was taking possession of his mind. Even now, in the midst of the raucous badinage of his customers, with ever greater insistence, his conscience had been bringing to mind the phrase he had read and reread because he could not tear his eyes away: *Thou shalt not kill. Thou shalt not kill. Thou shalt not kill.*

Should he have left the gun defective so that the bullet might be deflected? He could even have weakened it so that it would, very soon, explode in the officer's hands or his face. But that would only be taking sides. It would still be killing. Ramón brushed the metal filings off his scarred workbench and then pressed his hand against the pit of his stomach. He walked back into the kitchen.

"Have we got some milk?" he asked of his tiny, dark-eyed wife.

"You should see a doctor, Ramón," she said worriedly.

"You'd be sick too, Ana," said Ramón roughly, remembering the bent steel and the matted hair, "if you had to listen to the jokes of the police all the time."

"I sometimes wish we hadn't left Guamalito."

"Nonsense. We'd still be sleeping out in the mountains three nights a week."

"Sleeping out in the rain and cold was better for you than this tension—this trying to keep on the good side of both parties."

"Well, as long as they need guns—"

Ramón knew that as long as he had a suave tongue in his mouth he could play it safe. No, it was not fear of the two political parties that was causing this knot in the pit of his stomach; it was the nagging thought that somehow, by his trade, he was breaking one of those laws that God had written with His own finger on tables of stone. He kept repeating to himself that he was innocent of any crime, that he bore no one either hatred or rancor. Yet his conscience whispered that he was involved, and his soul was weighted down with a crushing sense of guilt.

I may need this gun before tomorrow. The priest wants us to do a little errand for him at Santa Inés.

Ramón moaned. "I'm going to lie down a bit until I feel better," he said. "If anybody comes, tell them I've gone out." He felt like retching. Even during the night, he got up time and again to drink a sip of milk.

He was to hear more of that sinister errand early the following morning as the news swept along the Aguachica grapevine.

"Ramón, oh, Ramón!" Ana Maria rushed into the house. She was pale as death, and her voice was shrill with horror. "They've burned a family alive—*a family,* Ramón!"

"Holy Mother of God," he cried, a hammer slipping from his numb fingers. Sobbing wildly, Ana had covered her face with her hands.

"Think of the children—"

Ramón heard again the casual statement of the police officer who, he knew now, was responsible for this brutal crime.

The priest has an errand for us tonight at Santa Inés.

"The Marco Francos—in Santa Inés!"

Ramón spoke the name as the knowledge was torn from his quaking conscience. Why hadn't he guessed this last night? He could have warned the unfortunate family. He would have. Though he had never tried to make his acquaintance, Ramón had secretly admired Marco Franco for his fearless evangelical stand. Suddenly Ramón Nieto, the man who was trying to play on both sides of the political violence, realized the plight of the victim of last night's raid. *Marco Franco had not been able to play on either side!*

"Why do you say Franco?" asked one of the men who happened to be in his workshop. "Isn't he a Conservative?"

"Yes," said Ramón, paling as he considered the trend of his own hidden convictions, "but Franco was also an *evangélico.*"

"Why don't those heretics keep their mouths shut?" commented another unfeelingly.

"Well, that one will," said a third. "It was Franco, all right. That's who they said they were after."

Anger boiled up in Ramón. "Maybe they don't keep their mouths shut because they've got something important to tell us."

"Such as?"

"That there is a law against murder, for instance. And that our priests are making disciples of hate!" His anger made him forget discretion.

"How many children were there?" asked Ana.

"They say they had eight," said the man who had already heard the news. "And Antonio had a friend staying with him—a Gómez boy."

"Eleven people!" cried Ana, with renewed horror. "Holy Mother of Jesus, have mercy on them!"

"They don't believe on the virgin—those infidels," said one of the men harshly. "She won't help *them,* you can be sure."

Another man, more thoughtful, commented, "Even good Catholics are dying without supreme unction these days."

"Yes," retorted Ramón bitterly, "and good Catholics are the ones who are doing the killing."

"Be careful, Ramón. You almost sound as if you're taking sides with the *evangélicos*."

Ramón spun on his heel. Was he becoming an infidel? Was he losing faith in the only religion he knew anything about? Day after day these questions had grown more insistent and his doubts more clearly defined as he had pursued his surreptitious reading from the Bible that he kept under his mattress. He regretted bitterly that he had not been at Marco Franco's side the previous night, openly fighting in the evangelical cause.

He walked to the back of his house, with visions of the holocaust and the final torment that had swept away eleven lives curdling his blood. He pictured the fire roaring above a family who had been caught unaware and had slept until overcome by the suffocating flames.

It was only after eyewitness accounts began to circulate that he learned that the family had tried to escape but had been driven back into the fire. So swift and deadly had been the conflagration that the crowd had been forced far from the blazing house by the heat. They had stood watching, secure—and probably a little ill—in the thought that they had consummated the evil of their horrible intention. Soon after the Franco family had tried to break out through the doors, there had been a deafening explosion. No one could have survived that.

At least they didn't have to suffer long, Ramón thought.

However he retched miserably the rest of the day and through the long night that followed. The horror of the perishing Franco family never left him.

I could have saved them—

4

Eternal Shadow

"What do *evangélicos* have, Angel, that makes them willing to die for it?"

Angel Pabón, a man who repaired radios and other electronic equipment, squinted at his visitor who had so abruptly opened a subject that, quite obviously, he would rather keep closed. Angel would have preferred to believe that nobody knew of his brother Armenio's open declarations of the evangelical faith. Ramón Nieto, who had asked the question, knew that Armenio Pabón had lost his political position and his security for taking such a stand, but Angel was far too astute to get himself involved by confessing that a member of his family was an *evangélico*.

Ramón shrugged and turned to go. He would get no help in this quarter. He dropped a casual hint that if Armenio ever chanced by his home, he would like to talk to him. Angel eyed him sharply, then twisted a double-edged blade into Ramón's conscience.

"I'll tell Armenio that you have a new design—in guns—that will interest him."

Ramón swung around to stare at Angel, who stood grinning widely—an inscrutable mask of pleasant geniality. What did the man mean? If he guessed at Ramón's interest in the evangelical religion, his thrust had been a deliberately malicious reminder that his trade and his whole manner of life were poles apart

71

from evangelical ideals. Perhaps Angel considered him a spy and was letting him know that he would warn his brother that Nieto had evil designs against him.

Unless one was rashly indifferent to consequences, even an interest in the evangelical faith was a hush-hush matter. One approached only those one could trust. On a number of occasions Ramón had allowed his tongue to betray his inner battle with tradition and his quest for truth. He was to discover that others shared his growing dissatisfaction.

He was standing in the Aguachica plaza one day, when a bleary-eyed derelict tapped him on the shoulder. The man was notorious for his drunken rages. One of the men he had knifed was dead. His wife often fled for her life. Almost anyone in town would take her in, with her children, even if it meant facing the menace of Felipe's revenge.

"Not a chance, Felipe," said Ramón shortly, trying to shrug the shaking hand from his sleeve. If he gave that family any money, it would not go to Felipe for liquor.

"Somebody tells me you have a Bible," Felipe quavered. "Is it an *evangélico* Bible?"

"What's it to you?"

Fear seared Ramón like a shock of electricity. How did this man know that he had a Bible? Was this general knowledge? Who had seen him? He knew his wife would never betray him. But an innocent remark by one of the children could have given him away. Felipe's faltering voice cut in through his fear.

"They say that *evangélicos* have the power to stop drinking."

"That's what they say," said Ramón, still suspicious.

"God knows I've tried to stop," muttered the man. "I need help. I just wondered—would you let me take your Bible for a few days?"

Felipe was serious and pathetically insistent. He came back to the house with Ramón, who was divided between relief and regret at losing the book even for a short time. Now he would not need to fear a search of his home. Now the persistent nagging of his conscience might die down.

But Ramón's quest for truth had been far from finished. He regretted his gesture of generosity, for Felipe refused to let him have his Bible back. As Ramón's frustration increased, he became more recklessly outspoken.

"Why can't a man be free to follow any religion he feels is right?" he asked of José Carrillo, a man whom he had hired to help him. "It's guaranteed by the constitution."

José was a good listener, but he made no comments..

"There was an *evangélico* in Santa Inés," continued Ramón. "The priest and Mayor Vallona threatened him several times. Told him to stop having services. Well, it was the man's religion. It was his religion—what he believed was right." Ramón turned to José to see if the other were listening. "They burned his house down. They burned him alive. And his family."

"Yes, I heard that too."

"Queer what you'll do when you're drunk and part of a mob. The man tried to get out, you know, but they were slashing at him with machetes. One of the guys who went along for the show isn't sleeping nights. He keeps hearing the way those Franco kids were screaming. I don't wonder."

"No, I'm not surprised."

"Sometimes I think Don Marco could have saved his family by coming out. The mob would have been so busy butchering him that the rest might have had a chance to get away." Ramón brushed a hand through his hair with a nervous gesture. "I keep thinking what I'd have done, but it's easier to imagine yourself a hero when you have a week to decide what you'd have done. He had a burning roof over his head and a yelling mob outside. He didn't have time to think."

"Maybe God didn't let him think because He wanted His name to be glorified by what happened."

"Does God ever involve Himself with people, like—" Ramón stopped abruptly. He had been about to refer to God's saving intervention in one of the Old Testament incidents, but it would not be a good idea to admit that he had been reading the Bible.

"God does involve Himself with people when they pray. Sometimes He allows us to get into trials and danger to prove Himself worthy of our confidence. Persecution brings us blessing."

"Us?"

José hesitated, then straightened his shoulders almost defiantly. "I'm an *evangélico* too."

José need not have feared that Ramón would expose him. José, it developed, knew many details of the burning of the Franco home. Ramón plied him with questions, and José told the story so graphically that Ramón almost felt as though he too had been there the night of the Carnival.

The Franco children had been allowed to sleep in the house because Marco had felt that the attention of most people would be occupied with Carnival festivities that night, and there had been no celebrating in Santa Inés. It was only two days after someone had tried to shoot Marco, so they supposed that the opposition would rest for a time.

About midnight Marco sat up in bed, listening. Then the dogs began to bark.

"It sounds as if they are going to steal our chickens, Rosa."

"Oh, dear, and they were almost big enough to lay eggs."

By this time the dogs were going wild until, with three pistol shots, they were silenced.

"That I don't like," said Marco apprehensively. "That shooting of the dogs I don't like at all!" He practically leaped from the bed and ran to the doors to see if they had been carefully barred. He pushed at the heavy poles to make sure that they were securely propped against assault. The killing of the dogs implied a more serious intention than the theft of poultry.

A subdued babble of voices suggested a number of people. Marco was straining to hear something intelligible when a sudden glow of light in the darkened room caused him to look up. The dry thatch roof above him was on fire. Flames appeared at all corners of the house at the same time. The voices outside now rose to a triumphant shout. The Francos knew their home was surrounded by an excited, sadistic mob.

"They're burning the house, Rosa!" Marco shouted a warning at the sleeping children, even while Rosa shook the toddlers awake.

"Quick! Quick!" he shouted. In the smoke and confusion, it was difficult to know where the children were. The youngest cried at first from sleepiness, then screamed with terror. Outside, the sadistic mob was now yelling triumphantly. The roof had caught fire as though saturated with gasoline, and the blaze added its furious roaring and snapping to the compounded din.

With the children crowding at his heels, Marco swept little Santa under his arm. He threw aside the heavy poles propped against the door, then tugged it open, crying as he did so, "I'll try to hold them, Rosa! Children—dash for the woods!"

Just outside stood the mob, staring up in fascination at the wildly burning roof. As Marco darted forward, a masked man leaped from the massed, roaring rabble and, framed in sinister menace by the leaping flames above, lunged at him, swinging a machete. Dodging the murderous weapon, Marco literally tumbled back into the house. Had his assailant not been revealed by the brilliant blaze from the fire, Marco would have been decapitated by the blow.

"The other way, Rosa," he shouted, even while he scrambled back to his feet.

Rosa had already thrown aside the pole from that door. Her baby over her shoulder, she flung the door wide to make a break through the back way. Here another masked fiend thrust a revolver at her chest. Marco pulled her back into the house.

"They want to burn us alive!" she screamed. "O God, help us. Have mercy on our children!"

The heat quickly became unbearable, and the children were shrieking in tortured gasps. While Marco threw up imploring arms to God, the door frames began to burn. The cane roof supports would collapse on them momentarily. Rosa, choking back her sobs, moved purposefully to the bed. Before she would allow her babies to burn she would strangle them. She gathered them to her, with her arms full of pillows, praying frantically that God would spare her this crime of mercy.

Emalina, the little minx, had an idea of her own. She alone knew how many times she had slipped between the knees of adults to get where she wanted to go. She tugged wildly at the door that was hot where her little hands grasped it. Though only a few minutes had elapsed since the first warning, the house had turned into a smoke-filled, blinding inferno. The door swung open.

"Come on!" shrieked Emalina. "They're not here!"

They raced barefoot across the brilliant glow that flooded their back yard and created leaping shadows in the woods toward which they fled. They felt neither thorns nor rocks. The clamor of the bloodthirsty mob and the roar of the fire seemed to pursue them. Just as they entered the cover of the trees, Marco's supply of gasoline for the store blew up with a thundering blast. Above the trees they could see burning debris sailing through the brightly lighted sky.

Although their racing heartbeats sounded in their ears like the pounding of pursuing feet, the mob never traced their flight into the woods.

"You ought to hear Don Marco tell it," José said to Ramón. " 'God,' he says, 'knew just how to get us out at the right time.' "

"You mean he hasn't turned from being an *evangélico*—even yet?"

Ramón's long-hidden thirst to know the reality of this kind of faith now became an urgent need. He bewailed losing his Bible.

"I can get you a Bible," said José.

"Is there anybody who could explain what it says?"

"Vicente Gómez. He's the one you ought to see. I'll get the word to him that you're interested."

Some weeks later, after José had left Aguachica, Ramón was visiting with some other men in the home of a neighbor.

"There's some man asking for you," he was informed. "He says he doesn't want to come in."

Ramón had never seen Vicente Gómez and was surprised to see a plain little man in ordinary if not shabby clothes, wearing a large brimmed hat and carrying two bags of books. Ramón was aware of a tired droop of Vicente's shoulders and of the intense black eyes in his swarthy face. He was impressed with the determined cast of the evangelist's jaw. Still, for some unaccountable reason—perhaps because he had built up a mental image of a distinguished figure in priestly robes—he gave Vicente very little encouragement.

"I was visiting—"

Vicente was used to such rebuffs. He did not remind Ramón that he had made a special trip to Aguachica at his request. "Here are some leaflets," he said. "Perhaps they will answer your questions. Keep searching. The truth will set you free."

"Thank you," Ramón said shortly. He swung on his heel; but before he went back to join his friends, he turned to watch Vicente—stooped with the weight of his bags of books, his big hat flopping with each step—until he was lost in the shadows of the poorly lighted street. Ramón was not to see Vicente again for over two years. Meanwhile, Ramón continued to be the sickly gunsmith of Aguachica who privately read a well-thumbed Bible every free moment.

Beyond three chains of mountains, and removed from Aguachica by many strenuous hours of mule trail, a coffee plantation clung to the steeply sloping sides of Palmira Mountain like nubbly green fleece. The owner of the hacienda, unlike Ramón, was a devout Catholic. Dashing and remarkably handsome, Manuel Contreras was at the heart of all festive gatherings on Palmira. He dined and drank and danced with wholehearted gaiety; he gave alms and hospitality with the same generous abandon.

Anyone in trouble sent for the affable plantation owner, who seemed always to have time for his neighbors. When Manuel was told of a serious illness in the home of one of his acquaintances, he did not hesitate to go, though his act of comfort entailed a ride of two hours down the face of La Palmira and scaling the crest of another mountain. He found the sorrowful family gathered gloomily in a corner of the front *sala*,[1] discussing in low tones ways and means of getting a casket made.

[1]Room, usually living room or parlor.

"Have you sent for the priest?"

A strained look came over the entire group. His hostess shook her head wordlessly and with an air of tragic resignation. Her husband cleared his throat in the brittle silence.

"Go on in, Manuel," he said, avoiding his visitor's eyes. "Maybe Pepito will listen to you."

Manuel looked about the room. Aside from the natural sadness, what was wrong here? Had the youth become unmanageable or belligerent through delirium? Was it fear he sensed? Or disapproval?

Manuel found Pepe propped up on several hard pillows. His eyes were brilliant with fever; his breath came in short gasps of pain. Still, he moved his hand toward Manuel with a gesture of welcome.

"Don Manuel!" Pepe's voice was weak, but his lips parted in a glad smile. "I wished—you would come."

"Why didn't you send for me then, Pepito?" asked Manuel kindly. Taking the youth's burning hand, he added with forced gaiety, "But never mind, Pepito, you'll be out of here in a few days."

The young man flashed his visitor a smile of understanding. "Don't kid yourself. I'm not."

"Now, now, Pepito—"

"That's why I—wanted you to come. Nobody here—can read."

"Should I ride to Aguachica for the priest? I have made it in three hours and a bit when I was in a hurry."

Pepe shook his head, still smiling. "What I want—is that you read—from the Bible." He was squeezing each phrase out between shallow grunting gasps. Each breath meant pain.

"Sure, sure—anything—"

Manuel stopped in midsentence. The shock of Pepe's request had just penetrated his own anxious preoccupation about the boy's condition. He leaned forward and whispered in startled disbelief.

"From the *Bible?*"

Pepe nodded, as though he were not aware that he was dying

and that the book was evil. Raising his eyes to the top of a dresser, he motioned to the book that lay there. With serious qualms, Manuel went to get the Bible and then sat down near the bed with it. He was not sure whether he should read that book. Would Pepe really want him to if he knew how sick he was?

"Read that bit—in John—about the mansions—will you?"

Pepe groped about on the chair near his bed. Glad for any pretext for delay, Manuel helped him lift the glass of water to the parched lips; the lad's hand shook with weakness and the glass rattled against his teeth. Then Manuel fumbled hesitantly in the thick book. Even after he had found the name John in the list of contents, he saw there were four such listings. Which one would be the right one? Pepe lay back quietly on his pillows, waiting with his fevered eyes closed.

"It's the beginning of the fourteenth chapter," he said finally, his eyes still closed.

Awkward because of the trembling of his own fingers, Manuel leafed toward the place. He would read a few sentences, he decided. If the words were sacrilege, he was determined to begin the *rosario*. Perhaps Pepe would not even know he was not reading from the Bible.

> Let not your heart be troubled: ye believe in God, believe also in me. In my Father's house are many mansions: if it were not so, I would have told you. I go to prepare a place for you. And if I go and prepare a place for you, I will come again, and receive you unto myself; that where I am, there ye may be also. And whither I go ye know, and the way ye know.
>
> Thomas saith unto him, Lord, we know not whither thou goest; and how can we know the way?
>
> Jesus saith unto him, I am the way, the truth, and the life: no man cometh unto the Father, but by me.[2]

Pepe lifted up a detaining hand from the sheet. "The sixth verse, Don Manuel—read it again."

[2]John 14:1-6.

Manuel reread the last sentence, then looked thoughtfully at the boy. A tear trickled from between Pepe's closed lids and down his flushed cheek, but a smile lighted his whole face when he opened his eyes to look at Manuel.

"I just found out about—this—a few weeks ago, Don Manuel," he said, his pain still breaking his speech into short phrases. "It's what Jesus did when He died for me—not your prayers, or the priest's—that brings me to the Father."

He closed his eyes again, exclaiming, "Thank you, Lord Jesus, for letting me know in time!" Pepe seemed to be speaking to the Christ with the same consciousness of His presence as though He, like Manuel, were there in the room. Marks of suffering on Pepe's face were replaced by an almost celestial radiance of joy.

Manuel was aware of a strange, painful constriction in his throat. He had seen others—frantic at the thought of imminent death—utter wild, terrified pleas for an extension of their lives. Pepe's prayer was gratitude, or better, it was worship. Was this right? Shouldn't he also pray for his soul?

"Can I say a prayer for you now?"

Pepe's long dark lashes trembled as he opened his eyes momentarily. "The prayer of—Jesus."

"Our Father which art in heaven—"

This was familiar ground again, but Manuel repeated the prayer with the peculiar feeling that he was really hearing it for the first time. Had he never thought about the words before? When he had finished, Pepe said, "The other one too?"

The *other* one? Was there another prayer of Jesus? He saw Pepe's hand wandering toward the Bible. The young man wet his finger and turned a few pages. He shoved the Bible weakly toward Manuel.

"Slowly," he whispered. "Read it slowly—the seventeenth chapter."

Manuel read thoughtfully and distinctly the prayer that Jesus Christ prayed shortly before He Himself was to die.

"What beautiful words," murmured Manuel, when he had finished. Pepe made no response. Manuel thought that he had gone to sleep, for his breathing was somewhat less labored, and he seemed to be resting quietly. Manuel was shaken by the ideas of this book he had been reading, and by the quiet peace in Pepe's eyes.

When Manuel had prayed for the dead or dying, he had always thought that his prayers would lessen God's fierce judgment on the soul in agony. His own intense fear of death drove him to say prayers for others in the secretly selfish hope that others would remember and come to his aid when his own time came in the burning pit where sin was purged from a soul. But Pepe was resting, it seemed, in the confidence of this divine and eternal love. He had no fear. Was he wrong? Was the lad refusing the rites of the church under a false security that was nothing but delusion?

But Jesus—he had read it now with his own eyes—had repeated that those who were His would be with Him. *With Him!* There was no mention of the fury and the judgment of God. On the contrary, Jesus seemed to commend them to a loving Father who even now loved them as He had loved His Son, Jesus. *And this is life eternal that they might know thee. . . .* But he had never thought that one could know God. Was not this why they approached Him through the blessed Virgin?

"Holy Mary, Mother of God—"

Manuel mumbled the prayer softly. He was distracted momentarily by the gentle movement of Pepe's hand as he took the Bible from his grasp, but he finished the familiar prayer before he looked up. "Have mercy on us now, and at the hour of our death—"

Pepe seemed to have sensed Manuel's anxiety. Hardly able to handle the book, Pepe turned to a verse he had previously marked, and lay back with a clearly radiant smile on his face. Manuel read:

> Verily verily, I say unto you, He that heareth my word,
> and believeth on him that sent me, hath everlasting life,

and shall not come into condemnation; but is passed from death unto life.[3]

The smile was there again on the lips crusted and cracked with fever. Manuel raised the youth's head and gave him a drink. Pepe thanked him with his calm, fever-bright eyes. He seemed to be studying Manuel's face. What did the boy want?

"If there's any other—"

"Could I impose?"

"No, Pepito. I have never read such beautiful words before."

Pepe asked him to read the Twenty-Third Psalm, which was also familiar to Manuel. But somehow it too had a new meaning that day.

Pepe had dropped into a quiet sleep when at last Manuel left his chair near the bedside. A strange turmoil of spirit caused him to excuse himself hurriedly from the others in the *sala*. His horse's hoofbeats on the rocky trail seemed to find the rhythm of the psalm that knew no fear of death, only the same quiet assurance that Manuel knew Pepe possessed.

Yea, though I walk through the valley of the shadow of death, I will fear no evil. I give unto them eternal life; and they shall never perish. He that heareth my word and believeth . . . shall not come into condemnation; but is passed from death unto life. And I will dwell in the house of the Lord forever.

Without ever having heard a sermon on the gospel and without an understanding of all the gospel provides, Manuel began talking to people about the love of God and death without fear.

Pepe's death had made a deep impression on him, for the youth had slipped out of his pain with a smile; and Manuel carried a deepening conviction that Pepe had been more concerned for his—Manuel's—soul than for his own. In the very moment of death, he had been secure and confident in his own eternal destiny. He had been spending the last ounce of his strength reaching out his hand to lead a blundering soul—a lost soul—in the direction of deliverance.

Manuel made earnest inquiries about where he might buy a

[3]John 5:24.

Bible, but in those days it was as difficult to acquire this book as it was dangerous to possess it. Months later, Manuel found a man who sold him a Bible, but by that time his normal round of revelry had dulled his great desire to prepare for death.

* * *

It soon had become known that the Franco family had, by some miracle, escaped from the flames of their burning home. Still, their leaving Santa Inés meant that the services there would cease, and Vicente himself had urged that Marco settle for a time in Ocaña, where fellow evangelicals had generously provided for the family's immediate needs.

Marco, since his home and business had gone up in flames, was again destitute, but for Vicente the burning of the Franco home implied disaster far greater than the destruction of his friend's property and livelihood. On his next excursion into the mountains, he stopped to survey the blackened ruins and knelt in the debris and ashes to grapple with a profound discouragement.

Santa Inés had been the focus of a ministry beyond his earlier vision of what could take place through just such a strategic meeting point. Now all lay in ruins. Would this spell an end to the tremendous sweep of the gospel through this territory? Had the enemy conquered?

Vicente groaned and bowed his face to his knees. Tears mingled with the black ashes of his hopes and labors. No man intruded while the pastor wrestled alone in prayer for the souls that had begun to bare their emptiness and their needs to him.

Hours later, Vicente brushed the ashes from his knees and set off to visit sympathizers in the area. He was astounded when several suggested—even urged—that the Santa Inés services should be continued in their own homes. On conferring together as a group, they decided that no one individual should draw the undivided hostilities on himself. The meetings would take place in first one home and then another.

Vicente, taking that first service, looked up from his Bible to announce his text. His face was aglow. With these stout-hearted people, who were risking their lives and everything they owned for the present and the eternal hope that the gospel offered, he would share the story of the fierce persecution of the first Christians.

"They scattered over all the then-known world, friends, just because they could no longer worship in Jerusalem. And wherever they went, they heralded the news that the promised Christ had come. Men had put Him to death, but He had risen. Jesus was still alive. Signs and miracles confirmed their message. People saw the evidence that Jesus was, indeed, still with His disciples.

"And now the great enemy of men's souls has used the misunderstanding of our neighbors—or their lack of understanding of the gospel—and has driven our witness out of Santa Inés, the Jerusalem of these hills. But it appears that burning brands from the Franco house have been cast in several directions. Let us pray together that in each place the fire kindled will increase, and the light from the fire will push back the darkness from other hearts."

Vicente's fervent prayer touched heaven, for the spot fires of gospel witness took hold and spread out. The wind seemed to be blowing almost due north along the Andean ridges between Santa Inés and El Carmen, except on San José, where Sixto Machado flung the message fearlessly into the teeth of a threatening storm of opposition that was concentrated against him.

The northward sweep of the gospel was due, at least in part, to the activities of Armenio Pabón, who knew neither fear nor fatigue as he shared with everyone who would listen the message that had given him peace of heart and mind.

The Pabón home, too far from the Santa Inés congregation to provide a place for their services, became the center of many excursions to the encircling areas. Armenio invited inquirers to his home. The readiness of his warm smile and the dignity with which he was proclaiming this unpopular message made people brush aside their prejudices and give him a hearing. He invited

Vicente to make Las Planadas the center for roving evangelism and accompanied him on these *jiras,*[4] furnishing the horses.

One of Armenio's old friends was Aurelio Sánchez. Together with his grown son Oscar and a friend, Víctor Téllez, Aurelio visited Armenio in his home.

"I'm curious about what my father wants to discuss," Oscar confided to Eliécer Pabón. "Let's stay around."

Presented with such a clear opening, Armenio lost no time telling his friends about his faith in Christ and what it had begun to mean in his life. He mentioned that it had freed him from liquor.

"That's what that old rooster, Marco Franco, keeps saying," muttered Víctor.

"Whatever he now has," Aurelio said, "he's sold on it."

"So am I," said Armenio. "And I'd like to sell you."

They talked far into the night, the two men asking questions, Armenio meeting their objections and answering their arguments. When they prepared to leave, Armenio invited them to return.

"Don Vicente Gómez is having a meeting here tomorrow night. You'll find many of our mutual friends here. Why not join us?"

"I'm coming," stated Oscar.

"Now, Oscar," remonstrated his indulgent father. "We haven't come to any decision about this."

"I've come to the decision that I want to hear more about it."

Not only did Oscar keep his word, but he made a commitment of his life to Christ the following night at the first public evangelical service he had ever attended. He rode home with a hymnal which he had purchased from Vicente.

Oscar went regularly to the meetings and often managed to cajole his fond parents into accompanying him. Soon he was leading family *cultos.* Each time Oscar would propound a new facet of this unfamiliar doctrine, Aurelio would ride across the ridge and discuss it with his friend, Víctor Téllez.

At the crest of Soledad the main trail forked to lead down op-

[4]Trips, journeys.

posite flanks of the mountain—one to his own coffee plantation and the other to Víctor's. At this point where their trails divided, it had been their custom to shoot off their revolvers in exuberant camaraderie and, with echoing shouts, announce to the slumbering neighborhood that they were returning from a night in Aguachica.

One day on the familiar trail Aurelio realized with something of a start that they had been drawn less frequently to the taverns in the valley that lay in magnificent panorama below him. Instead, they had been spending their evenings poring over their Bibles.

Aurelio checked his horse. He was a fine figure of a man as he sat his horse on the summit of the mountain. His strong, masculine features were molded after the regal dignity of his Spanish ancestry. His thoughts, however, were on the emptiness of the life he had been leading. Moses, he had learned from his Bible reading, had chosen hardness and danger, but he had chosen a life of purpose. He felt that he stood at the verge of making just such a choice.

He gazed unseeingly across the Magdalena River Valley. So level is the basin that the river, instead of confining itself to a narrow bed, meanders through the slimy marshes it has produced. From this height it reflects the sun from vast reaches of glistening swamp that extend as far as the eye can reach. Directly below him nestled the villages of Aguachica and Gamarra; La Gloria lay far to his right.

Letting his eyes wander to the left, he saw the ridge above Santa Inés. That was where the Franco home had been burned. He knew they had suffered this indignity and loss because of the gospel that was disturbing his own mind at this very moment. Farther along the mountain chain, beyond Aguachica, was that peak on which lived another of these dauntless evangelicals, Sixto Machado.

Too far away for Aurelio's sharp eyes to find them on the fine thread of trail, four horses were leaving the Machado ranch to dip for a moment behind the shoulder of another mountain only to reappear some time later in another community known as Guadal.

Sixto, at the head of the file, turned to pass a remark to the three men who were following. Arcádeo Mateus had joined Sixto on one of his evangelistic *jiras,* bringing with him Félix Quintero and Antonio Galán, two recent converts from La Esperanza. Arcádeo, a believer for a little over two years, held the seniority as *evangélico* in this group of missionaries.

Sixto pointed. "Down there, beyond that small ridge, are three haciendas. We must not miss them even if they turn the dogs on us. If we get into one house, we may get them all." He continued his briefing. "See that spot of taller trees in that small canyon? Marcelino Cárdenas lives beyond there. He has a Bible and may be reading it."

"You don't own a Bible these days unless you intend to read it," grunted Félix. "It's too dangerous."

"Well," said Arcádeo, "so far it hasn't rubbed off on Marcelino."

Sixto took off his hat. "While we have them in view, let's stop right here and ask God to go before us to prepare the way in those hardened hearts. And to lead us to someone who knows he's lost and is fumbling in the dark for the way to God."

The doors of the nearest cluster of houses were closed and barred from within. Knocking brought no response.

"They recognized us, I guess," Sixto said regretfully.

Before they arrived at the Cárdenas home, they met Marcelino's nine-year-old son Aurelio. The boy wheeled his mule to follow between Sixto's horse and that of Félix.

"My brother has a friend visiting us," he volunteered. "Inocencio Trillos. He's a *Nazareno.*[5] I'll bet he beats it when you come."

"A *Nazareno!*"

"Well, he's finished with that now. So now it looks to me like he's making up for lost time. While those holy guys are swish-

[5]A penitent who goes in processions in Passion Week.

ing around with their long white robes, I'll bet they never get changed inside like you said Jesus could change people."

"And you think Jesus could change his heart?"

Aurelio pondered that for a moment in silence. "Well, a real religious kind of guy like that— What do *you* think?"

"I think Jesus could do it. I used to be pretty religious myself."

Aurelio shrugged. He was not sure about Inocencio Trillos. "Even a guy that's spent seven years helping the priest and wearing robes—like a priest almost?"

"God looks right past the robes into the heart, Son," Sixto said gravely. "When He looks at you, what does He see?"

Aurelio fidgeted on the saddle. He flicked the mule's ears with the end of his reins.

"I think it's the truth, what you tell us. Papá didn't think much of it, but last week an old buddy of his came over and they got to talking. So Papá put it to him straight. 'You think this Bible is a sacred book?' he asked him. 'You think there's anything to this *evangelio?*' So he said, 'Yes,' and Papá said, 'Well, if you say it's the truth—' Well, he didn't come out and say he thought so too, but you ought to hear him argue with this Inocencio Trillos."

"And you?"

"Well, if Papá wouldn't whip the hide off me, sure."

He swung off his mule, for they had reached the Cárdenas yard. "I'll take your horses, Señor Machado." He gathered the reins of the horses in his hands, but turned back. "Señor—"

"Yes, Son."

"Could a person be an *evangélico* on the sly, like? Without people—without my father knowing?"

"There's another side to that question, Son," Sixto said gently. "Did Jesus, God's Son, die on the sly—without people knowing?"

Aurelio studied the serious, compassionate face of his neighbor, then shook his head. "I see what you mean, Don Sixto. He did it in public; and they beat Him up too."

Amelia de Cárdenas came out, warmly welcoming Sixto and his friends. She ushered her guests into the house where a young stranger swung carelessly around to meet them, as though he had not been watching them from a window.

"Inocencio," said Amelia, after she had introduced them, "will you take our friends into the *sala?* I'll have some *tinto* for you in a few minutes. In the meantime, you can become acquainted."

Inocencio wore a plaid flannel shirt jauntily opened halfway down his broad chest. A machete swung on the right-hand side of a brass-buckled belt, while the hilt of a slender dirk protruded from an ornate holster at his left. It was set at a businesslike angle of instant accessibility, and the hard cast of the young man's chin suggested an acquired knowledge of its efficient use.

While the men drank their *tinto* and spoke on various generalities, Inocencio—his chair tilted back at the wall—studied them warily. Suddenly he asked bluntly, "Are all four of you *evangélicos?*"

"Yes," said Sixto without hesitation. "And young Aurelio tells me that you have spent seven years as a *Nazareno.*"

"Not all in a stretch. I had my military service after I'd been in the brotherhood for three years. I finished my pledge when I came out of uniform. So you see," Inocencio grinned self-importantly, "you're not the only people who take their religion seriously."

"You don't look too much like a person who seeks seclusion for its own merit—or asceticism," said Sixto smiling. "Tell me, what made you become a *Nazareno?*"

"Asceticism?" Inocencio laughed. "A general concept carried in the minds of the piously gullible! All the brotherhood required of us was the robes—and confession on Good Friday."

"And so you spent seven years with no other motive than to wear a robe?"

Inocencio squirmed before the patent incongruity of his own story. "Well, I saw one of the priests with a white robe, and asked with what object he came. He said it was to serve God. This was what I wanted to do too."

"And?"

Inocencio hitched his chair self-consciously then exploded de-

fensively. "Well, who can think of purgatory without fear?
Doesn't a man do what he can to lessen this torment in the fire?
I thought—"

Sixto quickly leafed to a page in his Bible and held the place
with his finger. Here was the man they had prayed for—a man
who knew he was lost—who was fumbling in the dark toward
peace of mind. He waited for Inocencio to go on. The latter
glanced, as if for support, at Alfredo Cárdenas, a young man
about his own age who had come to stand in the doorway during the conversation. That young man shrugged and grinned
sardonically.

"I daresay," he said, with a glint of amusement in his eyes,
"that just one of the *parrandas*[6] in Guadal helps as much to make
a man forget hellfire as seven years of wearing skirts."

Inocencio flushed a furious red, and Alfredo laughed heartily
at his friend's discomposure. Just then Alonso, his older brother,
came in with their father. Amelia de Cárdenas went to a locked
cupboard and brought out a Bible. Inocencio found himself a
part of an evangelical *culto* before he was aware of what was
taking place. He sat with glum attention through the service,
obviously ill at ease.

Afterward, Arcádeo Mateus, who sat near him, tried to reopen
the subject of the young man's personal need. But now Inocencio
was unresponsive, even hostile.

Later, on the trail, the evangelicals prayed for the family, and
for the hard-faced young man who had given seven years of his
life to extinguish the terror of death and of the judgment of God.

[6]Revel, carousal, gay time.

5

A Pact with the Invisible

Two hundred and fifty people came to celebrate Christmas with the evangelicals on December 20, 1952, on Cerro Bravo, three miles from the main road and Santa Inés. The congregation had long since outgrown Don Cristóbal's veranda and patio. Paper festoons and flowers fluttered gaily from arched branches of a grove of trees. Board seats, laid across logs, completed the rustic meeting place. People had spent hours on the trails to come from distant communities in all directions.

Marco Franco and his family were present—this time as guests. Vicente moved from one cluster of visitors to another. He knew most of them, for he had visited them in their homes. For some, this would be the first evangelical service of their lives; for others, the presence of these newcomers meant a joyful triumph, the reward for patience in the face of rebuffs and discouragements, the answer to many earnest prayers, the wages for grueling hours in the saddle to make just these contacts for the cause of Christ.

During the afternoon service, people who had recently made a commitment to Christ were given an opportunity to make a public confession of their faith. Nine took advantage of that opportunity. Juana Lazzco and her consort, Germán Vanegas, were among the first.

After the service, the entire crowd followed the band from the Ocaña church to the river's edge where ten more made an open declaration of their stand by public baptism. As the sun lowered toward the west, the crowd dispersed, having been given a hearty invitation to attend the Ocaña program on Christmas Eve.

The Ocaña church had grown during the days of danger. Israel Navarro, soon to become one of the staunchest pillars of the Ocaña church, had begun to slip into the meetings a year earlier. Now a baptized believer, he had been instrumental in persuading many of his friends to come to the Christmas program. The building was packed.

An uninvited participant shuffled in during the last part of the program, however, and it became obvious at once that he had not come to enjoy the songs or the recitations of the children. He began talking without any consideration for the audience as he crowded rudely into a bench beside Francisco Velásquez and his brother.

"This is a bunch of Liberals, isn't it?"

"We really don't take any part in politics, Ramón."

Ramón Briquel shifted about and began talking to another man. Israel Navarro, seated near Francisco, whispered, "Let's pray. This man is here for no good purpose. He's dangerous."

They began quietly to pray. Ramón made a few more disturbing moves, but soon he got up, mumbling to himself, and left the building. After the service had proceeded normally to its close, Francisco moved over toward Vicente and the missionary, who were greeting people at the door as they prepared to leave.

"Ramón may be lurking around outside," he warned. "I didn't like his attitude."

No sooner had Francisco voiced his warning when Ramón stepped into the crowd near the door, growling a threat. Emma, Francisco's wife, knew the man. This otherwise retiring little woman imposed her small frame in his path.

"Look, Ramón," she said, "we're quietly celebrating a Christmas fiesta. We are pacifists."

Ramón, a tall, heavy-set man, thrust a belligerent face into hers. Though she clung to his arm and tried to get in his way, he brushed past her and struck the missionary a brutal blow. Then he drew his gun. Before the men near him could snatch it from him, he had pulled the trigger three times in quick succession.

As the missionary dodged to avoid the shots, the congregation fled into the patio or threw themselves under benches. Women screamed. Children shrieked with terror. Men yelled conflicting orders at Vicente who, with several others, pounced on Ramón. After a short scuffle, they shoved him out the door and barred it after him.

Slowly the terror subsided and people came out to join hands in quiet praise to God who had preserved them all from the blackguard's bullets which had been fired into the crowd at close range. Any or all of the bullets might have been fatal.

Had there been casualties, the evangelicals would have had small recourse for justice. Violence was commonplace. Members of each political faction now had brutalities and losses to avenge, and assassins were settling personal scores by committing crimes which were horrible beyond description, without fear of police intervention. In fact, Laurenista police, far gone in the habit of murder, were themselves so often responsible that they became known as Bluebirds—blue being the Conservative color, and "bird" the local slang for villain.

With the approach of the local elections scheduled for the middle of March, a wave of increased violence swept across Colombia. Military police and guerrilla bands roamed the countryside, bent on terrorizing Liberal voters—raping, murdering, and ruthlessly destroying property. Launches and canoes on the Magdalena River were loaded to dangerous levels with refugees packed together with any household goods they had been able to carry with them.

Among several of Vicente's acquaintances who were killed in those days was a Colombian pastor, Carlos Julio Tovar. Years before, Carlos, an orphaned bootblack, had wandered into the Cúcuta church. Because of his uncouth appearance—the boy spent his nights on park benches—some members of the church were less than gracious to him. Others doubted his motives for returning again and again. But he had found the peace he sought in the evangelical faith and had committed himself wholly to Christ and to sharing his discovery.

Already conditioned to public scorn and abuse by his trade and way of life, he was utterly devoid of inhibitions or fear. He used his shoeshine box as the pulpit over which he preached the gospel of Jesus Christ to customers or companions. He had had frequent encounters with police officers because he distributed tracts openly and had been jailed several times for this indiscretion.

About February 12, 1953, he left Barranca Bermeja for a trip downriver. On the boat, a national policeman heard him speak to a fellow passenger about the claims of Christ. The policeman would have killed this *evangélico* on the spot, but the captain of the launch would not permit it.

"If you want to kill him, do it on land!"

Arriving at Puerto Wilches, the officer took Carlos to the police station where they confiscated his Bibles. Without trial or sentence, they set him to carrying cruelly heavy loads of wood to the local slaughterhouse, where on the night of February 17, they stabbed him twice with their bayonets and threw him into the Magdalena River, whose waters, cumbered with floating corpses, ran red in those days.

Caught in the current, Carlos' body must soon have been carried into shallow water. At five o'clock the following morning, he appeared at the home of a believer in Puerto Wilches. Someone informed police of the wounded man's presence in this home. Police searched the house, found Carlos and clubbed him to death. This time the river carried his lifeless body downstream.

Since Liberals were again kept from voting, the elections changed nothing. Still, the four-day Bible conference that had been planned for the thriving Santa Inés evangelical groups took place as scheduled at the end of March. To prevent concentration of unfavorable attention toward one place or family, this conference was held at Marisonga, ten miles off the road, almost as near to the home of the Mateus brothers as it was to Armenio Pabón's.

One hundred thirty people gathered daily under a thatched roof erected to provide shade from the sun. During the year since the Franco home had been burned, scores of mountaineers had openly declared themselves evangelicals in the midst of determined persecution. Marco Franco, as chipper as ever, moved among his former customers, exchanging testimonies of God's grace and power in their lives or sharing the wonder of such a gathering in this place.

During the conference, Aurelio Sánchez and his charming wife, Ninfa, from Soledad, made a public committal of their lives to Christ, as did their son, Luís. Lorenzo Galvis, a new believer from Palmira, urged Vicente to visit his neighborhood. He was overjoyed that Carmito Ballina, whom he had brought to the conference, had made a decision for Christ.

"Now I won't be alone on Palmira!" exclaimed Lorenzo, tears in his eyes betraying the difficulty and loneliness of his stand.

The climax of the conference came on Sunday. Armenio Pabón announced that the elders of Las Planadas congregation had met with Vicente and the missionary and that they were to organize into a recognized church. They planned to build a chapel and had chosen the name Bethel for their congregation.

"Bethel," said Vicente, his tired face aglow, "means House of God. Bethel was a place of worship and sacrifice, a place of vision and a vow to serve God. What better name could a congregation choose for itself than Bethel? Bethel was the first step in claiming a whole country for God. Let it be so, here in this land."

Vicente remained in the area to enjoy another tramp through the mountains with Marco and Armenio Pabón. A new believer often opened up an altogether new neighborhood, so these *jiras* were taking them farther and farther into unreached territory.

Though most of the mountain people were unaware of the true causes, political tensions in Bogotá were reflected in increased guerrilla activities. Terror of attack or of reprisals kept many of the mountaineers locked up in their homes, suspicious of even the visiting evangelicals.

Colombian President Laureano Gómez had not only used

martial law to drive Liberals from the polls, but he had been
relentlessly using a bloody civil war to drive them clear out of
public life. Now he had scheduled a constituent assembly for
June 15, and it was known that he planned to revise the constitution along totalitarian lines. Colombians knew that without army intervention the powerful Gómez would win even more
power.

President Gómez suspected wrongly that the army chief of
staff, Lieutenant General G. Rojas Penilla, was plotting against
him. The Colombian army had been almost unique in its eighty-
seven-year record of staying out of politics. But when Gómez
suddenly demanded on June 13 that Rojas be fired, top military
men stuck to their general and flew him to Bogotá for a military
coup. When he arrived, his loyal troops had already seized control of public buildings and communications. That night the
national radio announced that Rojas had the support of the
armed forces, the police and representatives of both parties. In
a midnight broadcast, President Rojas appealed for "no more
bloodshed" and said the army had assumed power to prepare for
"clean elections."[1]

Rojas never kept his promise for elections; and by the end
of the year the second wave of violence, more brutal than the
first, had begun to surge through the land. Rojas became known
as "the dictator."

Throughout those tense months, the evangelicals had never
once ceased to go forth with their fearless witness. New converts
were quick to urge Vicente and other older Christians to hold
cultos in their homes so that the blessing might also reach to
their own circle of friends and neighbors.

One day Vicente and his friends, Armenio Pabón and Marco
Franco, took a trail that led them east of Los Cerros. Carmito
Ballina, their host for the evening service, had joined the *jira*
that would end at his home. They stopped at the coffee plantations within a few hours' ride of the Ballina home to invite every-

[1]"More than any other Colombian of this century he dominated his country's life. . . . Then—simply, surprisingly—Laureano Gómez, 64, slid like a
wilted leaf down history's drainpipe" (*Time* magazine, June 22, 1953).

Like colorful, segmented caterpillars, Colombian homes join in a solid front that follows the contours of the streets. Above the narrow doorstep that extends the full length of the block are bands of paint, red (Liberal) or blue (Conservative), identifying the political sympathies of the owners.

Liberal leaders were lined up on these streets and shot. Their corpses were left unburied, and the cobblestones became slippery with blood, while Colombian military police and guerrillas continued their fearsome search.
—El Carmen

Don Marco Franco, his family and a few visitors near his home at Santa Ines that was destroyed by fire. Little Santander, once victim of extreme clubfoot, is in the foreground.

Aguachica. Because terror stalked the streets during the violence, security became more important than light or air. Many windows were bricked in. A ten-foot wall, often spiked with shards from broken bottles, encircled patios at the rear of homes.

El Carmen. When military police invaded El Carmen on November 15, 1949, they proceeded first to the city square and tore down the newly erected statue of Liberal idol Jorge Gaitan. The base, with Gaitan's name effaced, still stands, monument of the Colombian violence.

Don Sixto Machado, martyred pastor of Nazaret Church. At San Jose.

Sunday at Belen Church—before the roof was up. At La Vega del Gusto.

Don Vicente Gomez, faithful pastor of all the churches.

Jose Pinzon with Manuel Garcia's oldest son in front of El Salvador Church. On La Quiebra.

Cane and thatch home of Don Andres Vargas. At Puerto Oculto.

ESSO Gasoline—delivery service.

Don Vicente Gomez, his wife Carmen and his three children.

Marco Franco family—First Row: Santander, Jonas; Second Row: Natividad, Dona Rosa, Emalina, Alicia, Antonio; Third Row: Don Marco.

Don Vicente Gomez near his home in Aguachica. The horse was presented to him by grateful parishioners.

Colombian newspaper accounts relate "Regime of Terror."

one to the service. The visiting evangelicals stimulated interest and curiosity, and prompted several to promise that they would attend the *culto.*

"We'll probably not find anyone at the Chogó place," said Carmito, grinning. "If you want to have a *culto* there, you have to sneak up on them."

"How's that?"

"Well, we have to come down this canyon wall and ford the stream before we can get there. If they identify my horse or suspect that we are *evangélicos,* they'll all make for the woods behind the house."

"Did you catch them at it?"

"No, but José Pinzón, a man who works at the plantation, told me that Don Salvador has given that kind of orders. This José told me about a group of men who are plotting to attack *evangélicos.* He was asked to join them."

"And was José warning you against attack?"

"No, I don't think that was his idea. They're not afraid of the likes of me, but they don't want you in Palmira territory."

"Then this José is friendly, is he?"

"I can't say he's so friendly," said Carmito, "though he says he argued that as long as the *evangélicos* weren't molesting anyone, he wouldn't join any attack against them. 'We'd better find out first what they're teaching,' he says he told them."

"Is that what he came to you about—to find out what we're teaching?"

"I suppose it was. He came over to my house with a friend. He was carrying a bottle and his guns that first time. I'm not sure what he expected."

"He was prepared, I'd guess, to accommodate friend or foe. Has he been back?"

"Yes. That man has something on his conscience. He kept bringing up the judgment of God. And so I told him, 'I've got a little book here that's wonderful. It tells about God's judgment, but it also tells about His mercy.' So he borrowed it—the gospel of Mark. He came back some days later and asked to buy it."

"So you sold it to him?"

"Well, no," admitted Carmito. "It was the only one I had, and he'd already read it through—"

Vicente nodded. "Well, we may sell him a Bible today, instead. He sounds like a man who already knows his need."

"Can a man who has sold his soul to the devil—can such a man be saved? If not—"

"What makes you say that?"

Carmito told his friends the story José had related to him. As a young man, José had entered the brotherhood of the White Nazarenes of El Carmen. His real motive, he admitted, had been to find a way of accumulating wealth without undue effort, and he had been advised that religious service in that order would give him the greatest prestige.

He also desired the blessing of the church. He had a superstitious idea that the handling of sacred objects would place some sort of supernatural power on him for life. He told Carmito about allowing his dagger and certain charms to lie in the sacred sepulcher so that the potency thus attained would assure their effectiveness in time of physical danger.

When he observed how deeply the priest of El Carmen was involved with the political intrigues and atrocious crimes committed during those first months of the violence, José became completely disillusioned and left the brotherhood. Convinced that all the teachings of the church were mere fantasy, he no longer attended either mass or confessional.

With the loss of his faith in God, he also lost all the restraints the confessional had once provided. His desire to become rich without effort remained his chief obsession and was to lure him toward his utter undoing. An avid reader, he devoured books on Communism and the Black Mafia. Finally he began dabbling in spiritism.

Here, at last, he found a book that not only promised power and wealth but outlined the secret, step by step, of conjuring up the presence of Satan. If he were successful in summoning the

Satanic presence, he thought, he would be shown ways and means to the riches he desired.

With this fixed intention, José closed himself up in his room, alone, and studied the book, taking pains to follow each detail of the evil instructions. At last, as hours passed, he became aware of a presence near him, and he began to shake in terror. At the same time, he grew conscious of fearsome, unearthly sounds. Whether or not they entered by way of his ears, he was too agitated to know. So evil were the insinuations of the demonic presence that José thought himself already in hell.

A pact with Satan, José began to understand, meant a committal of body and soul. This revelation shocked him to his senses. He would not be enriched, but enslaved! He closed the book with finality. He would break off the seance.

Quaking in every limb and still conscious of the presence he had invoked upon himself, he went to his room, hoping to sleep off the evil incantation as he would a bad dream. But his agitation increased; he wondered how he would live through the endless night. Having proven beyond doubt that the realm of spiritual personalities is reality, reflection on the possible consequences of his contact with the Satanic presence intensified his abject terror of the sinister, tangible, though unseen power.

"He's still afraid to be alone," said Carmito. "He's obsessed with the subject of the judgment of God. If the devil's real, so is God. And so is hell. I think that's why he told me so much—he's looking for help. I didn't know what to tell him. Is there hope for a man who has sold his soul to the devil? He seems to have gone too far to stop the evil powers."

"What do you mean?"

"Well, immediately after that night when he refused to go through with his pact with the devil, he began to have enemies. He had begun to drink more heavily, and one night he and some others were passing a cemetery when he got into an argument, and someone stabbed him. He got to the home of his sister, still drunk, and nearly unconscious from loss of blood. She spent the night doing what she could for him, but toward morning he knew the devil was bent on getting him, one way or another. His sister did not deny it when he told her he was dying.

"His head had begun spinning, and he started blacking out one time after another. So, while he was sinking like that, he implored God not to let him die without hope—to have mercy. 'If You give me life,' he said, 'I'll serve You from now on.' Well, he lived, though I guess it was touch and go for a long time."

"So he really desired to find his way to God?"

"I guess so, Don Vicente. I think he tried in the only way he knew. He had them send for the brothers of the Virgin of El Carmen. José did everything they told him. He made vows to St. Anthony too, since they felt St. Anthony had helped him in his illness. Then his sister brought a sacred heart from Ocaña, or tried to. The thing came apart during the jolting of the car on the road, and he could see that this sacred heart was completely hollow."

Carmito clucked encouragingly to his mule. The crumbling edge of the trail had given way under one rear hoof, and the animal clawed for new footing in momentary panic. The men could hear a rock's dwindling staccato as it bounded from one rocky eminence to another on the way to the bottom of the precipice.

"Don't let him graze, Carmito. They don't watch where they're going—"

"I know. I just wasn't paying enough attention." Carmito gathered his reins more firmly in hand. "Anyway, he told his sister that he had lost all faith."

"Still, he fears the judgment of God?"

"Yes, and he's convinced he is being revenged by the evil spirits. He's just been kicked off one plantation because of his advances to a girl there. He doesn't know why he made the advances. He says he has pleasure in nothing—that all he can think of is the judgement of God."

Vicente reined his mule where the trail broadened into a shelf. He slid from the saddle, and the other men followed his lead without comment. They knew, from many previous expeditions with Vicente, that he wanted to pray.

"Jesus cast legions of devils from a man who had been possessed for many years. He cleansed Mary Magdalene. Whatever pact José Pinzón has made, God's power can free him from it. I believe he is being harassed because he failed to fall into the devil's trap. May God help us to bring this man the message of release."

An aura of prayer and deep seriousness remained with them as they proceeded to the plantation of Salvador Chogó. As their mules clattered to a stop a few feet from the raised porch, they came upon a silent drama that was all too clear and not very encouraging.

José Pinzón, a pale young man of slender build, sat reading a book. His face was in shadow, but defiant obstinacy was chiseled in every unyielding line of his rigid body. His master, Salvador Chogó, stood near him, the scowl on his flushed face spelling out his impotent rage. A third man wavered just at the corner of the house around which, in all probability, the rest of the family had disappeared.

Ignoring the tense scene, Carmito hailed his neighbor heartily and swung from his mule. He mounted the hewn-stone steps of the porch and held out his hand. Salvador shook it. An expression of cornered helplessness slowly replaced the anger that still lurked in his rather curt reply.

"I've brought some friends, Don Salvador," prompted Carmito.

"Dismount, dismount!" said their host with forced heartiness, the innate hospitality of isolated mountain living overcoming his prejudices. José here will take your mules to water them."

The pale young man moved abruptly and slammed his closed book to the table with irate vigor. The other laborer came over also and nervously fumbled with the bridle of Vicente's mount while Salvador led his guests into the house.

"Sit down," said Salvador, swishing at a backless bench with his pocket handkerchief. Having seated his visitors in a row, like pegs in a shooting gallery, he pulled out a hide-covered chair and straddled it to face them. Carmito spoke awkwardly into the silence, for their host was not giving them any encouragement.

"We came to ask permission to hold a meeting."

"Well," said Salvador uncertainly, after a short hesitation, "if it's something good, you can speak."

"It's the Word of God that we wish to read," said Vicente. "And then if you have any questions, we will be glad to answer them."

He crossed over to the doorway where he had set down his bag of books and handed hymnals to his friends and one to his host. He was making time for the two laborers to come in, but it seemed that he was to be disappointed; for when they did come back onto the porch, he heard the timorous man urge José not to go in. Vicente was unable to hear what the latter replied, but José stood stolidly at the door, refusing to be drawn away but not deigning to enter.

Salvador ignored José deliberately—a transparent snub for the man's open insubordination. He moistened his finger while he turned clumsily to page sixty-one, the hymn that Marco suggested they sing. Vicente broke the awkward lineup of *evangélicos* by remaining on his feet at a place where the light from the open door fell on his book, although none of them needed to read the words except their host, who did not join them in singing.

Nor silver nor gold hath obtained my redemption. . . .

The seat Vicente had vacated was the one nearest the door where José still leaned against the frame, though outside the room. As Vicente placed his books on top of his other literature, he graciously invited the young man to take his seat.

"I'll be standing as I read the sacred words of God, anyway."

"*Gracias*, Señor," replied the young laborer, sullenly polite. "I'm all right here."

Vicente read the third chapter of John's gospel, and began to speak about the new birth, explaining the enigmatic expression Jesus had used in speaking to Nicodemus who, though a highly educated, religious man, had failed to understand what Jesus meant.

"Yet the expression becomes very clear when you understand that Jesus really was talking about a new life—a new spiritual life that wipes out the guilt and the fears and the inclinations natural to man and provides a divine power to live a life befitting the new, God-given nature."

As Vicente elaborated, with clear, pithy illustrations of lives revolutionized, of fears relieved, of peace that passes human language to describe, José moved into the room. He listened with great attention, but his face grew more and more distorted by some inner reaction. Was it animosity? Or conviction of need?

When Marco prayed, Salvador rose to his feet with the other men. Not so José. He sat rigidly erect, his lips twitching back from clinched teeth, the skin drawn white over the knuckles of his hard fists.

After they sang another hymn, Vicente hesitated over putting away the books. Should he offer this morose young man a Bible? Would he consider himself insulted? Would the animosity that showed in his face break into open violence? He withdrew a tract from his bag and offered it to José, who accepted it but quickly closed his hand over it as though to hide it. Did this furtive action represent the jealous guarding of a treasure? Or a determined move to prevent anyone from snatching back this piece of incriminating evidence against the *evangélicos?*

"Come to the service at Don Carmito's home tonight," said Vicente. He offered his hand to José, who ignored it. His host was far more gracious. Afterward, on the trail, they discussed the strange attitude of the sullen young laborer.

"I'm afraid we reached the conclusion that because *we* know what that young José needs, he'd recognize it too."

"The devil must still have a hold on his mind," replied Carmito. "He sure didn't seem receptive to anything. Just suspicious. By the way he acted toward you, I'm wondering if we should even have let him know about the meeting tonight. If he joins up with those others, it could mean shooting on the trail. I'd sure hate to have brought you into danger."

"We have to invite them all, Carmito," said Marco.

"You'll get used to antagonism by the time you've been an evangelical a little longer," counseled Armenio. "You'll learn to commit everything to the Lord. He can take care of us and the people on the trail. And He can change that young rascal's heart too."

At the Chogó plantation, as Carmito had suspected, the family reappeared from the woods behind the house as soon as the evangelicals were out of sight. They were bursting with curiosity.

"What kept you?"

Salvador glowered at José, remembering the latter's obstinacy in remaining on the porch.

"Couldn't get José to move. I thought he wanted to hear the *evangélicos,* but he sure didn't act like it after they got here. Just pigheaded."

José did not reply. His mind was in turmoil. What had the preacher meant by the new birth? Was there truly a way to escape the terrible judgment that haunted his days and made his nights long battles with terror?

Poking around among some old books not many weeks later, José found a small volume of the four gospels that had been soaked by rain and was warped and mildewed through neglect. He discovered that the gospel of Mark, which he had earlier tried to buy from Carmito, was a part of the contents. He reread it, then began on the other gospels. As he read on, the musty little book became very precious to him. He approached the señora, requesting that she sell it to him.

"I'm letting you read it for nothing. I want to keep it because the padre gave it to me." Though abused and allowed to lie in disuse, she was loath to sell it. At last, however, she yielded and took his money.

José took his treasure up to his room where he read and re-read some of the passages many times. He began to understand what the gospel could mean in his life, but he did not understand how he could appropriate its power.

As time went on, again and again he identified the evangelicals on the trails that laced together the isolated mountain plantations. As José watched them, knowing that these men would be driven from some homes at gunpoint, he pondered on the spiritual force that caused these men to risk their lives repeatedly.

Were they risking their lives so that they should gain the life Jesus had spoken about? What kind of life was this? Vicente had spoken about a spiritual birth. José did not understand how one could procure this birth—this new spiritual life.

Though Vicente, Armenio and other evangelicals became more or less frequent visitors at the plantation, some inner force restrained José from speaking. He did not stop to consider that the evil power that flayed his soul with fear and hopelessness was the spiritual enemy of the claims of Christ, and that he would have to withstand the one to gain understanding of the other. He only knew that he was often dejected after the evangelicals left, deeply disappointed that they had not chanced to speak on the subject of his own despair.

After the evangelicals' first visit to the Chogó home, the family did not flee to the woods as they previously had done. Salvador's attitude was that of baffled curiosity.

"What's so evil about the *evangélicos'* teaching?" he challenged defensively after one such meeting, responding to his wife's unspoken censure.

But when Vicente appeared at their home not much later, Salvador greeted him somewhat uncertainly. He studied Vicente's gaunt face, the hollow cheeks, the intense dark eyes that met his unflinchingly and with undeniable concern for him, personally.

"Come in and sit down," he said at last. "Maybe we can scare up a cup of *tinto* for you."

José sauntered into the room with his forefinger in his mildewed book of gospels. He was hoping Vicente would explain some passages he had marked. Both men were distracted by the rather heated quarrel that could be heard coming from the kitchen. Vicente got up hurriedly to meet Salvador, who entered quietly but red of face.

"Just a drink of water, Don Salvador. There is no need—"

"While I'm head of this house," growled Salvador, "there will be *tinto* for my guests!" Then, somewhat defensively—or to convince even himself—he pursued the subject that had brought on the family opposition.

"Didn't you say Eulogio Quintero went up to San José to make himself into an *evangélico?* He was *asking* for trouble, then."

"Not for trouble, Don Salvador. He was looking for peace. If he has trouble because he has accepted the gospel, it will not be able to rob him of that peace."

"I never thought you'd be able to trap any of the hombres in these mountains. First you got Lorenzo Galvis. Then Carmito. And Eulogio from La Esperanza. And Víctor Téllez—"

Vicente's eyes lighted. "So you've heard of Víctor Téllez? Then you know, of course, what a change the gospel has made in his best friend, Aurelio Sánchez. With that kind of a testimony of God's power right on the other side of the ridge, Don Víctor could hardly help being convinced."

"A testimony? *One?* Why Aurelio has taken that whole Franco tribe to live on his plantation. That whole family is a bunch of preachers. Aurelio isn't a talker like that Marco Franco."

"You do keep up with the news, don't you? Don Marco just moved there a few weeks ago."

"He got put off that farm in Algodonal, didn't he? He could have kept it, if he'd kept his mouth shut."

"When the gospel has brought a man into the very presence of God and the contact has completely changed his life, he can't keep from sharing it."

"If this gospel's as powerful as all that, maybe I'd better not let you read me any more out of it. I'm not sure I want to meet God."

"Do you think that by not meeting God now, you can avoid meeting Him to make an account of your life at the end?"

Salvador's face betrayed the conviction in his soul, but he was saved from the necessity of an answer by his daughter's haughty entrance with their *tinto*. She set it down near Salvador, then turned in silent disdain and swished out of the room.

José clenched his fists lest he scream out his own terror of meeting God. His need to understand more and to acknowledge his secret desperation tore at him from within, but the evil powers to whom he had once nearly bargained his soul away seemed to bind him. He remained glumly silent. His face showed only a clouded brow and an obdurate set of his lips.

Vicente could have no way of knowing that this young man, who so often appeared sullen and morose, was desperately longing for help. Even when José asked Vicente if he had a Bible for sale, it appeared that his question was merely to satisfy his curiosity about the contents of the heavy bags.

"Yes, Señor Pinzón," said Vicente in answer to his question. "And the Bible is the best Book there is."

José held the book in his hands, knowing that he must have it, but a perversity beyond his control caused him to blurt, "But I haven't any money."

"They don't cost much. I can sell you one for three pesos. That's not much for a book like this!"

The Bible José held had a good hard cover, made possible at that price because the printing had been subsidized. José knew it could easily be sold for twice that amount. Still he heard himself say, "The sum I have is two pesos."

"I can't sell you the Bible for two pesos, but I have a New Testament for—"

"Well, then," interrupted José curtly, "I can't buy it."

José's attitude did not invite further sales talk. He began firing questions at Vicente that might indicate he had never listened to anything Vicente had told them. Did *evangélicos* believe in God? Did they believe in a Holy Spirit?

Vicente met his rather rude questioning patiently, answered simply and with no bombastic show of theological superiority.

"This is what we teach—a triune God. God, the Father, is made understandable by the Son, Jesus, who was God incarnate.

The Holy Spirit is the Son's Representative in the hearts of those who have received the Son."

Vicente left without even suspecting the need that José had so successfully hidden. So urgent was that need that, when work on the Chogó plantation slackened, José found another job in the vicinity where the evangelicals were more active.

By chance—if there is such a thing in the eternal destinies of man—he found a New Testament in the home in which he next found work. From the time he took it to his room, he spent all his spare time reading. Now quite familiar with the Gospels, José found that the Epistles clarified what a man could become if he were controlled by the spiritual power of God.

What a contrast to that vile book that still lay in the bottom of his box of belongings under his bed! Surely, as he had once followed the demonic instructions toward a personal confrontation with the evil spirit through one book, he would be able to make personal contact with the Holy Spirit of God. If he could do that, would he not find release from his present torment of fear and guilt? Far into the night, hour by hour, he read on.

> This is my prayer. That God, the God of our Lord Jesus Christ and the all-glorious Father, will give you spiritual wisdom and the insight to know more of him: that you may receive that inner illumination of the spirit which will make you realize how great is the hope to which he is calling you—the magnificence and splendor of the inheritance promised to Christians—and how tremendous is the power available to us who believe in God. That power is the same divine energy which was demonstrated in Christ when he raised him from the dead and gave him a place of supreme honor in Heaven—a place that is infinitely superior to any conceivable command, authority, power or control, and which carries with it a name far beyond any name that could ever be used in this world or the world to come.
>
> God has placed everything under the power of Christ and and has set him up as head of everything for the Church. For the Church is his body, and in that body lives fully the one who fills the whole wide universe.

To you, who were spiritually dead all the time that you drifted along on the stream of this world's ideas of living, and obeyed its unseen ruler (who is still operating in those who do not respond to the truth of God), to you Christ has given life! We all lived like that in the past, and followed the impulses and imaginations of our evil nature, being in fact under the wrath of God by nature, like everyone else. . . .[2]

José's hand trembled as he put a marker into the Testament. He fell into his hard bed and stared up at the cane ceiling. His heart pounded, and he was shaken to his inner being. Yes, here was the promise that he had been seeking. To be dominated by the power of God was a possibility, and it would set him free. He recalled Vicente's earlier text; he had even marked it in his New Testament: "Ye must be born again." The unseen, fearful power he had contacted *was still operating in those who did not respond to the truth of God!* This passage declared that he was spiritually dead unless—and until—by this spiritual birth his life was wrested from the evil power that controlled him as well as all who did not have this spiritual life.

"If I keep on this road I'm on—I'm lost."

Months went by while José wrestled secretly with his problem. At last he began openly to say that he wished someone would talk to him about the gospel. He shrugged his shoulders at ridicule.

"You can't fulfill what they require," his friends argued, for the austerity of the evangelicals was generally understood.

"If they can—why can't I?"

Soon after he declared himself openly, he heard that the evangelicals were planning a meeting in the home of Lorenzo Galvis, and that anybody was welcome.

"Here's your chance, José," was the taunting challenge, "to try to make an *evangélico* out of yourself."

He did not reply. He had already struggled to make an evangelical of himself. He had stopped smoking and drinking, because

[2]Ephesians 1:16—2:3 (Phillips).

he knew that evangelicals considered both a vice. He had been staying away from the local *parrandas* and had been occupying himself with the reading of the New Testament. He was becoming known as a strange person, but nobody had ever mistaken him for an *evangélico*.

In spite of the wretched battles that had gained him a victory—at least for the time being—over his acute cravings, he realized miserably that he had no urge to persuade anyone else to share his bleak attempts at being an *evangélico*. The more he struggled against his habits, the more certain he became that somewhere he had missed the main issue. Lorenzo Galvis had found a dynamic for living—not a sedative against the fear of judgment. He emanated a contagious, exuberant joyousness; José had merely a deadly determination.

Why did St. Paul pile up his superlatives as he did in this New Testament? St. Peter spoke of joy inexpressible and full of glory. Something miraculous had happened to these men that had changed the quality and direction of their lives. It had enabled them to draw thousands with them into this new sphere of living. They must have experienced what Jesus called the spiritual birth.

Pondering this, José suddenly remembered the book that he had thrown into a box under his bed. To lay hold on that hellish power, one needed to summon the presence to himself by intense, determined concentration. To gain those promised supernatural powers, he must commit himself, body and soul, to the spiritual personality.

Was not that exactly what the evangelicals had done to acquire this supernatural power and zest for living? Was this new life a sign of a new birth—spiritual birth? That meant that they had gone through a spiritual pact that gave them entrance into a supernatural realm of living. Here was the clue to their power to step out from shackles of the same temptations he still continued to fight with grim desperation. Only this could explain their joyous victory where his fierce struggles left only emptiness and chagrin.

For a moment he was tempted to go back to the book that had

once opened the door to the spiritual realm for him. He could go through all those steps again, this time conjuring up the Spirit of God.

A leaden sense of apprehension clutched his heart; remembered horror at his encounter with spiritual reality and power made a chill creep up his spine. He shuddered.

No. He could never go through such an experience again. He reached for the New Testament. Somewhere in this book he would find the secret.

6

Give Me This Mountain!

On another mountain, the *Nazareno,* Inocencio Trillos, still came frequently to visit at the Marcelino Cárdenas home. Young Aurelio, eager for excitement or diversion, still kept an alert eye on the trails. He burst into the house one day with a breathless announcement.

"Hey, Mamá! Somebody's coming."

"We saw him, Son," said Amelia, with a smile.

They stood together watching the toiling speck on the trail that led toward the house.

"Wonder if it's an *evangélico,*" suggested Aurelio, with a glance at Inocencio.

"It's Don Vicente Gómez. Nobody else is as thin as that," said Amelia finally, when the man was but ten minutes away. "I'll start the fire for *tinto,* you go get Papá and the boys."

"No wonder he's thin," remarked Inocencio. "Look at the rate he's been climbing that trail. He'll be ready for that *tinto.*"

But Vicente had not planned to stop at the Cárdenas home, and did so only at Amelia's insistence. Aurelio had ridden to where Marcelino and his two older sons were working in the coffee plantings. They would be disappointed, she said, if they came home and found that he had not remained. Vicente followed her into the house while Inocencio loitered in the corral.

Inocencio went in with Alfredo and Alonso to find Vicente

112

in earnest conversation with his hostess. When Amelia became aware of them, she quickly wiped her face with her apron; but her face had a look of shimmering joy even while tears continued to trickle down her cheeks. When she walked toward the kitchen she appeared to be treading clouds.

As for Inocencio, though he was consumed with curiosity about Amelia's unprecedented betrayal of emotions, he joined the family *culto* merely as a matter of courtesy to his host and the young men who were his friends. He spent the time cleaning his nails with a pocketknife. He would sit with them; that did not mean he would listen.

When Inocencio next went back to the Cárdenas home, however, he became aware at once of a marked change. They were reading their Bible together as a family, and they were living by it. For the first time since he had begun coming to their home, his friends talked to him of what the salvation of Jesus Christ meant to them. And this time they refused to argue with him on the questions that once had occupied their attention. They were not interested in winning a point; they were interested in winning him to this faith that had become important to them.

"I'll be the last to accept the practice of *evangélicos.*"

"But Inocencio," exclaimed Amelia, "you have no idea what you're missing."

Recalling fleetingly the radiance he had glimpsed through her tears at the time of his previous visit, Inocencio knew the deep, quiet joy in her eyes dated from that conference with Vicente Gómez.

"I'll be faithful to my own religion," he said, making an oblique remark about untutored men who thought they could understand the eternal and divine thoughts of the sacred Scriptures.

"You mean, because Vicente doesn't wear skirts?" asked Alfredo, needling the onetime *Nazareno.*

"Leave him be, Alfredo," admonished his mother, but she turned back to their guest, beaming. "Don Vicente has been to

a seminary, and Don Sixto and others speak from their experience and by the Holy Spirit—I found that out."

The idea of the Holy Spirit was even less comprehensible. And
since his two friends seemed determined to sink themselves in
this Bible reading and had lost their taste for the *parrandas* in
Guadal, Inocencio withdrew himself from their hospitality.

The strange *evangelio,* he was determined, should not inter-
fere with his way of life, and he felt a queer premonition that if
he kept listening it would do just that. In fact, as time went on,
he realized he had already heard too much to remain neutral.
He was overcome by a restless compulsion to find out what gave
such peace and joy to people whom it robbed of what he considered life's pleasures.

His problem now became one of saving face. For three months
he had taken a supercilious attitude of aloofness toward the
whole family, and he had no pretext for resuming his visits.
Still, the urge was greater than his pride.

When he brought his horse to a lathery halt near the Cárdenas
porch, and stopped on the pretext of watering the animal, he
was amazed at the cordial welcome he received, considering his
own attitude and his prolonged absence.

Of course, he still had one hurdle to cross. Possibly by this
time, he thought, the gospel was not the all-absorbing topic of
conversation that it had been three months ago. He still had to
manage to bring the conversation around to the subject so that
they would not realize how much he actually wanted to speak of
it. They continued to talk of banalities.

"We've missed you," said Amelia, bringing a steaming cup of
tinto.

"I didn't have time," he muttered lamely, and realized at
once that they all knew he was lying.

"Haven't you been hearing the Word of God all this time?"

"No," said Inocencio, with an excited stirring of his pulse,
though he held his voice to careless indifference. How should he
proceed? He must not allow the opportunity to slip by, for he
must lead them to talk about their new faith.

Amelia erased even that difficulty. She turned to the table where the Bible lay. No more kept safely under lock and key, it was an open declaration of fearless faith. While he sipped his *tinto,* she turned to a passage with a confidence acquired since he had visited them previously.

"Here is a book written by the wisest man that ever lived," she said. "He was also a king, and he wrote it for a young man like you. You'll find it quite easy to understand." She placed the Bible on his knee, opened at the Proverbs. His eye picked up some lines, then he became absorbed in the reading.

> Reverence of the LORD is the beginning of knowledge;
> but foolish men despise wisdom and instruction.[1]

Engrossed in the lyrical beauty of the literature, he read on. Moreover, his indifference to the context was gone.

> How long will scoffers delight in their mocking
>   and fools despise knowledge?
> Turn to my reproof!
>   Look, I will pour out my spirit for you;
>   I will disclose my words to you.
> Because I besought and you refused,
>   I stretched out my hand and no one responded,
>   and you have treated all my counsel lightly,
>   would have none of my reproof,
> I also will laugh at your calamity;
>   I will deride when terror comes to you,
>   when terror strikes you like a storm,
>   and your calamity hits like a whirlwind,
>   when distress and despair come upon you.
> Then they will beseech me, but I will not answer;
>   they will seek me diligently, but will not find me.
> Because they despised knowledge,
>   and did not choose reverence for the LORD,
>   would have none of my counsel,
>   scorned all my reproof,
> therefore will they eat of the fruit of their way,

[1]Proverbs 1:7 (Berkeley).

will be sated with their own counsel.
For the waywardness of the simple brings their death
and the self-assurance of fools their destruction.
But the one listening to me will dwell secure,
will be quiet without dread of calamity.[2]

The upshot of the matter was that he was so late discussing the evangelical faith that he remained overnight and shared the family bedtime *culto,* in which each of them took part in a session of short impromptu prayers, very personal and specific. He was being mentioned by name.

He slept little during that night, and as he rode home he was tormented by the decision he needed to make. Was it the truth? He wanted the peace of this gospel, but could he pay the price? One remark of Amelia's kept coming to mind: "If the Catholic religion had kept faithful to the Word of God, it would be evangelical too."

Was she right? They had been able to answer most of his questions and protests with passages from this Book they called the Word of God. Some of those passages were diametrically opposed to his way of life and to beliefs he had held unquestioningly. Weren't they correct when they insisted that both his beliefs and his actions should coincide with the divine revelation of God?

He had to carefully examine this new and compelling religion, he decided. He considered vaguely that he would need at least four years of study, of weighing the pros and cons. So, with this secret resolve, he went with the Cárdenas family the following Sunday to the meeting in the home of Sixto Machado.

But Inocencio had reckoned in ignorance of the very words he had discussed with Marcelino Cárdenas: *"I will pour out my spirit for you: I will disclose my words to you."* As Sixto spoke very simply, the Spirit illuminated the words of God with convicting power, and the hard, proud *Nazareno* bowed to accept the eternal gift of spiritual life.

So wonderful was the release from his fear of death and judg-

[2]Proverbs 1:22*b*-33 (Berkeley).

ment, so amazingly rich were the promises in the Book which he devoured with hungry soul, that some days he could hardly lay the Word aside. In his enthusiasm, the thought occurred to him that he must go home. If his family could just hear the truth explained, they would share his glorious faith.

Although he could recall his own attitudes toward the gospel, he was surprised at the reaction of his family. Not only did they refuse to give him a reasonable hearing, but they told him to leave. He left his home in hurt bewilderment of his parents' rejection. A comforting thought penetrated his gloom. Jesus, who also had once been known as a *Nazareno,* understood what it meant to be hated by those He loved.

Even while Inocencio rode back sadly toward Guadal, far to the north, the *Nazareno* José Pinzón slipped his machete into place and slapped the fringed leather chaps that covered his best suit of clothes. On Palmira, word of the evangelical meeting at the Lorenzo Galvis home had been circulated by friend and foe. José was relieved that both were planning to attend—for their own separate reasons. He would be saved from openly revealing the full trend of his own convictions and the heavy reality of his need.

The people who had preceded José had gathered in the Galvis patio and were standing in tight little knots from which he caught fragmentary bits of subdued conversation. José could feel an indefinable thrill of expectancy. Whether drawn by curiosity or conviction, everybody was discussing what they understood of this *evangelio.* They spoke earnestly or jocosely about the mysterious changes that were taking place in the lives of its adherents, and of the persecutions that one would be bound to endure if one joined them.

José greeted one or two acquaintances. He could feel the speculations behind their strained greetings. They knew of his past and were aware of his open attempt to break with it. He realized that everyone here was being placed into a category according to his sympathy with or participation in this new evangelical movement, for a movement it was clearly recognized to be. This was no longer a sporadic desertion of old, accepted standards; large numbers of people seemed willing to risk their lives to join up with this revolutionary, if not heretical, teaching.

"Did you know about Manuel Contreras?"

José, standing with his back to one of the clusters of visitors, listened to their comments.

"What about Manuel? Don't tell me *he's* here!"

"He is here. Not only that, Edilia's here with him."

"Well, watch for fireworks. You know Manuel and his monkeyshines. He's planning something that'll be worth watching, or I miss my guess."

"Remember when he caused a lot of commotion in El Carmen? He just about beat down the door of the place where they have their meetings. I wouldn't call it a church, because it isn't."

José was restless. Against his deep need and his conviction, a strange power still bound him against taking an open stand as an *evangélico* sympathizer. He moved into the house where chairs and benches were being placed along the walls of the *sala*.

"So very glad you could come, José!" said Señora de Galvis, with gracious sincerity. "Don Armenio asked us if we had notified you, and we had to admit that we hadn't. You're not at the Chogó plantation anymore, are you?"

"Not for more than three weeks."

She inquired about his new work, and said she was glad that he had not left the community. "We want everybody to hear about the wonderful joy we have found," she said.

José studied her beaming face. She could not possibly be feigning this happiness that seemed to bubble up from her and put a lilt into her voice even when she was speaking of the trivialities that had made him feel welcome, even important. She flashed him another quick smile when she saw Armenio Pabón coming toward them.

"I was hoping you would come, José," said Armenio. "It looks like a houseful, doesn't it?"

"Yes, Señor," said José, conscious that his face had frozen into sullen lines of resistance. People were drifting into the room, and José edged away from Armenio and took an inconspicuous seat in a corner. Everyone would know now that he had had previous contact with evangelicals. He shrank back into the corner. When they began to sing he pretended not to know the hymns, some of which had become familiar to him.

During the singing, José noticed that Señora de Contreras plucked at Armenio's sleeve. She seemed to be asking a favor or reminding Armenio of a promise. She appeared to be sparkling with sheer delight. Or was it mischief? Had Manuel Contreras enlisted her to help him stage one of his practical jokes?

"Doña Edilia has something she is bursting to tell us," Armenio announced when they had finished singing the hymn. He tilted his chair back against the scarred wall, a wide grin spreading across his face. José was impressed, as always, with the spirit of these evangelical meetings. He could feel the very power of their worship, but it was so shockingly informal that even those who were in charge seemed not to have any set ritual in mind.

"Do you want me to stand up?" she asked, a bit flustered in spite of her eagerness.

Armenio shrugged his shoulders. "We're a group of your neighbors. Just tell us what happened."

"Before I knew the *evangelio*," Edilia began, "I would have said it was good—if I had heard what it was. But all I knew about it was that it was bad. When Manuel said that the pastor might come here to the mountains, I said, '*Ojalá*,[3] I hope they don't come to our place!' I thought that if the gospel were the truth, we'd know, wouldn't we? Well, then one day Manuel said, 'If the pastor comes while I'm gone, let him wait here.' But I didn't know what I'd do with him if he came.

"We're not strangers. You know what kind of a life Manuel led and the hard time he gave me. I myself was rebellious, and we were quarreling more and more about his drinking. Many days both of us were in despair. So I said to myself, 'Well, if he

[3]An interjection expressing wish or hope.

wants the *evangelio* to come here, and if it means I can rest from all this trouble—and Manuel can too—I shouldn't stop them.' And they did come. And we listened. I waited, of course, that he'd be the first.

"They came again, and we listened. They kept coming, but it seemed that maybe Manuel couldn't become an *evangélico* because his habits held him. Six months they kept coming. One day, when he was so depressed and despairing, he accepted the gospel. And so we both did."

The silence in the room became electric with suspense as every eye rested on Manuel Contreras' handsome face. In the minds of many listeners, Edilia's declaration that both had become evangelicals meant that they had become infidels. Manuel leaned over toward Armenio with a twinkle in his eye, and with the same easy humor that had always made him the life of a crowd, he inquired mildly, "You mean you'll let me have the last word?" At once the tension in the room was broken.

"You've really heard it already," said Manuel. "That I gave my wife a terrible time wasn't news to any of you. You all know more about me than I want to tell. Edilia didn't tell it all either. You saw me when I was high—at *parrandas*. Edilia saw me when I was low—on the morning after. But even she didn't see the emptiness and despair, nor did she feel the chains I was dragging, or the shackles that held me." He raised his dark eyes abruptly from his shoes.

"You've all seen me at *parrandas*. Many of you have called me to say prayers for your dead. When Pepe died—that was how I first found out that the gospel held out a hope after death. I talked to my brother Ricardo about that young boy's hope, and he told me he thought it was good.

"So that's when I said that the brethren could come to my place. Don Vicente was the pastor who came many times. He brought the gospel with love. As I read the Bible, I became convinced that the Saviour, Jesus Christ, is the One who can pardon sins."

Armenio received a good hearing for the message that followed these testimonies. The man near José leaned over during the service to ask under his breath, "What do you think of this?"

José thought the man was trying to get him into an argument or even to commit himself. He shrugged and remained silent. José had changed. People knew it, and they were watching him. But José knew beyond a doubt that his change, so far, was a matter of negatives. Even if he could create the effect of having become an *evangélico* for those who observed his actions—which he doubted—he knew that he lacked the living spark that made these other people glow from within.

With the vicissitudes of plantation work, José again sought work with Salvador Chogó, his previous employer. Finding the family now open to discussions about the evangelical faith, José invited them to go with him to the next scheduled service. He even urged that they accept the gospel, declaring that he proposed to commit himself to it. He argued so convincingly that they began to read the Bible seriously. José informed Lorenzo Galvis that when Vicente Gómez came to the Chogó home for another *culto,* he intended to make a public avowal of his faith.

Galvis did tell Vicente, but when the latter came, José, overcome by a powerful oppression, withdrew to the kitchen. So desperate was he to break the bonds of the evil forces that he fell prostrate to the floor, crying out bitterly in torment of soul, pleading with God to show him how to be released from his spiritual subjection to the Satanic powers that had driven him from the *culto* at which he had vowed to make an open committal to Christ.

"From this commitment I will not retract!" he cried.

When he went belatedly to the *sala,* Vicente was conducting the meeting. They were singing, "*O yo quiero andar con Cristo.*"[4]

José joined in the singing, knowing it was the cry of his heart. Suddenly he became aware of a sense of release, of the lifting of heavy fetters. Without the prolonged explanation he had determined to seek this day, without any external sign to

[4]Oh, I want to walk with Christ.

anyone else, he suddenly knew that he had been freed from the
demonic powers and had entered the reality of a new life. It was
so simple that he would have a hard time explaining it to anyone else. He tingled with a joy that was beyond words. This
was not the heaviness of acting *like* an evangelical. He had
achieved what he had nearly despaired of ever attaining.

Achieved? No, he understood now the truth of what he had
heard but had never truly comprehended until it became a
reality. It was a gift from God. He had done nothing. It had
just come to settle in his heart. And he never wanted to be
without this gift and the peace that had come with it. Why had
he ever hesitated because of what people would think of him
or the personal risks involved? Nothing could compare with
the sublime blessing he had gained.

"I commit my life to the Lord," José said simply, after Vicente
had finished speaking. "All that I am, all that I have. I am
His."

Three others made their decision for Christ that same night.
José knew their commitment was real, for he sensed a kinship
in the deep joy that shone in their eyes. No wonder the evangelicals called each other *brethren*. This was a kinship deeper
than blood.

José eagerly offered to accompany any evangelical on any
jira that was to take place in the community. "I want to learn
to share this great joy!"

Vicente accepted his offer with alacrity. On the long stretches
of trail, older Christians found opportunity to help or instruct
new recruits, to answer their questions. When Vicente discovered how carefully José had read and reread his New Testament,
he suggested that José come with him often so that he could
quickly grasp the depth of the evangelical message. He wanted
him to soon be able to conduct a Sunday Bible class.

"Many places are asking for a teacher," he said, "and we can't
go to all of them at once."

Now that realization had replaced his doubts, now that the

new spiritual life was no longer a theory but a living reality, all José's own questions had dissolved. The obscure places that he had marked in his New Testament were now perfectly clear, and all the Scripture glowed with new meaning. Before long, José was in charge of the Sunday morning services at the Lorenzo Galvis home.

Though the growing group of believers did not have a chapel, they chose a name, La Cruz,[5] for their congregation. It drew immediate hostility. One night, soon after his public confession of the evangelical faith, Manuel Contreras' neighbors attacked his home. Unable to break open the heavy doors, they hacked at them with machetes and finally began shooting. They left after stealing goats, pigs and chickens.

In spite of these distressing losses, Manuel kept witnessing to all his neighbors on Palmira. He eagerly offered to accompany Vicente and Armenio Pabón to *cultos* in other mountain settlements. When José Pinzón fell into a role of leadership on Palmira, rumors were soon afloat that José would be killed. The work of La Cruz would be brought to a halt.

"You shouldn't go out so much," a friend warned. "They're really laying for you."

A horseman on mountain trails can often be seen for hours before he arrives at his destination, and on one occasion José was ambushed on the trail. He escaped to the Chogó plantation without harm, though he was thoroughly shaken by this attempt on his life.

"We'll be right here next Sunday," his assailants had shouted after him. "We'll get you then!"

"You should always carry a machete," advised Señora de Chogó.

"But *evangélicos* don't—"

"Not that you have evil intentions; but if you carry something, they may not be so bold."

Admittedly nervous about the inevitable encounter, and persuaded of the wisdom of peace-by-armament, José wore a small machete at his belt when he prepared to go on his Sunday as-

[5]The Cross.

signment. Not a pacifist either by nature or by previous practice, he wondered uneasily whether he could carry this weapon and refrain from using it if he were cornered. Evangelicals, he knew, turned the other cheek in accordance with Jesus' law of love. Great as the change within him had been, José doubted if he had gained the courage necessary for meekness. He might fight back.

"I can't take it," he told the señora.

"Maybe you should not go this time. If they waste a day waiting for you, they may decide it's not worth the bother, and leave you alone."

No man faces possible death without fear. José toyed with the thought, then rejected it, because he knew that many would be riding or walking long distances: an entire day was involved in attending the services for some people. Still, every one would understand if he did not appear.

Then he remembered that Manuel could not take over for him. Manuel had promised to go to speak to a small new group meeting in La Quebradita. Was La Quebradita a safer place than Palmira? Decidedly not. But Manuel would be going, José knew, regardless of any threats.

José's failure to appear would amount to a denial of his own assurance of the Lord's reliability. Furthermore, if he failed to arrive at Palmira, a group of men would surely come to see if anything had happened to him. In that case, they would fall unsuspectingly into the ambush that was being set up for José.

"You read Psalm 121 while I'm on the trail, Señora," he said. "And I'll remember that you are praying for me."

José had faced angry and dangerous men before, but he had relied on his own skill with gun or dagger. He had relinquished these to depend upon the still untested weapon of faith in God. When he drew near the point where ambush would be most probable, his heart began pounding until it sounded like pursuing hoofbeats. He swung around. At that same moment his mule, seeking the edge of the trail as usual, loosened a rock. The impact, as it struck a ledge below, was like the report of a rifle. He whirled back again, shaking with fear.

Vicente had faced far more perils than a threatened ambush; Marco had survived numerous attacks. Both of them urged that in time of trouble or terror one should repeat some promise of the Lord's. He had asked Señora de Chogó to read Psalm 121. José began to repeat it aloud, and the clicking of the mule's hoofs on the rocky trail brought rhythm to the poetry; the awesome sweep of the majestic mountains brought depth and meaning to the words.

I will lift up mine eyes unto the hills. He had read the Psalms over many times for assurance, but now José felt a kinship with David, another young man who had been threatened on mountain trails and whose life had been in constant danger. In those rugged Judean mountains had lurked a mad king who had vowed to have David's life. He had had an army at his command. No wonder David felt there was no escape: *From whence cometh my help?* Ah, but David knew his God. The awe-inspiring Creator of the universe, whose word could bring worlds into being, was also his ally. So David looked up—not about him: *My help cometh from the Lord, which made heaven and earth.*

And while José contemplated God's personal involvement and faithfulness, he passed the area of danger. The rest of the trail ran more openly down the flank of the mountain.

Still, the God who had cultivated in David those qualities of soul that had enabled him to reach down through centuries with counsel and comfort, had employed the very dangers that David feared in order to accomplish His divine purpose. Neither did God remove the threats and dangers from the lives of the Palmira believers. José's persecutors did materialize on other occasions, though most often when he was not alone.

Sometimes stones were thrown merely as gestures of hatred or contempt; at other times they were heavy and well aimed, and the evangelicals did not always come out of the stonings unscathed. They suffered blows from clubs; they dodged rifle fire. But their burden to reach every home on Palmira had not lifted.

As they prayed for those who misunderstood them and their motive, the gospel they preached became more definite and intense.

They followed every spark of sympathy to fan it into faith. Often it meant many hours of tiring and hazardous trails, farther and farther from Palmira.

One November day José accompanied Manuel Contreras and Lorenzo Galvis, who had started on foot down the trail leading toward El Carmen. Coming by the ascent called La Esperanza[6] they ran into a man whose evil character and hatred of evangelicals was no secret. Recognizing him, Manuel, who was in the lead, uttered a quick cry of warning. There seemed no way of evading the encounter. They had time only for a few ejaculated words of prayer before the man came around the bend with a shotgun under his arm, pulling an unwilling calf behind him.

When the man saw Manuel, with whom he had spent many a wild, drunken night, he stopped in the middle of the trail and began to insult him with blasphemous and foul oaths. Manuel made no answer, but his meekness only added fuel to Rincón's animosity. He raised his shotgun, and his intention was obviously not merely to terrorize. He meant to kill. They were too near to dodge his fire; there was not time to push past Manuel to disarm Rincón.

Prayer does not require time or terminology when instant death is at hand. And God, at times, reveals His sense of humor or His contempt of the threats of men by completely simple means. The calf, quite oblivious to any soul-chilling drama, snorted with pure bovine independence, and took to its heels down the slope at the very second that the gun came to rest on Rincón's shoulder. Aiming would have been instantaneous at such close range, but the calf's rope, wound about Rincón's left wrist, pulled him around.

With another oath, Rincón clutched at the end of the rope that had slipped from his wrist, missed, then lunged at it with his foot just as the calf bounced down to terrain where it might take hours to capture him. Rincón paused a moment, vacillating be-

[6]Hope.

tween the lust to kill and the need to rescue his property. He postponed the former, lest the latter be too tedious. Needless to say, the men from Palmira did not loiter to watch him catch his calf.

"Praise God," exclaimed Manuel, wiping the perspiration from his still pallid face. "That was perfect timing. One second later—and it would have been too late."

"You said it, Brother. If I were still betting, I'd not have bet on God's chances that time."

After hurrying along to leave a safe distance between them and this avowed foe, they relaxed to resume their interrupted fellowship. They had been employing the hours on the trail for mutual strengthening. Each man had shared the blessings of his own diligent search of the Word and of answered prayers.

To their consternation, they suddenly realized that Rincón must have tied up his calf and was following them. This time the men left the trail, scrambling up the stony slope of the mountain on hands and knees to the shelter of a wooded area. Reaching that, they made their way over the ridge to run along a gully for some distance. At last, after the danger of being overtaken seemed remote and the men were panting from exertion, they stopped to catch their breath. They could hear no sounds of pursuit.

"We might as well stay here a little while before we go back to the trail," said Manuel. As usual, he quickly pulled out his pocket Bible.

Again and again in moments of trial these men had found the comfort of the Psalms a very real help. Now he read, his heavy breathing still accenting the truths as the sentences were clipped into phrases pregnant with practical meaning.

"Fret not thyself because of evil doers. . . . Trust in the LORD. . . . Delight thyself also in the LORD; and he shall give thee the desires of thine heart. . . . Commit thy way unto the LORD. . . . Rest . . ., wait patiently for him: fret not. . . ."[7]

[7]Psalm 37:1, 3-5, 7.

"Listen!" said one of the men, interrupting. They sat with bated breath but heard nothing. Manuel read on.

"The wicked watcheth the righteous, and seeketh to slay him. I have seen the wicked in great power, and spreading himself like a green bay tree. Yet he passed away, and, lo, he was not. . . . The salvation of the righteous is of the LORD: he is their strength in the time of trouble. And the LORD shall help them, and deliver them: he shall deliver them from the wicked, and save them, because they trust in him."[8]

A woman slipped into the clump of trees that had afforded them a screen.

"Daniel Rincón is up at our house looking for you. We could see you on the trail up there, so I came down to warn you."

The men were on their feet instantly.

"Thank you," said Manuel. "We'll just work our way down to the trail if Don Daniel is up your way. May God let His blessing rest on you."

"I sure need it," the woman replied wistfully.

"And may you find the peace of heart that God longs to give each one of us."

Tears sprang into the dark eyes, and the woman wiped them away with the corner of her apron. But she waved them away. "Go quickly, before my man finds out that I've been away from the house."

But Rincón too had spied them among the trees, and he came upon them at this very moment, fuming with fury and hurling the vilest insults at them. Still, he had left his gun, and the men escaped to the trail.

Instead of remaining in the immediate area to visit the homes of La Esperanza, they went on to El Salto,[9] to the home of Manuel's brother, Carmen Contreras. Having been notified of their arrival, Ricardo Contreras came to join them for a meeting. Ricardo, the brother with whom Manuel had first discussed the gospel, had become an evangelical not very long after Manuel had himself accepted Christ.

[8]Psalm 37:32, 35-36, 39.
[9]A leap, a gap.

Another day, when Manuel had ridden by to see if José could accompany him on a visitation jaunt, they started off toward the northwest. The community of Palmira was on the shoulder of a mountain and looked toward Los Cerros, a chain of peaks that reared themselves up on the opposite side of a profound valley. But beyond Los Cerros the majestic crown of La Quiebra towered head and shoulders above all other mountains. The early morning sun reflected from tiny white dots that the two men knew were whitewashed homes built upon the very brow of the seemingly bald, granite peak. They were also well aware that the rugged mountaineers who wrested a living from the almost perpendicular slopes were as fierce and unreachable as the pinnacle on which they had chosen to live.

"Some day we must go up there, Don Manuel," José said. Both of the men were challenged by the massive need presented by the great mountain.

"Don Vicente says it's much better to wait until we have one home where we can at least run to, if the worst comes to the worst," said Manuel, and then he corrected himself. "Maybe he didn't really mean that, but it was what I was thinking! He says it's best to find a sympathizer in the neighborhood before we can hope to have meetings. It's an imposition to expect an uninterested man to entertain us and his neighbors as well, if it ends in trouble."

That day they went to La Quebradita, a community named for the mountain stream that bounds along a gorge branching out of another vast and spectacular valley beyond Los Cerros. They had actually arrived at the foot of that lofty mountain, La Quiebra, around whose shoulders the day had draped a graceful veil of fleecy clouds. And they chanced to meet a resident of La Quiebra who also had come down to visit in La Quebradita. Manuel García was an old acquaintance out of Manuel Contreras' past.

"Come to our *culto,* García," invited Manuel Contreras.

"Why not?" replied the other quite readily. "I think I'll come."

"Did you hear that?" exclaimed Manuel triumphantly when

he was alone with the others from Palmira. "You never can tell
how they will react. So we just have to ask them all."

"If he listens once, we may have a toehold on La Quiebra,".
said José. As they rode from home to home, inviting people to
the meeting, both of them carried about with them a silent
prayer that García would keep his word and come to the service,
and that he would receive the message favorably.

Not only did García join them at the service, but he committed his life to Christ that night—the very first time he had
ever heard the gospel presented. García knew full well that his
committal meant a complete revolution for him and his way of
life. Involved with two women, neither of whom was legally
his wife, and entangled in vices that had brought him and his
households into constant turmoil, he could foresee some violent
repercussions ahead.

He waved aside Manuel's words of caution and counsel. García
was so exuberantly enthusiastic about the reality of this new spiritual dimension of life that he was completely confident that
everyone he met would accept the gospel as quickly as he had.
All he needed to do was to tell them, he assured Manuel. He had
gone home anticipating nothing less than an evangelical mountain.

When José suggested soon after that they climb the mountain,
Manuel agreed at once.

"No better time than right now," he said. "I have a feeling
that García may even need a bit of encouragement."

They could not have a chosen a better day for the long, dangerous excursion to the heavy brow of La Quiebra. Both were
on surefooted mules that had never known any other terrain
than mountain trails, so they clattered casually along dizzying
cliffs and easily followed footpaths that snaked gradually down
the precipitous slopes or forded the swift mountain stream below by jumping from one familiar boulder to another. If the
moss was slippery and their hoofs skidded, they had an amazing
agility in gaining new footing before a misstep proved disas-
trous. The men, like the mules, were accustomed to the routes,

and only rarely commented on the entrancing beauty of valley and mountain scenery. They took the peril of the trails entirely for granted.

"On Los Cerros we should make a stop," suggested Manuel. "Lalo Guevara's brother-in-law, Cristo Galvis, likes to hear the gospel. He works for Lalo. I've been there once with Lorenzo Galvis and young José, his younger brother."

"Is Cristo an *evangélico?*"

Manuel laughed. "No, he's a fighter and a drunk, like I was! But he listens, and usually Lalo does too. He has to know everything that goes on around his plantation."

"Does Lalo have other workers?"

"A score of them. Lalo doesn't even know how many hectares of land he owns. Just take a broad sweep from the top of the mountain down to the stream on that side. It's all his."

José whistled. "Don Armenio owns around a thousand hectares.[10] I thought he was a rich man."

"Armenio's isn't on such a steep slant as this, so the land is worth more. Whatever it's worth, Don Armenio—as well as Don Sixto—has dedicated all he has to the cause of Christ."

As they neared the plantation, however, Manuel hailed a woman who was wandering aimlessly along a side trail. Two little girls who were with the woman came dashing toward the men, and the woman joined them at a more dignified gait.

"*Buenos dias,* Señora. Is Don Lalo at home?"

"He's at home." Her tone bore an unpromising implication which was quickly endorsed by the smallest of the girls.

"He's on another rampage. He beat Mamá, but I got under the bed."

"A little too much brandy?"

"A little!" Lalo's wife shrugged her shoulders and said indifferently, "He'll drink himself to death one of these times."

"Señora, may we have prayer for you and Don Lalo right now?" The suggestion seemed to stun the woman for a moment. Manuel added quietly, "I think I know what you must be suffer-

[10]About 2,471 acres.

ing. And I know from experience what Don Lalo is going through most of the time."

"It can't do any harm, can it? If God can do anything about him, it's more than I can. And more than Lalo can. He fights it. He makes resolutions. It's all no good."

"The Lord can help him where he can't help himself."

"You were always good at prayers, Don Manuel."

But Manuel's prayers were not stilted repetitions of the *rosario* any more. He made a brief plea to an understanding heavenly Father to guide a lost son gently home, and to receive a broken-hearted daughter into the comfort of His love and the assurance of His salvation. Tears trickled down the woman's cheeks, but she brushed them away quickly so that Manuel would not notice that she had been stirred by the warm simplicity of his prayer.

The men found Lalo on the veranda, staring glumly across the valley they would be crossing before they began climbing La Quiebra. He barely responded to their greetings.

"Is Cristo around?" asked Manuel.

"Nobody's around."

"I'm sorry we missed him. I was hoping to talk to Cristo."

"Don't you go making an *evangélico* out of my brother-in-law. He'd get my wife involved with that heresy next, and I've got plenty of trouble as it is."

"The *evangelio* could get you out of your troubles, Don Lalo," said Manuel gently. "I know. I've been through it."

"I don't need any more religion. I go to mass. I attend the fiestas. When I calculate I've done wrong, I go to confession. That's enough religion."

"Maybe too much," commented José. "You should trade it all for a personal relationship with a living, loving Christ."

Lalo glowered at José. "You're that *Nazareno,* aren't you?" Then before José could reply, he said, "Where are you two heading for?"

"Manuel García's place on La Quiebra," said Manuel. "What's the best way up?"

Lalo chuckled with malicious humor. "From this direction,

there's only one way, and you'd better be sober." He stepped from the veranda to where his patio fell away into the awesome depths of a wide valley. Flowering shrubs, that had been planted along the edge to prevent a fatal misstep in the dark, framed the grandeur of the mountain they contemplated. Lalo pointed out the trail they would need to take, giving them landmarks where other trails branched off. Then he craned his neck toward the summit.

"Manuel García lives above and to the right of that ridge you can see following along toward the top."

The ridge indicated was a sharp spur of granite that fell almost perpendicularly down into the valley.

"The trail must be on the other side," said José.

"Of the ridge?" Lalo turned bloodshot eyes on José. Then he slapped his thighs and laughed heartily as at a great bit of humor. "That's the trail, *Nazareno*. That spur is just as steep on the other side. You follow that ridge up if you want to reach the top of La Quiebra!"

José turned to gaze up at the mountain, then swung back to eye Lalo suspiciously. The latter roared with enjoyment of the young man's incredulity. "You find us another route, *Nazareno*, and the rest of us will follow it."

Manuel nodded. "I've heard of that route. It's a wicked bit of trail up there."

José's mule preceded that of Manuel along the narrow trail that zigzagged down steeply from the Guevara hacienda toward a mighty mountain stream whose rumble came to their ears half an hour before they reached it. The hairpin bends that led along a precipitous ledge of clay were tedious, and Manuel's mule persisted in snatching at the tufts of tall grass that grew along the trail. The descent was too steep to apply spurs; and the mule seemed to have an obstinate preference for the softer shoulder directly along the edge, because the beaten path was harder.

Suddenly the clay collapsed under the mule's left hind leg. For an instant the animal pawed for footing, but too much of its weight had been thrown outward. It flopped from the trail and rolled to a sloping ledge some six or eight feet below, where it scrambled to its feet with the alacrity of fear.

Manuel lay prostrate just below the ledge, clinging to some exposed tree roots to keep from rolling down the sharp incline. José spurred a few feet ahead to a bend where he had space enough to dismount. Hurrying back, he threw himself down along the trail so that he could reach down toward Manuel, who had cautiously drawn himself up on his hands and knees by this time.

"Are you hurt?"

Manuel ran exploratory fingers gingerly along a scraped shin. "Nothing broken but the skin, I guess."

"It's a good thing you know which way to fall. I hate to think of what shape you'd be in if that beast had fallen on top of you."

Both men knew the statistics of accidental deaths on the hazardous mountain trails. They did not stop to discuss the sheer drop just beyond where the mule was still shaking its long head in solemn, stunned surprise. If Manuel had allowed the impetus of the mule's swaying fall to throw him on the far side, he would have tumbled beyond the reaches of that sloping ledge of safety.

When Manuel shouted at the mule, it shrugged its shaggy hide and started up toward the trail. After a careful check of the saddle fastenings, they were again on their way, recollecting similar mishaps.

"A friend of mine had the same thing happen to him," reminisced Manuel. "Only Jorge is heavier, and he fell to the wrong side. He felt sure the mule would fall on him. As it was, the mule fell below him, and he lived to talk about it."

"This Carlos who works on our plantation tells of something just like this. He threw himself free, like you did. His horse rolled down the mountain. When they picked up the saddle, they could see what would have happened to him if his foot had caught in the stirrups."

"Well, I certainly wouldn't try this trail with a horse."

The sound of churning water below them grew louder as they

continued their descent. Across the boulder-strewn meadow at the base of the valley, a meandering band of shrubs and trees outlined the stream's course. The curving border displayed in lavish profusion a divine artistry done in shades and shapes of living green.

The mules trotted down to the stream that swept over a gigantic boulder to tumble like a rippling veil to the rocky bed some twenty feet below. The animals drank thirstily and then proceeded upward along the steeply falling stream for almost an hour. Then, leaping from one mossy boulder to another, the mules crossed over to the other side, and the zigzagging climb upward began in earnest.

Finally they gained that crest of granite which had appeared utterly impassable from the summit of Los Cerros, now far below them across the valley. At a vertiginous height, well above the peaks of other mountains, they wove patiently from one edge of this steeply rising spine to the other. So narrow was this ridge of splintering rock that the men on muleback could get a dizzying view of both valleys at once. On either side of them the mountain fell in an almost unbroken line right down to the valley floor. The narrow trail, chiseled out of the rock, often sloped at more than a thirty-degree angle toward the depths below.

The mules, picking their footing with inbred caution, had to claw their way up some of the abrupt inclines. Once again, on one of the unavoidable steep rises where the men stopped all conversation and concentrated on the trail, the left hind hoof of Manuel's mule slipped. For one frozen moment, Manuel looked to the right to find a place to cast himself to safety. A vast breathtaking abyss yawned on either side.

"It might be wiser to leave our mules below next time," Manuel remarked evenly, when the mule had regained its balance.

"It makes me break out in a sweat—" said José, "the thought of climbing this trail on foot."

"Yes, it's a pretty steep grade—and a long one."

"That's not it. I can climb almost any mountain if I keep my eyes ahead or above me. But you can't take a step on this path without seeing down—both ways. Somehow it pulls me—this height. I can't explain it."

"I've heard of that. It wouldn't be safe for you to live on this mountain then, that's for sure."

"I don't see why anybody would isolate himself like this."

"Coffee, José. You can grow coffee up here."

Half an hour later the men swung wearily from their saddles. Manuel García was almost pathetically happy to see them.

"How are you getting along, García?"

The new evangelical shifted his feet and shook his head. "I'm glad I didn't know what I was in for. It's been a battle—all the way around."

"Your wife?"

"Well, she hasn't made it easy. It's been—"

Their host broke off the narration of his own trouble, remembering that his guests had come a long distance.

"You haven't eaten."

"We haven't come to impose on your hospitality, especially—"

The woman who had come to the door met her husband's glance. "It's all right," she said. "I'm just putting the plantains on to boil, and I can put in a few extra. I have *tinto* on too."

She retreated to the rear of the house. The men remained near the front veranda. Manuel let his eye wander to the slopes visible above them. They were studded with thickets of coffee plantings.

"How's coffee up here?"

"All right, if you don't fall out of the field," said their host. "Lost a cow yesterday. She fell out of the pasture. Sharing the meat gave me a chance to prove that becoming an *evangélico* does not make me a bad neighbor."

Later, they strolled along the small plateau, getting a glimpse of García's plantation and the spring, which was the all-important feature. Over twenty homes on this level lay within an hour's brisk walking. Manuel broached the subject of their purpose on La Quiebra.

"We were hoping to have a *culto* to which we could invite others. It's a long way up here; we want to contact as many as we can."

After a long pause, García said doubtfully, "It's strange, Manuel. I thought my friends would be glad to hear about it. They're not. They won't listen. I wish they'd even just listen!"

"Well, we'd like to try. Sometimes they come to hear a stranger. If there are twenty families here, we might get a few to come."

"The house is at your orders," said García, "and I'll come with you to show you where the homes are located. But I have to warn you that the people on this mountain are plenty fanatical. They've said—"

"That we aren't going to get a warm welcome?"

García, noting the quizzical look on Manuel's face, also grinned. "Or they might make it *too* hot for you."

When they were about to start on their tour of the mountain homes, García had another suggestion. "I wonder if you'd like to borrow a couple of machetes? I see neither of you brought yours."

"We'll steer clear of trouble."

"If you can. I'd just as soon not have to do all the fighting, if it comes to it." He was strapping on a wide-bladed machete when he looked up with a queer expression, a wavering between incredulity and comprehension. His hand still on the handle of the heavy knife, he exclaimed, "Is this something I don't know? Is it part of being an evangelical?"

Manuel nodded. "We have nothing to bring your neighbors but peace—and the love of Christ."

After a long moment's hesitation, García put aside his own weapon, though a distinct doubt or reluctance remained etched on his features. For many men the machete is as much a part of their attire as is a pair of shoes. Later, as they walked along the comparatively gentle trail together, they passed a clump of straggling trees in a shallow dip that had obstructed their view. García pointed ahead, though one hand strayed to his empty belt.

"Our trail goes right by, but we'd better not stop at that house."

"You think we might have trouble?"

"He said to me, 'If they come, we'll kill them. And their heads will stay right here in the house.' The three of us could handle him easy. But I tell you, straight out, I'm scared—now that we don't even have our machetes."

"God is more protection than a machete," said Manuel mildly. "I think we should pray."

They stepped behind a towering boulder and knelt in prayer. When they brushed the grass and dry leaves from their trousers, Manuel said encouragingly, "The Lord is with us."

"Let's go!" said José, a trifle too loudly. It was not hard to see that García's uneasiness had communicated itself to him.

In this rigid schooling of faith, these recent converts were not to be spared a meeting with their outspoken enemy. He was standing in the doorway of his home. José, who was in the lead, felt his knees go weak; he bit down hard as he became conscious of the chattering of his teeth. It was unthinkable to pass a mountaineer's home without speaking, so he lifted his hat and called as casual a greeting as he could muster through vocal cords that responded more to his fear than to his will. To his surprise, the man returned his greeting with the normal courtesy of the mountains. Thus encouraged, they spoke to him for some minutes, telling him of the service in the García home.

"I'll come."

He did come to the service, as did forty others from the community. By God's guidance, Manuel led them in the Lord's Prayer, familiar to all of them. However, many had always repeated it unthinkingly as part of a ritual. When José asked some questions about it, the people looked to a local schoolteacher to give the answers for them. When she sat silent, someone asked her to speak up.

"Why don't we pray our prayers as it says here that Jesus taught His disciples, to the Father which is in heaven?" the man asked, repeating José's question.

"I don't know."

"Well, we can't let these *evangélicos* say we could not answer such a question."

"There must be a good reason why we don't do as Jesus said here," commented another. "You've been in school. Surely the sisters taught you—"

The teacher flushed. She was conscious that all eyes were on her. "Well," she said, somewhat testily, "they just didn't teach us about it."

"Don't embarrass the señorita," said Manuel. "We will just read some of Jesus' other teachings in the New Testament to discover the wonderful blessings that can be ours as we appeal directly to the Father."

At the end of the service all the tracts that they had brought were taken and all their literature had been sold. José even sold his own Bible. They left La Quiebra next morning in jubilant spirits. José voiced their feelings.

"This mountain is the Lord's!"

7

Circular 310

LUCILA MARIA PINO, beautiful in spite of the straggling black hair that fell to her shoulders, leaned heavily on a homemade broom. She crushed out a cigarette on the corner of a table before she waved her sister Carmen back from the kitchen.

"You stay right there and cast your usual spell on Gratiniano," she said maliciously. "It's a pity he didn't marry you in the first place."

Having made both her husband and Carmen very uncomfortable, Lucila flounced heavily to the kitchen, her thong sandals flapping resentfully with each awkward step. Carmen turned to her brother-in-law.

"You mustn't take her too seriously. In her condition—"

Carmen stopped in midsentence. Gratiniano had moved out of the doorway to a place where the sunlight from outside struck his face.

"Whatever in the world have you done to your face, Gratiniano?" she cried.

Gratiniano fingered his battered face gingerly. His bruised eyelids, once purple, were now a greenish brown, as was one cheek. Across the left side of his forehead was a livid scar where a flap of flesh—never stitched or even properly bandaged, protruded in grotesque and swollen distortion.

"You mean Lucila hasn't told you?" His tone was bitter, and it

140

was clear that he did not believe Carmen when she said she had not heard about it.

"You've been fighting again, Pino," she said. "Your luck won't hold forever. One of these days you'll be killed."

"And who would care?" he growled. But Carmen detected a break in his voice, and his glance wandered toward the kitchen. He opened his mouth. Carmen spoke before he had time to begin the bitter declamation she feared, for Lucila had confided in her sister that, though pregnant, she was determined to leave her husband.

"I'm going to ask one favor of you—quick, before you do get yourself stabbed, or worse," she said in a half-bantering tone.

In spite of himself, Gratiniano grinned feebly. "Well, talk fast. I'm not promising you anything though."

"I want you to go to a service at La Quiebra—a service of the *evangélicos*."

"A service of the *evangélicos!* Whatever for?"

"To show you that there's another way out of desperation," Carmen lowered her voice, "besides getting yourself killed."

Gratiniano's eyes searched Carmen's serious upturned face. "Lucila has told you—"

"Lucila has told me nothing new. Both of you are unhappy."

"And you think the *evangélicos* can do something about this hopeless mess?"

"*They* can't, but the faith in Christ that they preach of can change your life—even if it can't change your circumstances."

"How can it change my life if things aren't changed—here?"

"It can give your life a new center as well as a new goal. Then these other things won't be so upsetting."

Gratiniano began to wrinkle his forehead at Carmen, winced, and drew a careful finger across his healing scar. "The *evangélicos*, eh?" he said, still staring at his sister-in-law in incredulous amazement. "Well, what do you know!"

"Promise?"

"I have now reached the straw-clutching stage, Carmen. I have nothing to lose. Why not?"

Lucila entered with a steaming plate, which she set before Gratiniano. That she should serve him alone was not strange, for Colombian women often do not eat with their men. The children, who had been playing in the yard, began clamoring for something to eat, Carmen followed her sister to the kitchen, where Lucila began to peel yuca and plantain to boil.

"How did you manage to get a meal for Gratiniano so quickly?"

"Men are stupid. He'll never taste the difference between what I heated over from yesterday or fixed fresh today."

"You're not trying very hard to make your marriage work, are you?"

"Sometimes I hate myself," said Lucila, "only—"

"Only what?"

"Only, it always seems to be at the wrong times—when the damage has already been done. Just as soon as I'm with Gratiniano again, I'm on the defensive."

"Or maybe even—the *offensive?*"

"Well—"

"Lucila," said Carmen with sudden energy, "Christ could change all this. He could make your marriage beautiful."

Lucila went to the stove to shove aside the lid on the pot of plantains that was boiling over. She came back, still without speaking.

"Gratiniano says he'll come to a service at La Quiebra," continued Carmen. "You must come with him."

Lucila was glad Gratiniano had made the concession to Carmen's new faith before she needed to. She admitted to herself that she was curious to know what they taught, but in her heart she knew that her desire to go to that meeting was far deeper than curiosity. She guessed that her husband's was too.

Carmen had told her it was three hours "coming down" from La Quiebra, so it would take a bit more than that to reach the meeting, as the greater part of the trail would be climbing. But she noticed that next Sunday, without any urging from her, Gratiniano was getting ready. He seemed relieved that she too had decided to go, and he offered to carry their youngest son.

The children were excited at the prospect of a family outing.

The mountain trails naturally pass by the various homes along the way, and they called a greeting to their neighbors. They also passed a man working in his yuca patch with his son.

"Where are you going?"

"To La Quiebra," said Gratiniano.

"On Sunday morning? You don't mean to say you're going to one of those *evangélico* meetings!"

Gratiniano shrugged. "What's the harm?"

"Why that's a faction without shame!"

The man's referring to the evangelicals as he would have spoken of a political party revealed his own ignorance, though he was determined to argue with great conviction, and did so at such length that they knew they would surely be late. Lucila decided not to go on, since in her condition she could not hurry. Nor could the children climb fast enough to arrive in time.

"Well, what was it like?" she asked Gratiniano when he came back home in midafternoon.

"It was all over by the time I got there," he said noncommittally. In a moment, however, he took a small tract from his pocket. "They said I should take this, so I did."

He placed the tract before her. She knew that his pride would not permit him to ask her to read it to him, for she had often made him writhe under the knowledge that she could read and he could not. She looked at the title: "The Heart of Man." Because of her own desire to find out what it said, she offered to read it to him.

What she read was God's own verdict of a man out of touch with his Maker. "That's me," Gratiniano said bluntly. "I'm in that fix."

When Gratiniano told her the next Sunday that there would be another service and that he intended to go to listen again, Lucila was irritated. Who could show a man like her husband a faith such as she had glimpsed from what Carmen had told her? Admittedly, they gained peace of heart, but didn't that come from their asceticism? Why, they didn't even smoke cigarettes, these *evangélicos*. Imagine a man like Gratiniano among them!

Perhaps Gratiniano himself had similar misgivings, for he again allowed some of his acquaintances to waylay him and argue with him until it was too late for the service, though he still went on. Once more he arrived after the preaching was over. He came back with the comment that his friends had warned him that the *evangélicos* were gaining all humanity.

"That means that we're not the only ones who want to listen!" he said with some defiance. "And I've told them they could come over here to hold a service."

"You *what?*"

"Told them to come here. What's so wrong with that?"

On further reflection, however, Gratiniano must have realized what their friends would say when the news got around that they had entertained heretics. To Lucila's chagrin, he found an excuse to leave the house when he caught sight of the evangelicals on the mountain trail.

"It's just like you to invite these men over here—a whole day's trip—and then run when you see them coming!" Lucila was furious. "What am I going to do with them?"

"Tell them what you like," he said. "I'm getting out of here."

When José Pinzón and several of the men from La Quiebra arrived not much more than ten minutes later, Lucila was in no mood to entertain any of Gratiniano's friends.

"He's in Mahoma," she said shortly when José came to the door.

"That's strange," said José. "He asked us to come here today."

"You mean he asked you to come on a certain day?"

"Yes," said José. "He was very definite."

"All right," Lucila said indignantly. "I'll just tell you the truth. He's gone out to the pasture to fix a fence. You can just stay until he gets back!"

Having invited them to remain, partly to place her husband in an embarrassing situation, Lucila was at a loss about how to entertain them. The same spiritual resistance that had driven Gratiniano to leave the house now caused her to leave them alone in the front *sala* while she excused herself with the false pretext of having a great deal of work in the kitchen. The men wandered out into the yard. About noon she called them to come in and eat.

The men took the chairs she had placed about the rough table over which she had spread a clean cloth. She set bowls of piping soup before them, but they did not begin to eat.

"Let's thank our Lord for this good food," said José, "and we also thank our hostess for preparing it for us."

Because the men bowed reverently, she found herself also standing with bowed head. She had never been in a home where grace had been spoken before meals, and she was deeply affected by this young stranger's prayer—an unrehearsed, personal word of thanksgiving to a God he seemed to feel was right there in the room.

"What a beautiful thing," she murmured to herself when she had retreated to the kitchen. "I'd feed them again, just to hear them pray once more."

When in midafternoon her husband had not returned, she brought the men some *tinto*. She offered to bring cheese and *arepas,* but they said the *tinto* was all they wanted. But even for that, she saw they were going to pray. She found herself wishing urgently to be included in their prayer.

Lucila's sister Carmen, who had been informed that the men intended to visit the Pino home, also came to visit. Carmen's presence greatly relieved Lucila, especially when the men said they would have a *culto.* Carmen joined in the singing. She seemed to be familiar with the words, which were as beautiful as the prayers of José.

When Gratiniano returned, to slink shamefacedly into the kitchen for a plate of food, Lucila had no desire to berate him as she had earlier determined to do. He was there in time for the message from the Scriptures. They talked until late, and even after they went to bed, Lucila was not able to sleep. She kept wishing that she could hear the message again.

In the morning she was torn between the need to prepare breakfast and the longing to hover near so that she would not miss anything the men were saying. She was intensely relieved when José said that they would eat first and then have a short *culto* before they left. It was at that morning devotional time that she committed her life to Christ. Gratiniano said nothing, but she sensed that he was under deep conviction, as she had been during the night.

As is often the case, a man facing the full implications of God's conquest of his soul is often rebellious, and takes it out on those about him. Gratiniano was no exception. So fierce was his struggle that he sometimes left the house to wander about in the mountains all day. He came back hungry and often viciously ill-tempered. Several times he beat Lucila and abused the children.

So serious was Gratiniano's brutality that when José and the same men from La Quiebra came again, Lucila asked them not to speak to her husband, for fear that he would beat her again. José acceded to her warning, and they went on after pointing out some promises for her encouragement. Five days later, Gratiniano came home to mention that he had met José out on the trail. He had come home with a Bible—a mute and humbling admission of his need of her help.

"How does it strike you," he said, "if we all accept the gospel of Christ?"

By his complete reversal of conduct and attitude, Lucila knew that the miracle of transformation had already taken place.

Gratiniano continued to go to La Quiebra for meetings, though Vicente Gómez as well as the men from La Quiebra often came by to strengthen them in their faith and to counsel with them.

Meeting with other evangelicals on La Quiebra, where José Pinzón had begun holding regular services each Sunday, Gratiniano noted the earnest labors of the other brethren. Before long he sold his farm on La Osa and moved his family to his more productive farm so that he could occupy himself with the gospel rather than with the upkeep of two plantations. However, the trails to La Quiebra, always difficult, became completely impassable during the rainy season.

Vicente was delighted with the number of interested neighbors in the new area. Some had even then accepted the exuberant testimony of the Pino family and had become evangelicals.

"You had better concentrate here," Vicente advised Gratiniano. "La Quiebra is too far away for most of this flock that needs feeding regularly. I can come only occasionally, and José Pinzón will soon be entering a Bible school. So he will not be able to visit these people here either."

"That leaves us on our own."

"You seem to be doing very well."

"But I can't even read."

"Well," said Vicente, "that will put the responsibility of the teaching on Doña Lucila. But you must do all you can to bring the truth to the people in this community."

Such an assignment in the Colombia of those days required faith and courage of a high degree. The evangelical teachings of Lucila became the vortex around which raged a swirling eddy of fanatical antagonism.

Having ignored the Aguachica mayor's notification that the meetings would have to cease, Gratiniano was hailed to court. The judge could not be located, so Gratiniano was put into jail. When the judge at last appeared, he released Gratiniano on condition that he pay a ten-peso fine.

"For what?" asked Gratiniano.

"For holding *evangélico* services."

"For reading the sacred Scriptures to neighbors who came to our home to listen? For this you are fining me ten pesos?"

"Don't argue."

"I will pay no fine until I am told plainly what is the charge against me."

The upshot of the matter was that Gratiniano spent that Saturday night in jail. Early Sunday morning the judge came to ask him if he had reconsidered his refusal to pay his fine.

"Why no," said Gratiniano. "If I pay a fine, I admit I have done wrong. I have not even heard any constitutional charge."

"You've got to stop spreading your confounded propaganda."

"I'll be faithful to God unto death."

"If you were faithful to God, you wouldn't forsake the Holy Virgin."

"If you are so much in contact with the virgin," retorted Gratiniano, "tell me how she has helped you or given you peace of heart."

The demand seemed to confuse the judge. Gratiniano helped him out. "The virgin brought the Saviour into the world. It is this Saviour, the Lord Jesus Christ, that I worship. Is this a crime?"

Having no answer to Gratiniano's challenge, the judge released him to return home without payment of a fine. After all, this was only one incipient point of evangelical activity. The Aguachica mayor was busy enough trying to stamp out the embers of revival that threatened to flicker into flames right around his own doorstep.

Armenio Pabón had not been content with his activities in the foothills. Every time he came to Aguachica he was impressed with the fact that this rambling valley town needed a witness for Christ.

"Try Ramón Nieto," said his brother Angel, possibly to ward off a personal involvement with his brother's desire to hold a service in Aguachica during the Easter holidays. And so, on Good Friday of 1954, Ramón Nieto came out openly as a sympathizer with the evangelical cause by permitting a service to be held in his home.

Not much later, Armenio Pabón and Encarnación Galbán—brother-in-law to Aurelio Sánchez of Soledad—were called into court.

"You will be fined five hundred pesos each if you continue to preach in Aguachica."

"But we're doing it in private homes, at the request of the people who live there," said Armenio.

"That's the reason you are being warned. We have a circular here that forbids Protestants to make any public manifestation of their religious faith outside of churches and chapels. Protestants may not engage in any proselytizing." A smirk of triumph settled on the judge's face as he permitted Armenio to read the entire context of the infamous Circular 310, which was so restrictive that many missionaries left Colombia in discouragement.

Armenio handed back the edict. "This isn't our work; it's God's. And God's will is not only to preach the gospel by means of our own lips, but to proclaim it with *parlantes.*"[1]

Neither intimidated nor deterred by the printed prohibition and the threat of large fines, Armenio proceeded to hold services fearlessly. He was never forced to abandon these services by legal action, but the homes in which the services were held were often attacked by angry mobs.

By this time Ramón Nieto had come out openly as a believer, together with his wife and sons. As a sympathizer, Ramón had cautiously concealed the fact that he was reading the Bible and seeking to understand the doctrines of the evangelicals. Now that reality had replaced the search, he seemed to have a gleeful pride in the fact that he had found the truth; he advertised it everywhere.

In the services held at the Nieto home, Señora Carmen Sánchez, sister of Aurelio Sánchez, became the first Aguachica resident to share the faith of the Nieto family. After that she too offered her home for evangelical meetings.

About this time, Francisco Liévano, the fiery, young Colombian evangelist, again announced meetings in the Santa Inés area. As a concession to Circular 310, the local evangelicals had constructed a sanctuary of branches. The crowd that gathered from the now widely scattered groups of evangelicals and sympathizers

[1]Sound trucks. In Colombia, public ordinances and business advertisements are frequently announced along all city streets by mobile public address equipment.

made the arches of their primeval sanctuary resound with triumphant singing.

Local believers had also butchered a cow. At noon the great amounts of food were served on banana leaves—homegrown disposable plates. People from remote areas compared notes about their personal trials and victories. They gleaned encouragement from this sharing, finding it a great comfort to know they were not alone in trouble, and that someone had found the way through to victory.

A sudden ominous hush fell upon the noisy, friendly chatter when the Aguachica inspector of police and several of his lieutenants stalked into the noontime festivity. Purpose was written on their brutal faces; their guns were at ready. They had come to enforce Circular 310, though it was constitutionally unsound.

These policemen had massacred armed men as well as helpless women and children without compassion. They had tried to burn the Franco family in their sleep. Surely there were enough men there to overwhelm the police before all would have to die, but the evangelicals never forcefully resisted their persecutors.

In the dreadful silence that had paralyzed them all, the scratching of a hen among dry leaves made a startling sound. Then a tiny woman, her voice shrill in the tense atmosphere, broke the silence.

"You're just in time," she chirped. "Come on in. Get in line."

The food smelled appetizing. The inspector stepped into line and received a generous serving. His men followed his lead. The formidable detachment of military police had been disarmed by a tiny slip of a woman. Having eaten, they delivered their warning, though their tones were somewhat mollified by the warm food under their belts.

"We cannot guarantee you any protection if you are here by nightfall."

Real fear again held the whole company in its chilling power. The people seemed almost to hold their breath until the policemen were safely out of sight and hearing. Then Vicente strode to the center of the shaken gathering. He held up his hand for attention.

"Isn't God good?" he said. "I thought we were going to be dispersed. Instead, we have liberty to proceed unmolested. The afternoon service will take place as scheduled."

Instantly the tension was relaxed, and there followed a rumble of thanksgiving and worship. Everybody was well aware that their leafy bower would offer no protection in case of attack, and they knew that the original purpose of the police had been just that. The reality of the violence was ever with them, and they knew better than to take the warning lightly. Not long before, José Canónigo, from El Caño in the Betel church area, had been murdered.

A few people fled from the scene at once; but though the low talk in the visiting groups was less hilarious, most of them remained for the afternoon activities.

"Did I do right?" Vicente asked, joining the evangelist, Francisco Liévano, and a few of the older evangelicals who were chatting together.

"Certainly," said Sixto Machado. "We can't let their threats stop the work of God."

"The threats sometimes *make* the work of God," said a young man from the edge of the group. "I doubt if I'd be here today if it hadn't been for the troubles."

"How is that, León?"

"Well," said José León Duarte, "I work for Don Manuel Contreras. You've been there, Don Vicente, when the neighbors attacked his house, and you know how often they've done it. One time they came when we'd killed a hog, and those thieves were taking the pork and lard—and onions that were stored in the same place.

"Well, some of us plantation workers weren't going to put up with that sort of thieving. We decided we'd go and fight them off. If necessary, we intended to kill them. But Don Manuel wouldn't let one of his men even open the doors. For Don Manuel, the only important thing was the Word of God and his own witness for Christ, and every one of us knew it. That's why I became an evangelical."

"Santos Flores is the same," said a man from La Quebradita whom Manuel had also contacted for Christ. "They can come in and make a tremendous disturbance, calling him names, but he just keeps on preaching with love. Don Sixto, you were with us when they stoned us one time. Santos was hurt—bad. But he never changed. He always prayed for the ones who wanted to kill him."

"Well," said Sixto, "we have a good example to follow. Don Vicente always seems to be around somewhere about the time they're going to attack, or they attack because he's there. By his love and gentleness, he has set an example. Like father, like children."

"Nonsense," said Vicente, reddening. Then to withdraw attention from himself, he turned to young Duarte and asked him where he had first heard the gospel.

"Well, when Don Lorenzo Galvis started coming to our place, we didn't have the slightest idea what it was to be an *evangélico*. Then one time, when I was real sick with a fever, you came. None of the doctors had been able to help me. You said, 'Believe in Christ. He has power to heal you.' I said I didn't know if I could believe. So you knew I wasn't a believer, Don Vicente. You said, 'The blood of Christ can save you from sin. It can heal your body too.' And that's the way it was. Soon I knew by your love and by your teachings of God's love that Christ is our Saviour. And I could see the love of God in Don Manuel."

"Can you read?"

"I'm trying, Don Vicente. And God is helping me."

"One day, León," said Vicente seriously, "God will call you to preach for Him. José Pinzón is getting ready to go off to Bible school. God needs many more pastors for these mountains."

As they watched, the bashful young man's grin faded from his face. Into his eyes crept a shadow of hardship and great responsibility, and his chin seemed to be strengthened by an inner determination. Under the loving counsel of Vicente, revered man of God, a vision had been born.

Vicente and the evangelist moved off to speak to Armenio Pabón, then the trio approached a group of young women under the trees.

"That's the daughter of Elena Sánchez," said Armenio, nodding toward the vivacious girl whose gleaming dark hair streamed over her shoulders. Vicente's eyes twinkled.

"I remember her."

"Mamá didn't want us to go to those *cultos* at Julio Bartolo's," Victoria Sánchez was saying. "But we went anyway."

"You didn't act as though you'd come to listen," chimed in another of the young women from the Betel area. "All you did was chatter and disturb."

"Yes, and I thought I'd irk Don Vicente by describing a frivolous carnival picture that we had at home. Instead of being annoyed, he became so interested I asked him to come over next time he was near—to see it."

The young woman laughed hilariously at the rather guilty look on Vicente's face. However, the bachelor evangelist's motive was understood better than he feared, for one of the young women asked, "Did he remember to look at the picture when he got there?"

Victoria swung to face Vicente. "I can't even remember. Did we ever get around to showing it to you?"

"I saw it."

"Well, you know what happened, of course. We had a *culto* right there in our house. Mamá gave consent before she knew she'd said it."

Again everyone had a good laugh, knowing Victoria's mother. They all recognized another of Vicente's strategies for achieving openings for the Word of God.

"How does your father feel about the *cultos?*" asked a girl from another district.

"My father never did get to hear the gospel," said Victoria. "He came to the home where Mamá lived and wanted to leave after it was night even when he knew about the guerrillas in the hills. She asked him not to go, but he went. They shot him with a shotgun, and then cut off his head. They found the head far from the body."

This younger generation spoke casually of violent death and marital laxity. Both were part and parcel of their lives. The two men wandered on to where Marco Franco was entertaining a sizable crowd with some sort of animated account, if one were to judge by his vigorous gestures. The circle opened to admit the men.

"Don Marco is leaving us to live in the jungle," said Aurelio Sánchez, who had provided the Franco family with living quarters for some months. Vicente nodded. He had already heard that the Canónigo family, fearful of another attack by those who had killed José, had moved to a place called Puerto Oculto.[2] The government was making free land available to any person who staked claims in the uninhabited swampland of the Magdalena River Valley. Marco was considering the same move.

"And he's already gotten acquainted with his neighbors," said someone.

"Neighbors?" Vicente looked from one laughing face to another. "You mean the Canónigo family?"

His guess was greeted with a roar of laughter.

"Howler monkeys," someone explained. "You weren't here in time to hear Don Marco tell about them."

"Yes," said Marco with a chuckle. "They were having a *culto*."

"But it doesn't seem to me," interjected Aurelio Sánchez, "that they are *evangélicos*."

Marco obligingly repeated his story.

"I wanted to pray about this move, Don Vicente, so I was sitting there quietly, when this red monkey leaped into the branches of a nearby tree and set up his howl. Monkeys came swinging through the trees by the dozens, and pretty soon that tree was alive with monkeys. It seemed like it was choir practice, since they didn't have any congregation. The leader gave a pitch,

[2] Hidden Port.

and they all joined him. He'd change, and the chorus would follow his lead. Things were going right well until in swings this female carrying a young monkey. She was all out of breath, and with one toss of her long hairy arm, she plopped the small one down on a branch and then jumped to what looked like it was the place the choir had saved for her.

"She tried to come in without stirring up any fuss, but the choir director pulled his eyebrows together and glowered at her."

Marco chuckled. "Maybe this one had missed choir practice before! Anyway, he stopped the practice and cuffed her—screaming and in a terrible dither—off her perch, right to the end of the limb. Then he went on with the meeting."

"That's a good story to tell our choir members then," said Vicente. "Just so the directors don't hear it. Did you make up your mind to move into the jungle?"

"Sure did. I'd much rather live among howler monkeys than some of the people I've had for neighbors. It's safer."

"And Don Víctor, how's your building program coming?"

Víctor Téllez, who had recently become a believer, put his hand on the shoulder of his friend, Aurelio Sánchez. "It's above the foundation now, Don Vicente. Betania[3] will be a church they'll see from all directions."

"Yes," said Vicente, "a church up there on that ridge is a testimony of your changed lives to everyone who knew you."

He turned to Gratiniano Pino, who had arrived wth some of his neighbors. "How are things going at your end?"

"Just fine, Vicente. Just fine."

"Is there no persecution in your area?" inquired Francisco Liévano, almost incredulous, since most reports began with an account of local reactions. Gratiniano shook his head.

"No persecution. No real persecution."

One of the men whom Gratiniano had brought with him began to laugh heartily. "No persecution," he repeated. "Just a few people have tried to kill him, and keep swinging machetes at him. Otherwise, no persecution."

[3]Bethany.

Gratiniano grinned. "Knife play? I've always been very familiar with that type of negotiation." He passed his hand over the ugly scar on his forehead. The disfiguring protrusion of a flap of flesh now healed remained as a vivid reminder of Gratiniano's turbulent past.

"You should have seen the last bout when Gratiniano stood up to a guy with a machete. He said he'd come to kill Gratiniano. So Gratiniano said, 'For me to live is Christ, and to die is gain!' You'd think Gratiniano had hit him. He backed away and said, sort of stammeringlike, 'This work of the *evangélicos* has got to stop in this district.' Gratiniano said, 'If it is the work of men, then it will stop. If it is of God, it will stand.' He left with his drawn knife in his hand and has not come back to bother us since."

Together with Evangelist Francisco Liévano, Vicente strolled from group to group, listening to stories of victory or danger, encouraging, counseling, admonishing to faith and holy living. He knew all of these isolated mountaineers personally. Such a gathering as this demonstrated to them that they were not alone in their severe testings. Far more important, they needed to know that they had joined a movement that God was blessing in a phenomenal way. So appreciative were these people that many urged Vicente to disregard the police threat of attack and continue the conference as planned.

At two o'clock, the scheduled time for the afternoon session, the blast of a trumpet called the throng once more into the leafy chapel. In one corner young Duarte was bending over a guitar, strumming the theme song of the conference—a catchy jubilant melody that would soon be ringing out in the mountain air, a robust testimony of God's transforming power as these very people had experienced it.

Yo soy testigo del poder de Dios. . . .[4]

The sun was well to the west when the meeting closed.

"We have asked the Lord to protect us as we continue our

[4]I am a witness of the power of God.

conference," Vicente announced. "The believers from Ocaña have invited us to their church, and we will be guests in their homes. Now we will look to the Lord to provide us transportation before the sun sets."

The only transportation service, of course, was that afforded by vehicles that passed by on the highway, so the congregation broke up and started down toward the road. Moments later the vanguard, coming to the bend in the trail, saw a detachment of police waiting at the roadside. Obviously they had been loitering here until the time they had chosen to fulfill their orders.

"Al monte!" ordered Francisco Liévano sharply.

Had they been seen? The word passed back quickly from mouth to mouth until the last straggler knew what had to be done. In a short time the great crowd had melted into the shadows of the silent woods. Then, avoiding open trails, small groups wandered out to various points in the road to hail passing trucks or cars.

Miraculously the entire congregation was able to obtain transportation. So the conference trickled into Ocaña and proceeded to the church in the same discreet manner, breaking into segments of two or three as they walked along the streets. Astutely inconspicuous, the conference progressed without further interference right to the end.

8

Blessed Are Ye . . .

A STARFISH embodies a principle of life strikingly demonstrated in Santa Inés. Chop the starfish to a dozen bits and cast them overboard, and soon each fragment—as well as the original organism—has developed into a complete and robust star.

Emissaries of religious ignorance and bigotry had sought to stamp out the evangelical movement at Santa Inés. This body of believers, harassed and persecuted until its scattered members met in widely separated locations, had reproduced a number of stalwart congregations, each with the same vigorous testimony and the same living faith. With an unquenchable ardor of Christian love and the exuberance of people liberated from a deeper fear than that aroused by terrorists, the gospel became good news that was gossiped abroad in the land.

How the intrepid evangelists could take care of their plantations and conduct their own regular services and still continue to pioneer into unreached areas, will probably remain incomprehensible except to those who began working long before dawn, who spent gruelling hours on trails in fair weather or foul, who faced crushing discouragement and mortal danger with the same resolute faith and tenacity of purpose.

Santa Inés, the original congregation, had virtually become a great-great-grandmother in the five years since Vicente's arrival in 1949. Fourteen congregations had sprung up into robust life, some of them having produced offspring congregations almost at once. So enthusiastic and powerful was the witness of new converts and so great were the distances covered in their enthusiasm that separate meeting places became a necessity.

Betel in Las Planadas had been the first congregation to organize formally, and their church building had been dedicated on December 31, 1953. Now, a year later, its daughter congregation in Soledad had outgrown the haciendas of Aurelio Sánchez and Víctor Téllez, and the Betania Church now stood on a peak, a gleaming white testimony of the power of God to cleanse and to change.

As the gospel spread, other white chapels seemed to spring from the stony crests of the Andean landscape like the white blossoms of edelweiss that shoot up on the cold heights of the Alps. Besides Betel, Betania, and a new church building in Ocaña which had been built in April, two more—La Cruz on Palmira and El Redentor[1] in Santa Inés—were under construction at the end of 1954.

Three more were in prospect, for Sixto Machado planned to build a church, Nazaret, in San José, and his brother Juan and others of La Vega were planning to build Belén[2] Church. In the budding development on the Magdalena River at Puerto Oculto evangelicals were now gathering for regular meetings.

The band from Ocaña Church and some others of its hardier representatives planned to make the Christmas week a memorable holiday for the scattered groups of believers in the mountains. Having come from Ocaña to El Carmen by bus on Monday, they climbed out of that picturesque valley by a steep winding trail to the home of Ricardo Contreras in El Salto, where the isolated evangelical community that had no ordained pastor made the most of the missionary's visit and that of the band by celebrating a Christmas program, a wedding, baptismal and communion services.

Ricardo Contreras then joined the procession the following day

[1]Redeemer.
[2]Bethlehem.

as, by muleback or afoot, they threaded their way to La Yegüera, the next small community of evangelicals. Here they celebrated another wedding with Christmas music, and then the wedding ceremony dissolved into a baptismal service. On Wednesday the Christmas *jira*—now swollen to around a dozen—took to the mountains again.

The trail to the home of Ricardo's brother, Manuel Contreras, on Palmira, was steep and dangerous, often a mere scratch along the nearly perpendicular wall. Where a dip in the trail brought them to a small plateau, a group of men accosted the evangelicals and scuffled with them before they could pass.

Two hours later they descended the western mountain slope near the community of La Esperanza, so notoriously lawless that even government police and troops did not venture beyond the pass that led to the district. Here the procession met another party of holiday celebrants, two of whom carried shotguns, another a rifle. As soon as they realized that this was a company of the despised *evangélicos,* they became abusive, cursing the Protestants and pelting them with stones.

The group could have escaped quite easily by making a dash for a bend in the trail, but Ricardo Contreras was following with pack mules. He had come almost abreast of the belligerents before they became aware of his approach. Then one of the men swung toward him with a yell of hatred, and raised his heavy shotgun.

Ricardo cast a glance of dismay toward his friends who were waiting for him, but he saw they were too far away to help him. Then he looked up. Automatically he repeated a Psalm that had been a comfort and support on other occasions of danger.

> He that dwelleth in the secret place of the most High shall abide under the shadow of the Almighty.[3]

With a stunned expression, the drunken mountaineer dropped his gun. Ricardo passed safely by him to join his friends, who lost no time getting on their way. Once more their God had intervened in an utterly simple manner.

[3]Psalm 91:1.

That afternoon a large congregation met in the roofless chapel of La Cruz. The believers of Palmira had hauled all building materials, except locally felled logs, up those same perilous mountain trails. They had done all they could to have the building ready for dedication at this time, but heavy rains had washed the adobe walls down three times.

On Thursday morning they headed for the real goal of the expedition—Soledad. About an hour and a half from La Cruz, Vicente stopped to gesture over a magnificent gorge to their left. Along the far canyon walls, miniature houses looked like gems stuck haphazardly to a shield of tarnished copper. A cluster of houses huddled at the valley's narrow base. Vicente's face was aglow with the light of his burning vision and total commitment to the cause of Christ which he had, by his own dedication, communicated to all his followers.

His companions stood with uncovered heads while Vicente bathed that populous valley of Honduras in prayer. For some time, as they resumed the trail, nobody spoke. They had been drawn into the throne room of the Majesty on high, and the place whereon they trod was holy ground.

Later José Pinzón called attention to the near wall of another valley just one ridge removed from Honduras. The clumps of dwellings on the mountainside were not as large as the one in the valley's bed, but there was no mistaking that there too were scores of coffee plantations.

"It is Caracolí," said José.

There too they stopped to claim God's blessing on people who entertain murder in their hearts for the people who would bring them news of this hope.

Shortly after resuming the trail once more, at the summit of a high ridge, they were greeted by a spectacular view of the foothills that fell sharply down toward the Magdalena Valley. The sunlight reflected from the meandering convolutions of the great river that appears to sluggishly intend to make the whole level valley a swamp. Seventy miles beyond, the central chain of the

Andes formed a dramatic boundary. But the eyes of these men were fixed on Betania Church, which gleamed like a white beacon on Soledad Mountain, still hours away.

At Betania too a wedding was part of the Christmas festivity, and it seemed very probable that there was another one in the offing. Marco Franco's daughter Emalina, who had led the family to safety out of their blazing home when she was just a girl, had grown up into a vivacious young woman. Though she was still in her early teens, it was very plain to see that Aurelio Sánchez' son Oscar planned to make her his wife. Even while the Franco family had been living in Ocaña, Alicia, the oldest of Marco's daughters, had married Manuel Gómez, the young man whom she had encountered on her flight from El Carmen. Natividad had married Arturo Vanegas, son of Germán Vanegas and Juana Lazzco. Antonio had married Rosa Mateus of La Vega.

The final day was rounded out with the dedication service of the newly organized church, the baptism of new believers, and dedication of children. The annual business meeting concluded with a watch-night service, during which time the believers took communion.

Not much more than an hour's hard ride from Betania, the Ocaña band and the rest of the evangelicals gathered around the walls of the Santa Inés church, just a few bricks above the foundation. In this community where the believers had suffered much for the sake of the gospel and had survived to win their enemies for Christ, Carmito Elías was in charge. Armenio Pabón and Antonio Franco often helped out in taking the services.

A few nights after the new church in Santa Inés was completed in January, a hurricane lifted the roof from the chapel and flung it into a nearby field. For this poor congregation that had already suffered so much, it was a crushing disaster.   Still, this was no time to whimper or give way to defeat, but to set the roof back onto the church.

People who came from curiosity or malice to view the *evangélicos'* catastrophe, left with a sense of awe and wonder. These *evangélicos* were singing! Even as they wondered about it, the catchy melody of the chorus was drumming these words into their consciousness: *Si Cristo no cambia tu vida. . . .*

> If Christ doesn't change your life,
> Don't think you can do it yourself;
> If Christ doesn't change your life,
> Your life will never be changed.

They found themselves unconsciously humming the triumphant tune that carried its challenge of faith and personal victory right into their own empty, defeated hearts.

At the end of March, the new chapel of La Cruz was completed and became the focus of a three-day Bible conference that drew crowds from near and far. On Sunday, March 27, 1955, the chapel was filled to capacity at the dedication service. Again new converts gave their testimony to faith in Christ and commitment to His cause.

After Marco Franco moved his family to Puerto Oculto in the Magdalena Valley, Aurelio Sánchez retired to a quieter life in Aguachica, where he was immediately involved in the evangelical activities. Services were held alternately in his home and in that of Ramón Nieto, the most progressive believer in town.

The evangelical meetings were attacked repeatedly. The roofs over the Nieto *sala*—earlier his gun shop—and the inner veranda were destroyed by stoning. The Sánchez house was attacked in the same way. Mayor Lucio Vallona notified both of the men that services and teaching of the gospel must cease in their homes. He cited Circular 1785 as his authority to forbid religious activities in private homes.

Some time later, a copy of this restrictive circular fell into Ramón's hands and, acting much like the audacious Marco Franco, Ramón marched to Mayor Vallona's office with the edict in his pocket.

"Thank you for calling our attention to Circular 1785!" he said.

The mayor glowered. "What do you mean, 'Thank you'?"

"Because, Señor, this paper clearly gives us freedom for services."

Men who customarily loitered in the office to pass the time of day now pricked up their ears. Sensing excitement or diversion, they formed an interested ring around Ramón, who had pulled a sheet of paper from his pocket. The mayor cleared his throat belligerently.

"On the contrary, that circular forbids Protestant services."

He looked about at the animated faces of his staunch supporters clustered about the slight figure of the former gunsmith. "Not only does the circular forbid it—I do. And these law-abiding citizens here in my office will help me carry out the law."

"That's all right with me," insisted Ramón, "because this circular clarifies our right to hold meetings in our homes. Listen!"

Ramón, whose eyes were not at all good, moved toward the window and read, " 'Religious acts or non-Catholic services may be performed in temples, chapels, or private homes that have been declared places of service. The essential—' "

"Where did you get that paper?" demanded the mayor, his voice strident with anger.

"It's a copy of the circular, Señor Vallona. I got it after you said we were to obey it. We evangelicals are law-abiding citizens, so I wanted to know what the law says. And this is what it says."

"That's a lie!"

Ramón, the man who had once cowered at the thought that people would discover he had a Bible, now grinned and calmly beckoned to the men already breathing down his neck. "Follow the paper, please," he requested, continuing to reread the section, " 'The essential stipulation is that the pastor indicates in writing to the first political authority the place where the meeting—' "

"Stop reading that nonsense!" shouted the mayor, purple of face.

Ramón looked at the mayor soberly over the top of his steel-rimmed glasses. "Nonsense, Señor Vallona? But this is the government circular, number 1785." Ramón glanced at the men

who had been reading over his shoulder. "Did I read it correct-
ly?" A glint of mischief crept into Ramón's eyes and his lips
twitched. "Perhaps you would like to read it to us?"

"I can read my own copy," growled the mayor. "You're dismissed."

Ramón folded his paper carefully and tucked it into an inner
pocket. He bowed and muttered the usual formalities, adding,
"Thank you again, Señor, for calling this law to our attention."

Ramón left, exulting that the law was on the side of the evangelicals, somewhat oblivious to the fact that though the law of
Colombia had always stood for freedom of worship it had not
deterred the opposition in its violent attacks on Protestant work.

This law demanded that evangelicals hold services in recognized chapels; the opposition was making those chapels its special target. In the "holy" crusade that had formed against evangelical activity in Colombia, forty-three churches had been destroyed by fire, dynamite or bombing. Besides this, one hundred
and ten primary schools were closed, fifty-two evangelicals had
been murdered, still others stoned, beaten, tortured and jailed.

Newspapers denounced religious leaders for their part in the
violence—political and religious. Communism was capturing the
minds of the educated public that rebelled against bigotry and
discrimination. In the rural areas, however, few men thought
for themselves, and illiterates became ready tools of religious
hate.

Among the many men who were watching the evangelical
movement from beneath brows furrowed by perplexity and an
inner storm was Lalo Guevara, the wealthy plantation owner of
Los Cerros whose wife and children often fled to the woods when
his drinking turned him into a ruthless tyrant. Besides ruining
Lalo's marriage, drink was damaging him physically. As his wife
had told Manuel Contreras and José Pinzón, Lalo had tried to
quit drinking, but he did not know how.

Cristo Galvis, Lalo's brother-in-law who worked for him, was
like Lalo in that he often turned belligerent after too much
liquor. He often joined Lalo in making trouble. The dances

that began quite gaily around Lalo's phonograph with an amplifier—the mountaineers' substitute for a band—often ended in a free-for-all fight.

Then, almost suddenly, Cristo had committed himself to Christ. Lalo watched Cristo's life change from purposelessness and defeat to spontaneous joy, constant peace, and a zeal to share his new faith.

Vicente Gómez made a visit to the Guevara home during those days, though Lalo was still heartily opposed to the evangelical infiltration in the area. But the trail from La Cruz to La Quiebra led by Lalo's house, so Vicente often had stopped by to talk a bit. Lalo would admit that it seemed a "good system," but he would always change the subject before Vicente could get personal. Manuel Contreras and the Galvis brothers, Lorenzo and Trinidad, also stopped to speak to him when they visited Cristo. On one of those visits, Lorenzo asked if he could arrange for a *culto* to be held in Lalo's house.

"It's more central," said Lorenzo. "Everybody knows where you live, and you have a room that will accommodate a good crowd."

"Well," growled Lalo, "just so I don't have to drum up trade for you."

"Not at all," said Lorenzo, smiling. "We'll probably get some 'customers' here that we might not get anywhere else though."

"Well, just don't give out that I'm an *evangélico*," said Lalo. "I don't want anybody to think I'm an *evangélico*."

"Oh, that's quite evident to everybody," retorted Lorenzo quickly and without much thought. Then, realizing the implication of his first statement, he blundered further by adding, "They know that we often have *cultos* in the homes of sympathizers."

"Me? A *sympathizer?*" snapped Lalo. "Where in the world did you get that idea?"

Still, he was surprised at the group that Lorenzo had been able to interest in the meeting in a short afternoon. Lalo found himself wondering whether the *evangélico* had actually gone to the local tavern. It seemed that most of his intimates had come. More probably, he concluded, Lorenzo had contacted one of them, and that one had spread the word around.

Lalo was not too surprised when one of the men tried to stop the meeting. He seethed with disgust, however, that his acquaintance should have chosen to do so while Lorenzo was reading from the Book that Lalo had secretly begun to respect as the sacred Word of God. But he sat back in his chair, not quite willing to identify himself with the *evangélicos'* cause.

Another time, however, when Vicente had a *culto,* and his own acquaintances again became the ones who disrupted the meeting, Lalo openly took Vicente's part.

"You came to this meeting," he growled. "Well then, listen!"

Vicente, quickly perceptive, asked the gathered people to recite the Lord's Prayer. This was familiar ritual for all in the audience, and one that forbade ridicule. The meeting was finished without further trouble. Lalo even bought a Bible, and some force within him compelled him to read it seriously.

Lalo had truly intended to go to La Cruz for the dedication of the chapel, but because of his inner conflict he had begun to drink during the day. When it was time to go, he realized with self-contempt and real disappointment that he was not sober enough to ride that perilous trail. He wandered dejectedly to the point of his property that looked across the wide valley about the time for the meeting. His gaze swept upward to La Cruz.

He envied the people, visible as tiny moving dots, who were streaming up the trails toward the bright new chapel. Then, across the wide expanse of clear mountain air came the notes of band music, and Lalo knew the words. They were words that he had forbidden his small daughter Edilia to sing.

> If Christ doesn't change your life,
> Don't think you can do it yourself;
> If Christ doesn't change your life,
> Your life will never be changed.

If Christ Jesus doesn't change my life! he thought. *Why, I've*

been trying to change it myself, hoping to make myself present-
able to God. If Christ doesn't change my life—I'll never get it
done. I'll never be able to do it.

And so, far away from the evangelistic services in La Cruz
Church, the gospel began to be clear to Lalo. Still, when he went
to a later meeting, a sense of his own unworthiness caused him to
hesitate when urged to make a definite decision for Christ. He
had not the courage to face the disgrace of defeat as an evangelical. He still did not quite understand that the power to change
would not be his but God's.

Lalo was surprised at the understanding and patience of the
men who remained with him until his last doubt had been met
by God's own Word, and he knew that his past failures were
forgiven, that God Himself was committed to provide all he
needed to live this new life. The wonder of such a gospel turned
him at once—as it had done to so many in that area—into a fiery
evangelist, an enthusiastic salesman.

Friends and relatives came to battle with him over his infidelity. But Lalo knew that he had found reality, and no pleadings
or threats could turn him back to the emptiness and despair of
his former existence. Two weeks after he made his public confession of faith, his wife made hers. Very soon their home became the center for meetings for the Los Cerros community.

Meanwhile, many hours away and four to five thousand feet
below the robust congregations of the Andes, courageous evangelicals were attacking the jungles of the Magdalena River Valley with machetes and fire. Between the blackened skeletons of
majestic eucalyptus trees, still erect and proud in their denuded
state, the men carried on a monumental struggle against the
stubborn jungle.

Vigorous undergrowth fought to reclaim the fields planted to
yuca and corn, and to erase the trails that connected the few set-
tlers. Papaya and plantain shoots that had been thrust into the
oozing soil of the surrounding partially cleared land soon assumed the aspect of having always belonged to the jungle that
crept up around the quickly growing trees.

Régulo Canónigo, one of the first of the evangelicals that had come from Betel area, began working on the farm of Alejos Durán. Alejos' curiosity was aroused by Régulo's avid reading of a Bible, and he demanded that the latter read something to him. Soon Régulo was explaining the meaning of the gospel message.

When Vicente scheduled an intensive Bible *cursillo*[4] at Betel, Alejos accompanied Régulo to his old home community. During that conference, Alejos committed his life to Christ. As more of the Betel families moved to Puerto Oculto, Alejos opened his home to the evangelicals for meetings.

Other pioneering Colombians began to stake claims round about them. Swinging wide-bladed machetes at the rank verdure that would trip them up and engulf their holdings, the rugged evangelicals took to the trails with their Bibles and their ringing testimonies of what God had done for them and what He could do for all. The words they read from their well-worn Bibles were endorsed by their generous sharing of yuca and plantain cuttings, by calloused hands that were offered when it came time to erect a cane dwelling or a thatched roof.

So hard was the struggle to wrest a living from the new claims that only the poor made the effort. Homes were built from the materials at hand, and living was primitive in its simplicity. Because of the danger from snakes, scorpions and vampire bats, many erected sleeping shelters on stakes—just a cane floor with a low palm-leaf roof very near the sleeper—a sort of spacious cocoon on stilts. A fire built under the shelter might cause the sleeper to cough, but it would also deter the invasions of thick swarms of mosquitoes.

Battling the slugs and monkeys that would pilfer their plantings, fighting against hordes of ants and destructive birds, chopping back the encroaching jungle, and cultivating the ground that had been exposed by such grueling toil—these activities filled the long, hard days. Meetings were held on Sundays or at night, though to travel alone was almost foolhardy. Yet a spiritual hunger prompted them to brave the danger of meeting wild

[4]Course.

animals, snakes and alligators that lurked in the dank, tangled vegetation.

Since many of the believers came from Betel, Armenio Pabón often made the long trip to Puerto Oculto to hold services. Then Marco Franco arrived with his family and, shortly afterward, Antonio brought his wife to the new development. Naturally, each of them was eager to hold *cultos* in any home thrown open to them.

Bottles filled with kerosene with wicks of corncob gave light for the meetings. In one of the services led by Vicente, a snake coiled itself about a man's leg while he stood up to sing. In one of those backwoods meetings, Andrés Vargas, who had spent years roaming the countryside as a member of a guerrilla band, became a convert to this new evangelical faith.

Marco again secured a supply of items vital for living, and stocked a small store. His strategy was the old one he had discovered in Santa Inés. He drew customers to buy his wares, then witnessed to those customers of the love of Christ.

"He doesn't let one escape him!" remarked one of his acquaintances.

As in Santa Inés, such an audacious witness was not casually tolerated. One day on his way to Aguachica, Andrés overheard discussion of a murderous plot against the Franco family. Conditioned as a guerrilla to life that hung precariously by a raveled thread, Andrés knew that to disregard any threat could end in tragedy. He abandoned his own business and sprinted to the nearest evangelical home. Of Ramón San Juan he demanded a horse, explaining the situation.

"I have to go to warn Don Marcos!"

"Do you want me to come with you?"

Andrés knitted his brow in worried concentration. "If they had only said anything about when they plan to attack—or ambush—the family. Would it be at their home?"

"They've had their roof burned up over them twice. It could happen again."

"Well, we've got to warn them."

Ramón hastily sheathed his machete and shoved his plantain cuttings into a heap under a bush. He got two horses, and the men sped down the trail in the direction of the Franco holdings.

These men had learned to ride the hazardous Andean mule trails and so took in stride the obstacle race which led the horses in flying leaps over the smaller fallen trees and around the gigantic trunks that lay in profusion across the partially cleared yuca fields.

In mountain descents they had learned to lean back in their saddles to prevent their weight from pulling their mules into a somersault. They now learned to lean far forward in their saddles, with their hats down over their faces, when they passed under heavy overhanging limbs. Usually they kept whacking away at the foliage above with their machetes. Today they dispensed with that gesture of defiance against the energy of the jungle.

"Watch it!"

Ramón barked the warning back to Andrés as he passed by a tree with delicate, feathery foliage. Andrés pulled his horse to the left quickly, but not quite in time. Vicious hooked thorns concealed under the deceptive fragility of the fernlike leaves clawed at Andrés' shoulder, ripping a gash into the flesh of his arm. Ramón reined his horse; Andrés waved him on.

"Keep going," he said. "We can't stop for a thing like this."

"Have you got something to tie it up?"

Andrés had no such luxury as a pocket handkerchief, but with his machete he swung at a vine along the track, and placing a folded leaf over the profusely bleeding cut, he quickly made a pressure bandage, which Ramón fastened deftly with a special loop that was used in tying these vines.

Arriving at the Franco home an hour later, they found the place deserted. Now truly apprehensive, they raced back toward the home of Jorge Durán, one of Marco's sons from the "other" woman, whom Marco had won to faith in Christ. Jorge had followed his father to Puerto Oculto and had taken up an adjoining holding. His young wife came out of the house as the two men galloped into the yard.

"Where is Don Marco?" cried Ramón, bringing his horse to a spiraling halt.

"He went to Santa Inés with my husband. They all went. The whole family."

"Are you alone?"

"With the younger Franco children. Carmelo is here."

After a brief consultation, the men decided to send someone to watch the farm and protect this household, too, since Carmelo Franco was only about fourteen years old. Within an hour they had organized a general alarm. When the Francos returned, concerted Christian love had provided such a force of nonviolent resistance that the attackers, though armed, slunk away to their holdings. The Francos continued their aggressive witness without serious trouble.

Vicente went as often as he could to visit the thriving congregation which had chosen for itself the name of Ebenezer.[5]

Perhaps Vicente often encouraged himself with the same challenging thought—*hitherto hath the Lord helped*—to spur himself along on the boggy trail toward the new settlement. The five leagues from the end of the rutted road could be covered in four hours on horseback, but took much more time and energy afoot.

He arrived at the Vargas home one day in late 1955 after the rains had made the locale's more common name, El Barro,[6] completely appropriate. Vicente stopped, as usual, to pay a visit to friends on his way. Characteristically inclined to being less concerned for his own welfare than for that of his spiritual charges, Vicente got a very late start as he proceeded toward the Franco claim, still a good two hours' walk from the Vargas' clearing. Andrés had warned him that the jungle route now was a veritable bog.

Preoccupied with a local problem on which he had been asked counsel, Vicente had already entered the fringe of forest when he suddenly became conscious of a prolonged and strident growl.

---

[5]"Samuel took a stone, . . . and called the name of it Ebenezer, saying, Hitherto hath the LORD helped us (I Samuel 7:12).
[6]Mud.

He began to regret that he had been detained until almost sundown. Any animal was bolder after nightfall. He slapped his pocket. Yes, he had his flashlight, but he still wavered between turning back and facing an angry *tigre,* as he thought of the several species of jungle wildcats.

Then he began to laugh, though a bit shakily. Howler monkeys! They were passing along the signal that their territory was about to be invaded by an alien type of animal. As Vicente advanced with quickened step, the furor ceased, with only a few snarls to let him know that his every move was under watchful surveillance. He knew there must be scores of the creatures overhead, invisible among the leaves.

A colorful bird swept to the branches ahead of him, screaming an angry warning. Not much farther on, a sudden rustle in the underbrush made him halt once more. If it was a snake, it was very important to locate it before he went on. It would be the height of indiscretion to allow a cobra to strike him when he was entirely alone. Then he caught sight of the iguana—a jumbo-sized lizard built on the pattern of prehistoric dragons, armored with a horny carapace like a coat of mail, with a tight-fitting, spiked helmet. Fantastic purple wattles on either side of the reptile's jowls waggled ferociously as he nodded his head as though giving some sort of ominous signal of readiness to an ally hidden out of sight.

Vicente slashed at the ugly creature with his machete, partly as a reaction to his alarm, and perhaps just as much a gesture of disgust that he had not recognized the abrupt rustle as typical of this huge lizard, for it fled with the same violent rustling of dead twigs and leaves.

Insects chirped and buzzed in such volume that Vicente paused once to make sure whether it was not a distant sawmill, for there was one somewhere ahead. He walked on with a strange sense of deep quiet and isolation, though a vibrating spectrum of sound betrayed the presence of multitudes of creatures all about him.

A butterfly with a span of five inches caught a ray of the lowering sun and flashed by, a beautiful iridescent blue. Vicente gave it far less attention than the trees that stood in a pool of stagnant water ahead of him.

When he had gone through weeks earlier, it had seemed that all the trees in the area had literally leaped two feet upward from the soil as if to escape the strangling underbrush. All their spreading roots shot fantastically from the trunk base at the same level above ground. These slender trees were all of one species and stood on stilts of a kind, for the tapering roots were rigidly holding up the trees. With the level of swamp mud having crept up to cover these roots, the mystery was explained. These trees had begun a rapid growth from seeds drifting on the swamp's surface, and he had first seen them in the unnatural nudity of the dry season.

About that time, Vicente removed his shoes and rolled up his trousers, as his trail led into an extensive boggy area around which he could find no detour. He had not counted on the delay of the mud, which was laced with vines underneath the surface and made walking very difficult.

Only then did he begin to understand Andrés' emphasis on the mud. Was he to wade through three kilometers of this slush? He quickened his pace when he slogged once more onto leafy mulch that oozed and squished underfoot. He coughed and sputtered, then flailed with his arms at a cloud of gnats that hovered densely about his head and followed him with the seeming intention of being inhaled.

When he reached the second stretch of swamp, he came down so rapidly to knee depth that he waded back to the edge to remove his trousers. These he tied securely to his hat, which he shoved down firmly on his head.

The setting of the sun had left him abruptly in the dark, and the night air was chill against his naked, mud-plastered thighs. He began saving his flashlight when he noticed that the batteries were running down. At last, as he floundered out from an exhausting expanse of waist-deep mud and stood shivering in the dark, he realized that he was completely lost. He shone the feeble light of his flashlight in all directions without finding any familiar landmark. Even his sense of direction had dissolved in his circuitous stumblings.

Swarms of fireflies were bustling silently about on their own errands, lighting their familiar ways with their own pocket torches, the light of which was reflected in the fetid sludge, but which did not give him a clue to where he should be going. All around him toads were tinkling their little bells like a hundred thousand voluntary guides to places of interest, and bullfrogs blasted a startling bass note at him from unexpected nearness, their bloated throats just above the slimy ooze.

Night sounds of the jungle differed from the cheerful chirpings of the day, making a melancholy five-note call of a nightbird sound eerie in the distance. Nearer, another bird muffled a scream. A cautious cough reminded Vicente of very real danger lurking, perhaps not farther away than his elbow. He tried to shine his flashlight in the direction of the suspicious sound, but it glowed only feebly, not making much more impression on the thick darkness than one of the larger fireflies.

Wandering back and forth in the dripping forest, Vicente found a trail which led him to an abandoned shelter that had been used by loggers. He still did not know which direction to take, so he determined to spend the rest of the night there.

He found a plank that had been placed across the crude rafters of the open shed. After he had shoved it to one side, near the thatched roof, he felt he would be able to sleep on it without too much danger of falling off. Chilled to the bone and still shivering violently from his efforts to cleanse his body with handfuls of wet grass, he pulled on his clothes, deeply thankful that he had kept them comparatively dry.

Vicente had almost fallen asleep when he was wakened by that strange dry cough that had alarmed him earlier that night. The last, tired beam from his flashlight reflected from two green eyes spaced far enough apart for Vicente to know it was no small kitten that had him treed.

Vicente lay quietly on the rafters, tensely waiting for the animal to attack. He tried shouting to frighten it away, then he removed the dead batteries from his torch and threw them at the glitter of the creature's eyes. It moved to a new position, but Vicente was ever aware of the watchful presence below him. The *tigre* did not leap, neither did it lose patience. The gray of dawn made the outlines of the wildcat visible, and at last it turned, snarling with frustration, to slink into the jungle.

9

Marching to Zion!

Come, ye that love the Lord,
  And let your joys be known

. . . .

Let those refuse to sing
  Who never knew our God;
But children of the heavenly King
  Must speak their joys abroad!

WE'RE MARCHING TO ZION! Few who sing this militant challenge
to total commitment to Christ's cause would be able even to
imagine the hardships of terrain and of terrorization that faced
the rugged evangelicals of the Andes. Still, they kept increasing.

Lalo Guevara had built a new house as a temporary place of
worship. Almost at once the thriving congregation of Sión had
outgrown it and had expanded itself out onto the open veranda.

Except for those times when Vicente Gómez or Armenio Pabón, who early in 1955 had arrived at the spiritual age of three
full years, came to hold meetings, all who gathered in Sión were
mere babes in reference to this new dimension of living. They
had a normal, God-instilled hunger for the Word that would
bring them growth and maturity. When Vicente came—no matter
what day in the week it might be—people ignored both distance
and time involved, and they flocked to Los Cerros.

A delightful informality pervaded the meeting in Sión. The

177

leaders were simply intent on sharing the realities of a new life and of release from fear or despair. The fervent heartiness of their singing indicated joyous participation of old and young in the service. The moment one hymn or chorus had been finished, someone in the congregation would bounce up from the backless bench and lead off in another. This self-appointed leader remained on his feet, singing a lusty lead. The fact that all evangelical families habitually sang at least one hymn at each of their daily *culto*s was readily apparent in the shrill piping of children's voices joining those of their parents or leading off without self-consciousness in a favorite chorus.

No uncomfortable lags marred the spontaneous spirit of worship during the prayer session. Since every member of an evangelical family took part in their own devotional periods that often began as early as four o'clock each morning and were held again at bedtime, the children participated in this quaint but completely orderly prayer service. As all voices united to rise like incense to the Father's throne, a spirit of unmistakable reality shone in the faces. They were people checking out with a living God the lives they had been living with relation to the new truths that they had just heard. If a skeptic had remained indifferent through the preaching, this torrent of earnest prayer would have left him shaken.

Santos Millán, a young man with blue eyes and a mop of curly blond hair, came from San Joaquín to hold services in all the mountain congregations. He gave his testimony in Sión as well.

After describing the conditions in his home during his boyhood days, Santos said, "Evangelicals were beginning to have services around there too. One of our family explained this activity by saying, 'It's of the devil.' So, of course, I was very afraid of the evangelicals' work. One time I heard them play some musical instruments, and I took another route to avoid a possible evil influence. I had heard that they had a black figure of a devil with horns and tail, and that they worshiped this image. I closed my eyes as I walked along so that I would not even see these wicked people."

A few sympathetic chuckles swept the audience.

"One time I was visiting in the home of a friend. He had gone out, and his wife was very busy, she said. So she gave me a book to read. I read it with great interest. By the time I had read seven chapters of it, I was thinking deeply of my own life as it measured up to what was in the book. I put a mark in it and went to the señora and said, 'How did you get this wonderful little book?'

" 'I bought it from Señor López.'

" 'Not Señor *López?*' I said. I knew Domingo López was one of those *evangélicos*. 'Señor Domingo López?' I said.

"I was stunned. I was holding one of those evil books I had been warned about. I had even read in it.

" 'Why do they say these books are so evil, and this one speaks of the good Lord Jesus Christ and the miracles that He did, and other very precious teachings. How can this book be evil?'

"I began to meditate about it and to ask questions. I also bought a New Testament. After some time I even went to a *culto*. I decided to reform and did give up gambling in card games; but when I was tempted to drink, I couldn't withstand the temptation. Then I reached the place in the New Testament telling about Jesus coming back the second time to earth. That scared me."

Again a ripple of sympathetic laughter swept his audience.

"I had been drinking since I was fourteen and had been an alcoholic almost that long. I wanted to know about the kingdom of God and to get myself ready for it, but I couldn't. In despair, I discussed these matters with a friend.

"Together we went to Cúcuta to the home of Joselín Acero, who explained that becoming an evangelical was not so much imitating Christ as receiving Him. 'We cannot live the Christian life,' he said—as I'd already discovered—'but Christ can live His life in us.' Both of us committed our lives to Jesus Christ after the first sermon we heard there in Cúcuta. That was two and a half months ago. I'm here to share the wonderful joy of knowing that what he said is true. Jesus has broken all my fetters and has given me a goal for now and for all eternity."

Young Santos enthusiastically joined the local evangelical *jiras* into surrounding communities and shared Lalo's desire to contact every home on Los Cerros, no matter what the reception might be. He also shared in some of the narrow escapes the local evangelicals had begun to consider a part of their blessings.

The impersonal *they* had become a badge of a Christian's love and forgiveness. His neighbors might hurl insults and invective at him, stab him, or beat him with heavy clubs or leather thongs. The evangelical must resist personal resentments as he resisted the natural inclination to fight back. *They* had come, *they* had done what they wanted with him and all he had. It was for him to forgive *them*.

Santos was recounting a disturbance in one of the local meetings as he discussed the week's evangelistic efforts with Lalo.

"Don Sixto Machado came for the meeting too, but it was Santos Flores from Quebradita who was doing the preaching."

"I know Flores," said Lalo. "He wouldn't let Manuel Contreras and José Pinzón into his house at first. Now that he's a believer, he's sure getting a taste of his own medicine."

"And he takes it in such a spirit of understanding and love," said Santos. "They made a terrible disturbance at the meeting, and when he just kept on, they brought in sticks to beat him up. So we got mixed up with it. That's when they began to throw stones."

"By the number of purple welts all over you, you got mixed up in it pretty thoroughly!"

Santos grinned and ran his fingers carefully across a bruise above his temple. "Well, we couldn't just stand by and let them beat him down. He was the one who got the really hard blows."

"Here in Sión we had about eighty at our service," said Lalo. "And I built this place thinking that maybe—sometime—we would get fifty to come to special occasions."

"Thank God, then. Getting a beating now and then is worth it if the church grows beyond our dreams."

"I'm beginning to have a new dream," said Lalo. "Would you like to know what it is?"

Lalo took Santos across the summit, less than a half mile back of his house, to where the mountain fell steeply down into the eastern valley. Opposite them, on the next range of mountains, La Cruz gleamed like a pearl. La Quiebra, the peak that faced his home, towered above them to the west.

"Here, where Sión can be seen from both of these evangelical communities," said Lalo, "I hope to build a proper chapel."

"They are planning a church on La Quiebra," said Santos. "So that will make three chapels in a row, one on each mountain range."

"When they build on La Quiebra, we'll have to help. Think of getting building materials up that trail. Manuel Contreras did most of the work on La Cruz, but that was before we knew what he was about."

"The other believers helped, of course?"

"Yes, but Don Manuel had sixteen benches and a pulpit built in El Carmen. He brought them all up there himself."

"Benches!" exclaimed Santos. "Sixteen of them! It gives me goose pimples just thinking about it."

"Don Manuel has suffered very much for the gospel," said Lalo. "They keep robbing him of his goats, hogs and chickens. They've killed his dogs now, so he won't know when they're there. They've even stolen pots and pans from the kitchen. I don't know how many times they've had to snatch up the children and run for the woods."

"Everybody tells me of that man's humility and patience."

"One night they didn't have time to get away, and they were shooting into the door and chopping at it with machetes. Manuel gave the children each a Bible, and they read Psalm 91 lying on the floor."

"On the floor?"

"To dodge the shots. They kept shooting through the door."

"And no one was harmed?"

"Don Manuel has spent whole days with Don Vicente, praying

and fasting. I believe it is God that always protects him and his family. Don Manuel has been beaten on the trail and stoned, mind you, but God has saved his life. And the man radiates. He preaches all over his mountain and often here in Sión. He's been on La Esperanza, and lately he's been going down to Honduras."

"Why don't we just stop now and pray for him?"

"You sound as though you've been making some trips with Don Vicente!"

Santos grinned again and nodded. "It's the first thing you notice when you're with him. He covers these mountains with prayer."

"God bless that man. God bless him!"

"He doesn't talk much about it, Don Lalo, but Don Vicente is often sick. I guess he eats too irregularly and is often too tired."

"Well, he goes down to El Barro where the heat and malaria thin his blood. Then he comes up to the mountains. That's what makes him come down with those chills."

"And fever. I've nursed him through two bouts of it."

"When José Pinzón finishes Bible school, it will be much easier on Don Vicente."

The younger man was suddenly silent, and the glow seemed to fade from his eyes. Lalo eyed him thoughtfully.

"You want to go too, don't you?"

"There is nothing else I want to do with my life but give out the good news of salvation in Jesus Christ."

"You are doing a good work here."

Santos said nothing. Lalo studied his handsome young face, usually lighted with a wide smile.

"Well, why don't you?"

"I couldn't. I haven't any money."

No one knew better than Lalo why Santos had no money. From the moment of his conversion he had been giving all his time to heralding the message of the glorious salvation that had set his own heart free. There in the mountains, Santos had received free hospitality wherever he went, but his clothes were becoming ragged. The youth could be earning money to fulfill his dream of Bible school, but he saw the need of the mountaineers as greater than his own need. He had never complained. He was not complaining then.

"Why don't you make a project of this for God?"

Santos' blue eyes widened as he met Lalo's challenging glance. A gleam of hope and determination appeared, and then Santos bowed his head. Lalo joined with him in his prayer.

When José Pinzón returned to his Andean parish during school vacations, Santos concentrated his activities around Sión and the valley congregations. José, who still found the climb dizzying and fearsome, worked on La Quiebra where the sturdy congregation was growing in spite of severe opposition. Manuel García, the man who was carrying the brunt of the persecution since the services were held in his home, was almost pathetically happy to see José. He confided in José the difficulties of his first days as a Christian.

"I went home so happy," said García. "I just thought everybody would accept this gospel right away. But my wife said, 'If you've gotten into that—'"

José nodded in understanding when García paused.

"Well, she was critical." García's understatement was somehow more eloquent than an account of her tirades. Besides his private harassments, troublemakers had come to every service during those first two years. The doors and even the walls of the house had been hacked with machetes and badly damaged. Fanatical neighbors had chopped down fences; they had slaughtered a milk cow, slashing off the meat they wanted and leaving the rest to rot. García had never gone to battle for his rights, but he prayed instead for his neighbors.

Once a friendly neighbor discovered that some of García's cows were in the possession of a man who had been persecuting him.

"Go to law, man," the neighbor urged. "You can't just let them rob you like that without fighting back. I'll go with you and swear they're your cows."

Though sorely tempted to do so, García had refused to go to law. Now he confided, "I didn't know how to pray, but God taught me through these things. There was a canyon—there I learned to pray and praise. I couldn't pray at home, you know, because I was getting it there too. Still, I kept speaking about this way."

Several times his life had hung by a hair. More than once he was attacked with *rulas*—the broad machetes used in coffee plantation work—and again with stones. García's stand had meant great loneliness.

"When these things came, I opened the Bible and asked God in secret to give me grace in my peril."

Now however his wife was a believer, and it was she who told José about Ramón Becerra, who had drawn his dirk to stab García right there in his own home. "He didn't like it because I had changed my political ideas," explained García, who had been a Conservative until he saw the senseless and legalized butchery of the prolonged civil war.

"Ramón had my husband in a corner," said García's wife, "and was about to plunge the knife into him. Instead of whining and begging for his life, García began to talk to him of God's love. Ramón started raving at him, but he drew away just the same. That's when García fell on his knees and prayed for him, with tears. So Ramón began to see that it isn't the *evangélicos* that are evil."

"He even asked my pardon, José," said García. Then he added, beaming, "And today he's an *evangélico*."

"They don't all end up believing though," said García's wife. "Two of the men who attacked brethren who came here from Soledad have themselves been killed."

"You have been through a lot since you made your decision for Christ."

"Yes," said García, "but through the testings, I've found out how faithful the Lord is. What hurts most is that my best friend has turned against me. When I invited him to come to a service, he threatened to kill me—like the rest of them."

"It's easy to see they don't just come to make threats," commented José, examining the splintered door.

"God protected us," García said simply. "They want me to leave, but I am not about to forsake this congregation—voluntarily. If they kill me, they kill me. The ones I'm concerned about are those girls of Evaristo Martínez."

"Evaristo is really making it hard for them."

"Not only that, but there's always a gang of roughnecks hanging around Evaristo's canteen, and the stand the girls are taking is breaking up the *parrandas* they used to have down there. You can depend on it, the neighborhood isn't going to take that peacefully. Those girls are having a bad time."

"First from their father, and then from their friends. Have they made a public confession of their faith?"

"The older one has. Maybe now that you're here, José, the other two will also."

One Sunday morning Célida, Evaristo's vivacious younger daughter, excitedly declared that she was going to make a public declaration of her faith that evening in the evangelistic service.

"Why not now?" asked José, amused at her effervescent enthusiasm.

"At Sunday school?" cried the girl, who quite obviously had been weighing the propriety of making her public stand at that hour. "But we can come tonight! Doña María is visiting with us, and so Papá is letting us come with her." So delighted was Célida at the prospect that she pirouetted unconsciously.

Célida's exuberance had probably caused her tongue to betray her to the wrong people. When someone pounded on the door of the García home later that afternoon, José followed his host to the door. The manner of knocking had boded no friendliness.

The young man who had beaten on the already battered door seemed far from sober, and he had himself painted to suggest the face of the devil. Two cow horns protruded from a skull cap apparently made of knitted underwear. A tail, probably salvaged from the same cow, bobbed from below his coat. Two other masqueraders, with bony knees and elbows extending in hairy nakedness from below feminine frills, looked grotesquely angular as they waited on their skittish horses. By using lipstick and eye shadow over heavy white powder, they had achieved a rather weird and evil effect.

"Oh," muttered García over his shoulder to José, "I'd almost forgotten. It's a festival day."

"Where are the Martínez señoritas?" asked the man at the door.

García chuckled. "You don't think I'd turn them over to the devil, do you? I'm an *evangélico!*" The men on the horses roared at their companion's expense.

"Never mind the funny business," growled the horned man who was impersonating the devil. "Where are they?"

"They're not here."

At first the man was inclined to argue, then he declared, "It's a good thing for them they're not here. If they're not at the dance—"

"If you're going to make Protestants of them," yelled one of the others, with an oath, "we're coming to the meeting."

"And that will be the end of their Protestantism!"

"Or it will be the end of *them*."

"Why don't you pick on somebody your own size?" said García. "What have those girls done to you?"

"They're breaking up our dances, *that's* what they've done," said the devil emphatically.

"Well," said García, "it looks as if you have two girls here with you. Why don't you dance with them?"

Unable to think up a tart response to García's reference to their disguises, the youth strode back to his horse, sputtering invectives and the veiled threat, "Just wait!"

García shrugged his shoulders. "That's the way it is. If we paid any attention to their threats, we'd get nothing done. Half the time they're just blowing off steam. These fiestas are bad enough here in the mountains. If they can't think of anything else to entertain themselves, they're likely to pick a fight."

In spite of the fiesta, enough of the community was now truly evangelical that a rather good crowd turned out to hear José preach. José could not help thinking that he hardly blamed the young men of the mountain for their resentment. The loss of the three attractive Martínez sisters would make a great deal of difference to a party in these sparsely settled parts. That resentment came to fruition as the evening wore on.

José, intent on his sermon, was not aware of anything until García went abruptly to the door and bolted it. One of the other men helped him set a heavy pole against it.

"They're all masked," cried one of the women.

"They're all drunk," retorted one of the men. "That's what worries me."

The party collected around a huge boulder at the bend of the trail. Amidst shouted ribaldry, they struck up a popular folk tune. Several of them carried guitars, two had drums. Others however carried stones, knives, poles. Familiar with the menace of mob action, the evangelicals made a dash toward the windows, fastening the wooden shutters with every available bolt and hook.

Then, locked up in the darkened house, they listened tensely. A clamor of voices rumbled above the approaching beat of drums. The sound would have chilled the blood in a land of law and order. In Colombia, brutal violence had been a part of national life for seven horror-filled years. A massacre, such as seemed the mob's intent, would hardly make news headlines.

Children screamed in wild fear as the yelling crowd began beating on the door. García turned to his wife.

"Get the children into the bedroom—and the women. And set the poles against the door. We'll hold them as long as we can, Dear, but it's a big crowd. Pray for us."

The terrible battering continued. The evangelicals prayed for the people on the veranda as much as they prayed for their own safety. Some of their warmhearted neighbors, in a calmer moment, would deeply regret having any part in whatever violence might occur.

At last, having spent his fury vainly beating at the door, one man struck up a tune on his guitar. Distracted, the others began to dance on the veranda. When José opened a shutter a crack, one of the men, ludicrous in woman's attire, raised his skirt.

"Look, *Hermanito*,"[1] he bellowed, using contemptuously the word that was a common form of address among the evangelicals. "Look, *Hermanito*. This is where I keep my knife."

"God is with us," said one of the evangelicals. "He has restrained their anger."

Shortly afterward they heard someone on the veranda shout for someone to leave. As quickly as they had appeared, the crowd withdrew.

After a few choruses of fervent praise, the evangelicals dispersed. Manuel and José escorted the Martínez girls toward their home. As they had feared, some of the masquerade party had formed an ambush beside the trail. They sprang out to give the girls a terrible fright. However, in spite of the earlier threats, a scare was all that had been intended, and the girls were soon safely in their own home.[2]

Vicious attacks on the Martínez home caused Evaristo to become sternly antagonistic toward the girls' evangelical faith. However, when the harassments continued with deadly intent, Evaristo began to take his daughters' part. Finally convinced of the reality of their faith by their dauntless adherence to it, he began to share it himself. Soon the entire family believed.

José was not to escape to the security of his second term at Bible school without further demonstration of how a pastor would fare if he ever reached the day of his ordination. On his way to visit the congregation of Jerusalén that met in Gratiniano Pino's home, José had no choice but to follow the trail that passed directly by the house of a man he had good reason to fear. To José's dismay, the man stood glowering in his doorway. José began praying fervently.

The mountaineer snarled sullenly as José rode by, and turned abruptly back into the house. *Was it to get his gun?* José had been shot at from the back too often to wait and see.

---

[1] Diminutive of *hermano*, brother.
[2] Eight years later, when this story was told, every member of that masquerading party had become a baptized evangelical.

He spurred his mule sharply and was still shakily voicing his gratitude to God for helping him to pass unmolested when a bend in the trail revealed two other sworn enemies of all evangelicals at some distance. Both were carrying shotguns. The moment they recognized him, he saw them exchange a few words.

They allowed José to approach without any show of animosity; but when he was too near for retreat, both of the men raised their guns and covered him. His trail lay between the two men and the two guns that were trained directly on him. One of the men swore foully, and so evil was his facial expression that José expected him to pull the trigger of his gun at once. Strangely, the man whipped out a bottle instead.

"Have a drink."

His assailant seemingly wanted some legal justification for violence, should it get as far as a court. To refuse a drink, José knew, would be considered an affront. José looked at the thin lips drawn back against the man's yellow teeth in a sadistic leer.

"You may want an argument, Señor," he said, "but I don't." He was right between them. If only there were a bend in the trail ahead, or a chance to make a dash for the shelter of the woods.

"Answer me something," said the man, intent on an excuse for discharging his weapon.

"Why, yes," said José, edging his mule back onto the trail. He permitted the beast to begin to amble past the men at its own gait. "I'll be glad to answer any questions you have. In fact, I'd be glad to have you come to one of our *cultos*." He spoke evenly, playing for time.

Once beyond the man, with his back toward their cocked shotguns, José succumbed to sheer panic and, though he knew it might be fatal, spurred his mount. Even the mule seemed to sense his danger, for it adopted an erratic course as it sped down the slope. José was certain that God had caused these men to hold their fire.

Still shaking from his experience, he arrived at Jerusalén, where the congregation joined him in thanksgiving. Not one of the evangelicals there had escaped persecution. Gratiniano Pino's casual attitude toward knife play had not prevented his suffering many and frequent indignities.

These hardy brethren were speaking then of their advance in witnessing to people on La Osa[3], another peak, higher and colder than La Quiebra. They were having occasional *cultos* even then in the home of Mauricio Rangel.

One Saturday José started from La Quiebra, having accepted the invitation of Manuel Contreras to have the Sunday service in La Cruz. He spent the night at Lalo's home at Sión, and reached the new La Cruz Church, with its tiny flower garden in front, just in time for the service.

Afterward a boy burst into the Contreras home in wild excitement.

"Where's Don Manuel?" he panted.

"He's not here. He went to Corralitos."

"They're coming!" the boy shouted agitatedly. "I saw them! One has a pole, and the other a heavy club. And machetes!"

Everyone knew the temperament of the Palmira mountaineers, so no one wasted time trying to ascertain the identity of the enemy. There was no discussion about the assailants being outnumbered by the people in the house. The unflinching attitude of all the evangelicals was that of turning the other cheek, and new converts were less afraid of the inevitable blows than they were that they would revert to the old retaliatory instincts of their inflammable Latin blood. Their pacifistic stand naturally encouraged cowards to sadism and thievery. Moreover, as Christ's own meekness incited outraged reactions by its convicting contrasts, the excesses of passionate brutality often stemmed from a tortured conscience.

Windows had quickly been barred in all rooms. But just as the door was being pulled shut on its previously battered hinges, Viviano Real, taking one last estimate of the situation, held out a restraining hand.

"I know those men. Daniel Rincón and I used to be good

[3]The female bear.

friends. I think I can save us all a lot of trouble if I go out and talk with them."

"Now, Don Viviano," said one of the women, "you know that 'used to be' has nothing to do—" She stopped talking, because Viviano had already left the house.

"Then I'm going out too," said José. He started for the door, but two pairs of hands clutched his clothes and pulled him back.

"It's you they're after," the women insisted almost angrily.

They were quite right, for the men walked right by Viviano and demanded that the door be opened. They could hear Viviano remonstrating with Rincón.

"We want Manuel. And we want that *Nazareno!*"

When no one opened the door for them, they deliberately set about tantalizing Viviano by ruthless vandalism against Manuel's property. They chopped the posts holding the veranda roof; they hacked at the wooden trough in which Manuel washed his coffee beans. Perhaps, having known the fiery Viviano in former days, they were hoping to inflame him to the point of open anger or violence.

Inside, everyone was far more concerned over Viviano than the damage the two ruffians might inflict on the property. A single savage slash of a machete could end his life.

"Lord," prayed Doña Edilia, "you've so often turned aside their wrath. Do it again!"

But even while she prayed, Rincón picked up a heavy pole with a roar of evil inspiration.

"Come on, Chepe! Take hold of the other end. We'll ram it through the door."

"Did you hear that?" shrieked one of the women. "They're coming in. We can't stop them."

Her fears were not without foundation. The door, too often broken down, and hacked up by machetes, could not withstand ramming. They could hear Viviano pleading with the men for reason and for mercy. Rincón's voice rose above Viviano's.

"Come on, Chepe. We'll beat the door down, and then we'll let the rats have it. Let's get with it!"

"No." Chepe's voice sounded peevish. "Leave them alone."

Rincón swore foully at his companion; the latter retorted in kind and became all the more stubborn.

"We've done enough."

"What did we come here for? Come on, I'm breaking down this door."

"Leave them alone!" snarled Chepe.

Viviano, who later reported his view of the attack, said that Chepe appeared to have completely reversed his attitude. He stood glowering truculently and dared Rincón to push him aside.

"Try and stop me," roared Rincón. He jabbed the log viciously against the door, and the weakened boards crunched at the impact. A few more such blows would smash the door to kindling.

"Confound you!" shouted Chepe. "Look what you've done."

"That's just a start," Rincón growled through gritted teeth, accenting the words by slamming the battering end of the pole against the door. "Wait till I get through to the *evangélicos!*"

Viviano, bound by his pacific beliefs from intervening even though he saw the door being demolished, watched just as helplessly while the two men began to scuffle.

"You'll kill them over my dead body," snarled Chepe savagely when Rincón dislodged the heavy bolt with a few more shattering blows at the door, and started into the house. Chepe snatched up the pole Rincón had dropped, swung it over his head as he lunged forward, then brought it down over Rincón's head. The latter, who had advanced to the middle of the *sala,* staggered and almost fell. Then steadying himself, he raised a chair with which he held his assailant at bay.

Taking advantage of the diversion, the trapped evangelicals made a wild dash for the door, rushing down a steep incline that led to the woods. Children and one of the women lost the precarious footing in their headlong flight and started rolling and bouncing helplessly down the slope until, happily, the underbrush put a stop to their tumbling descent.

As they picked themselves up, ruefully fingering their bruises, they could hear sounds of a frightful scuffle going on above—

thuds, curses, roars of fury or pain. While the women and children scurried farther down and into the covering woods, José and Viviano stopped behind a boulder and listened.

"What happened?"

"I don't know," admitted Viviano. "I was standing there praying when he suddenly changed his mind."

"What did you pray?"

"That God would turn aside their wrath."

"The very words of Doña Edilia!"

The two men bowed their heads to thank God for His unexpected and literal method of answering their prayers. This they corroborated when the tumult and the shouting had come to an abrupt end and they made their way up the slope to investigate. Both of the men were still on the premises, though Rincón had been bludgeoned to insensibility. His battered body sprawled limply on the patio. Chepe, bloody of face, was sitting on the edge of the porch.

"He's not dead?" whispered José apprehensively.

"Just you leave him be," growled Chepe. "He'll come to."

Inside, the house was in total disorder. Dishes had been broken. The tablecloth was chopped up where a Bible had been left on the table. The Bible was in shreds. Blood was spattered all over the *sala*.

Chepe rose, his effort accented by an angry groan, and followed the men in to view the desolation. "I pulled him out after I clobbered him. He was bleeding." He waved a bruised arm. "It's a mess."

"We owe you our lives, Chepe," said José gratefully.

"Don't you be afraid. What they've done to you, they'll have to do to me."

The prediction was made with a tongue still thickened by liquor and in a voice anything but meek, but the two evangelicals understood that once more the Spirit of God had turned a persecutor into an inquirer.

Across two valleys, but always visible from La Quiebra, the congregation of La Cruz was enthusiastically preparing for its first Christmas after the building of its chapel in spite of renewed persecution throughout the mountains. Manuel, waylaid on the trail, was brutally beaten. (Just a year previously, Ricardo Contreras, Vicente Gómez and the Ocaña band had been menaced with shotguns at La Esperanza on the way to Palmira.) Eulogio Quintero, the first believer there, had repeatedly been threatened with death. Once a neighbor went into his own home to kill him. When he escaped from the house, the man shot at him on the trail just as coolly as he would have shot a cougar.

"He's not a bad shot," admitted Eulogio, "but God distorted his vision."

Jorge Quintero, of the same Quintero family, whom Sixto Machado had led to faith in Christ, had begun a dynamic witness in the community of Corralitos.[3] Together with one other new convert, he proceeded to literally corral the neighborhood for Christ. Their faith was almost epidemic, for their church grew in one year to almost the size of Nazaret.

Vicente, who constantly visited all the churches, found that instead of encouraging his "lambs" to go out and do exploits, he sometimes had to counsel discretion to modify their reckless ardor. Manuel García and the believers of La Quiebra were eager to build a church. Vicente had counseled patience after a series of attacks indicated the opposition's determined intent to kill the leaders. He was able to restrain their enthusiasm for several weeks, but their undiminished evangelization continued to swell the congregation that met in the García *sala*.

The phenomenal spread of the evangelical faith was general in those mountains. It was as though the burning of the Franco home, two years and nine months previously, had actually been the fuse on a keg of spiritual dynamite. Fourteen recognized rural congregations were now sending out teams into surrounding areas as well as holding their own regular Sunday services. Scattered brands, burning with conviction and faith, had set three mountain chains afire where they fell. The storm of deadly persecution seemed merely to fan the blaze of zeal.

[3]Small corrals.

During the night of the fiesta of Santa Rosa on Sunday, December 13, 1955, eight drunken rowdies set fire to the La Cruz Church. First they poured gasoline on the pulpit and benches that Manuel had so laboriously hauled up Palmira Mountain. They soaked the roof from the same receptacle, then they threw in a match.

The men, still drinking after they had accomplished their atrocious act, fell to battling among themselves with guns and machetes. Seven of them were wounded.

La Cruz burned like a torch. Inhabitants of those mountains— even two chains away—saw the flames, and a light began to burn in their own personal darkness. Satan had again outmaneuvered himself.

On Palmira the evangelicals shoveled aside the ashes of their church, and people thronged past the pathetic little plot of scorched flowers to a special meeting previously announced. Candidates for baptism stood on the charred ruins of the platform and told of the transforming power of a living Christ. During the service that followed their baptism, the reality and the very presence of Jesus Christ became evident in an awesome manner.

The audience had been standing attentively, listening to a message from the Word, when the Holy Spirit moved them. People fell to their knees in the ashes, and those Andean apostles were filled with renewed power and boldness. The prayer that went up amidst those ruins demonstrated that the Spirit had shed God's own love abroad. "Father," they cried, "remove all bitterness from our hearts. Save those who, through blindness, destroyed Thy house of worship. We claim them for Thy kingdom!"

On January 9, 1956, less than a month later, the sturdy-hearted evangelicals on another mountain, undaunted by the threats of their own foes and the troubles of their fellow believers, invited everyone for the public dedication of their chapel, Nazaret.

Sixto Machado, on the steep mountain overlooking the Magdalena Valley, had had such success during the last of his three years of untiring witnessing that his house could no longer hold the throngs that came to hear the gospel that had so transformed his life. Just one week before the dedication service, a neighbor demonstrated his hostility by shooting at Sixto as he stood in the doorway of his own home. The same man, with recruits of his own kind, came to the dedication services, setting up a stand behind the church building to sell liquor, cigarettes, bread and notions in an attempt to arouse outraged reactions from the believers.

The disturbance created by customers of the makeshift bar warranted both disgust and action. The land belonged to Sixto; the offenders were trespassing. Their conduct disregarded the desires and rights of all who had gathered to worship. In a land of law and order, they would have been thrown off the premises.

The only law of the San José district was the gun or the knife, and the evangelicals were not using theirs. When their enemies began to stone the church, making the continuation of the service out of the question, the evangelicals literally prayed the rabble from the premises. Without a word, they packed up their wares and quietly left. The evening meeting—always the most dangerous—was completely peaceful.

Ignoring advice and defying danger, the La Quiebra believers began to build El Salvador[4] Chapel on the granite brow of that towering mountain. La Cruz, the focus of equally menacing bigotry, they argued, had been rebuilt at once.

Theirs was a monumental task of transporting timber and cement. One mule fell to his death carrying a load up the treacherous trail. Mayor Vallona of Aguachica raged and sent word that the heretics would be exterminated. But the swelling congregation, crowded out of the García's large *sala,* began to meet in the chapel even before the roof was up.

To the southeast, across that picturesque canyon, Lalo Guevara, whose congregation on Los Cerros now numbered about eighty, prepared to build Sión Chapel. Women helped, carrying poles and bricks. A wall tumbled, but they rebuilt it. When neighbors hacked at the new doors, ruining the padlocks, they

[4]The Saviour.

quietly replaced the padlocks with larger ones and kept on working.

On Palmira the congregation of La Cruz had had even more severe reverses. Their new chapel had stood only six months when a hurricane lifted the metal roof from the building and hurled it into the canyon. Rain melted the adobe walls into mounds of desolation. However, when the churches of El Salvador and Sión were dedicated in March of 1957, the stalwart evangelicals of Palmira had nearly completed building the third chapel of La Cruz.

In that springtime of burgeoning congregations, the Ocaña band arrived for the dedication services. Hardy mountaineers followed them from one to another of the new churches and on to services at Betel, Betania and El Redentor.

To arrive at La Vega where the Belén Church was to be dedicated, the *jira* had to cross forty-three mountain streams. In youthful exuberance, the Ocaña band members invented a novel way of avoiding the tiresome necessity of repeatedly taking off their shoes and rolling up their trousers. Instead, they cut long poles and vaulted across. A few accidents ensued, most of which ended in a drenching and a good deal of laughter.

Newly slaughtered meat provided food for the throngs that had come for Belén's three-day celebration of accomplishment and advance. Three weddings were crowded into the days of worship and fellowship; new converts were baptized, children dedicated, and the entire membership shared communion service.

Two weeks later, part of the band took to the trails again, this time to the even newer congregation that was meeting in the home of José Santana. Jorge Quintero, the firebrand who had been engaged almost exclusively in contacting his neighbors since his conversion nine months previously, was beaming. Over a hundred people came to the Corralitos service, and though no one had been baptized as yet, they were contemplating the building of their own chapel. They even had a name for it: *Buen Pastor*.[5]

[5]Good Shepherd.

Vicente and the band also visited a new congregation at El Cerro over a trail so steep that those who were riding mules dismounted. Then, after another four-hour climb, they reached San José, seven thousand feet above the Magdalena River Valley.

The arrival of the band on Good Friday, April 22, was a momentous occasion for the believers of Nazaret Church. True to custom, local ruffians stood outside the church windows repeating everything that was said in the chapel in a jeering and offensive manner. During the serving of the sacraments commemorating the sufferings and death of Jesus Christ, they became even more obnoxiously disorderly.

At the evening service one individual in particular repeatedly disturbed the worship. The visiting missionary paused in midsermon and requested reverence to be observed in the house of God. Sixto went to the missionary at the close of the service and warned him that the offender had been enraged by his public reproof.

"He's threatened to settle the score with you. We'll have to watch him."

The rowdy was at the door at the close of the service with his wicked-looking knife unsheathed. Alert believers quickly surrounded the missionary, shielding his life with their own bodies. As they started down the trail toward the Machado home, Jorge Quintero—once Sixto's recruit and now leader of his own congregation—led the way with the gasoline lantern.

A chilling fear followed the group along the steep trail. The light of the lantern that Jorge was swinging was unable to penetrate the roadside thicket. All that anyone knew was that the man who had made the threat had disappeared into the night. Every shadow moved. At every turn of the trail they anticipated a lunge from the dark. They came to within a few yards of the house and then gasped in dismay, for the man was waiting for his vengeance at the Machado doorstep.

Again forming a bodyguard, the evangelicals brushed by the

baffled villain, who fingered his machete in impotent fury. Six men blocked the doorway while they waited for others to arrive.

Defeated by love that sacrifices itself for another, the man stalked off to his own hacienda.

10

Where Angels Tremble – Velásquez

IN THE ANDES MOUNTAINS east of Ocaña, on the trail that Marco Franco once followed on his way toward Aspasica, is a village known as La Playa. Slouching with listless and dejected bearing along one of its narrow footpaths, a handsome young man paused before a door. Bitter lines of disillusionment, almost of hopelessness, belied his youth.

Manuel Velásquez leaned against the door frame. The boisterous splurge of the previous night had left him with a splitting headache and the shaming knowledge that he had spent the money he needed right now. What if his parents had nothing in the house to eat? What if they asked for something from the market? They were both ill. They would ask him to go for it. Whom else would they ask? They had nothing. He had had one hundred sixty pesos the night before, but he had spent it all.

He flicked a hand angrily across his forehead to push back a lock of his disheveled hair. The door, sagging in disrepair on inadequate hinges, scraped the pounded-earth floor as he put his shoulder to it. He shuffled forward a few steps, while his eyes became accustomed to the dismal interior of the two-room house. His mother, on the bed just before him, raised her head weakly from her hard pillow. Her eyes, sunken in the transparent pallor of her face, brightened with relief at the sight of her son, and she held out her hand. She managed a smile.

"Oh, Manuel! I'm so glad you've come. I've been suffering so all night, and Papá is too sick to go to town for me. I have the prescription in the top dresser drawer, Manuel—"

Stinging from the guilty knowledge that he had squandered in folly that which could relieve her pain, Manuel interrupted her almost savagely with a rough tirade about the way he always had to run errands for them. His mother cringed as though he had struck her a physical blow.

He lurched out into the street again, sick with shame and self-reproach over his senseless outburst. Why had he gone to see his parents at all if he could do nothing but make their lot worse, he wondered morosely. His mother had never shown him anything but love and concern when he had needed her. He had not even spoken to his father.

"*Hola,*[1] Manuelito!"

Manuel turned. His friend, Rodolfo Pérez, sprinted to catch up with him.

"We're having a private dance at my place this evening. Eduardo Palonel will be there, and a few others. You must come. Bring your guitar. But don't let the word get out."

"Why not?"

"It's sort of exclusive."

"Sure," said Manuel without enthusiasm. They would serve something to drink though, and then he would feel better. He would forget this heavy remorse that filled his chest with a dull ache and even now clutched at his throat.

Arriving later with Eduardo, he was taken aback to note that one of the guests was the local priest. He whistled under his breath.

"So that's why this dance is so exclusive. Padre Velásquez must have confidence in us to be here."

Actually, Manuel was not happy about the priest's presence there. He had come hoping only to drown his problems in the drinks customarily served at dances. He sat down and strummed

[1]Hello.

his guitar, scowling. A few friends gathered about him, but Manuel's mind was on his disappointment.

Padre Velásquez removed that uneasiness promptly by pulling a bottle of rum from the pocket of his cassock.

"Come on, boys," he invited cheerily. "Let's drink."

"Mother of God," exclaimed one of the men, bending near Manuel's ear. "Do the holy ones carry their own bottles?"

"Well, this party may not turn out so bad after all," muttered Manuel. But in his heart he recognized that the frustration and disillusionment of this morning were deepening. He had failed himself, would his faith fail him as well?

He had always felt that the despair—the desperation—that had begun to burden his soul could be canceled as he sought forgiveness and counsel from the holy man who said masses for him, and to whom he could go to confess himself. Somehow, as the evening's revelry proceeded and everyone present became thoroughly intoxicated, his reverence for sacred matters became pointless and futile.

At two o'clock in the morning almost all the guests had passed the stage of hilarity and were dozing drunkenly or had succumbed completely and sprawled in sodden stupor here and there in the house. Eduardo and Manuel, who had been furnishing the music, were still on their feet, and the last couple on the floor was the priest and the wife of one of the men who had sunk into comatose indifference. At four-thirty they carried their host, Rodolfo, to his room and dumped his limp body onto his bed, dead drunk.

"I need to be propped up, Manuel," growled Eduardo, trying to make himself comfortable in his straight-backed chair. "They're sleeping on all the comfortable seats. Look at Padre Velásquez!"

"Let's get out of here," said Manuel. "Maybe a bit of cold air will sober us a bit."

Outside, Eduardo said thickly, "What do you make of this carousal?"

"You mean—the padre?"

Eduardo grunted.

"I'm forming a new concept of things. I'm not even sure I want to think what I'm thinking. Let's go get something to eat."

"Who's going to take charge of the mass this morning? That's what I want to know."

"Me, too."

They were sure the padre wouldn't dare touch the holy chalice and the sacred sacramental body of Christ until he had prepared himself spiritually. Would he confess to another curate?

At five-thirty the bells chimed the hour of early mass. The two men were still nodding over the *guarapo*[2] they had ordered in lieu of breakfast.

"Listen, Eduardo," said Manuel. "I'm curious to know what happens in a case like this. We left the priest in the house, drunk. Does the sacristan take over?"

"Let's go see."

They ordered another glass of *guarapo*. "Come on, then," said one of them, "it's time to go to mass."

The girl who had served their drinks laughed. "What? *You* go to mass? You're not only drunk—you're soaked!"

"She doesn't think we're really going to church in this condition," chuckled Eduardo. Then he sobered. "Well, it is the first time I've gone like this."

They knelt, without their usual reverence, and then took seats fairly far to the rear of the church. They had not come to worship this time, but to see how the mass would be conducted.

"Holy Mother!" whispered Manuel's companion of the night. "It's him!"

It was, indeed, the priest whom they had left sleeping soddenly at the Pérez house, bleary of eye, a bit unsteady of hand, but nevertheless going through the sacred ritualistic service without obvious difficulty, unless it was the thick slur of some of the Latin phrases. Nobody seemed to notice.

"He made it!" said Eduardo almost triumphantly, as they stumbled out of the church into the morning air.

[2]Home-brewed intoxicant made from corn.

Manuel did not answer. From that day on he absented himself from masses. He never went to confess himself. But his loss of faith increased his hopelessness. He drank more than ever and often engaged in pernicious squabbles. At last he was convinced that he would be killed in a drunken brawl or would himself commit a senseless murder. Occasionally someone invited him to one of the ceremonies of the church.

"Everyone has his own private god," he would say indifferently. "I've tried religion—rosaries, masses, penitences, communions, novenas. It's all false. Does it seem to you that there is a God? He doesn't exist. Or if He does, He is a God that is completely deaf. He never hears prayer. I've been deceived by this lie. I'm not deceived any more."

In a state of melancholy bordering on desperation, Manuel found himself one day in a rural area known as Montecito. Here he came upon a youth, Ramón Rodillo, who was completely absorbed in the reading of a small book. An inner compulsion caused Manuel to strike up a conversation, though he was aware of no interest in either the young man or his book.

"Hombre—where are you from?"

"From Ocaña."

"What's this you're reading here?"

"It's a gospel. By Matthew."

"Oh," Manuel jeered, his skepticism flashing out in bitter harshness against this stranger, "you're one of those religious nuts, are you?"

"Maybe you're the one who's not all there," retorted the young man mildly. "By the look of you, you're beside yourself with hopelessness. You're fighting alcoholism, aren't you? And you're not getting anywhere."

Manuel looked at him sharply. How did he know? Did his despair show to a complete stranger?

"Don't think you're going to hook me with any of this religious talk. This God doesn't exist. I've sought Him every way imaginable—and every day my life has been worse. This God simply does not exist."

"Look, Velásquez," said Ramón, for by this time they had exchanged names. "God—"

Manuel waved him to silence. "There is no God, I say. God just does not exist. I've stopped being deceived about this for about two years. These fake saints have deceived us—taken us in—to make a gain of us."

"Let me finish what I was saying. Maybe you have been tricked. You say you searched for God. You've not sought for Him as this little book tells us to do. God is Spirit, and those who worship Him must do so in spirit and in truth. You've tried to find Him by means of idolatry—by means of superstition. I'm *sure* if you find God, He'll change your life."

"Rot."

The youth did not argue, but handed him the book. Manuel, having nothing better to do, began to thumb through it. Then he began to read without much attention to the words. He read the whole book that day, and the only sentence that left any impression on his conscious mind was the statement of Jesus that one can tell a good or bad tree by the kind of fruit it bears.

What's a good tree—in the sense that He meant it? he wondered. *What's a bad tree? What tree is the book referring to?*

Later, Manuel did not even know what he had done with the book. Time passed. Manuel spent a couple of months in the coastal city of Barranquilla, taking a course in music. Then his restlessness drove him back toward home, but he did not want to go back to farming. His cousin, Luis Durán of Ocaña, consented to teach him tailoring. When Manuel came in drunk one Monday, he expected the worst. He was amazed at his cousin's calm. Luis, unknown to Manuel, had become a sympathizer with the evangelical faith.

"Why, he's taking it better than I am myself!" thought Manuel.

During the day he discussed with Luis this strange peace of mind and patience over his delinquencies at work.

"I'm learning," said his cousin, "that the Lord Jesus taught love and patience. It is the way of the *evangélicos*." Manuel recalled the small book then. Luis was right. Jesus had been like that.

"If you want to meet a man who's really an *evangélico,*" Luis remarked one day as they passed Ocaña's Parque Santander, "go and talk to that tall skinny man there on the plaza." He pointed. "There, near the cement park bench."

Manuel, being who he was, went over to investigate.

"How are you, Señor?" he said casually, as he reached Marco Franco.

The latter swung around with the alertness of accustomed caution. His face, however, broke almost instantly into a genial smile. Manuel recognized him as a born extrovert—a kindred spirit.

"I'm Marco Franco—*a sus órdenes!*"[3]

"Manuel Velásquez of La Playa." Then Manuel eyed Marco sharply. "Say, haven't I seen you in La Playa?"

"Could be. I used to live in Aspasica."

"Then you're the *tipo*[4] they ran out of town. An *evangélico.*"

"Marco grinned. "The same. They burned me out of Santa Inés since then and squeezed me off a farm in Algodón. But let me tell you something, Friend. When you've learned to know God personally such things are just incidents, and nobody can touch the thing that really matters."

"Look, Señor, don't talk to me about God. I don't believe in a God."

"Sit down," invited Marco, motioning to the cement bench. "Let's talk that over for a bit."

Someone had once remarked that Marco had been built for the gospel. Garrulous by nature, Marco could paint a vivid picture of a life that Manuel recognized all too well—its public roistering, its private despair. Marco recounted graphically the transforming miracle that his commitment to Christ had wrought, and the ensuing peace of heart in the midst of ceaseless persecution.

[3]At your service.
[4]Fellow.

Even as Marco talked, Manuel felt a strange lightness of heart. Was it possible, after all, that there was a God? It was as if the heavy despair of his doubts had begun to evaporate. He rejoined Luis, who seized the occasion to invite him to attend a church service. When Sunday came, however, instead of going with his cousin, Manuel went his own way and staggered home so drunk that he was not able to work the next morning. Again Luis was so patient that Manuel felt doubly mortified.

If these evangélicos are so evil, he thought, *how come my employer is less upset than I about this drunkenness of mine? He's working tranquilly. I'm in complete desperation.*

Luis' quietness was a far greater testimony to Manuel than haranguing about sin and its consequences would have been. Manuel already knew something of the despair of hell in his own soul. He had never known the peace that was being quietly demonstrated.

It was growing more and more important to Manuel that he gain mastery over his habit and over his moods. He was soon to be married. He hoped fervently that the new responsibility and the love he bore Isabel would provide the incentive and ability to change, and he wanted with all his heart to be the kind of a husband that Isabel deserved.

They both overlooked the fact that he was drunk on his wedding day, but later—try as he would—Manuel remained the same melancholy failure. His new relatives grumbled, but they did not have too much to boast of themselves. A brother-in-law who had settled a drunken argument with a dirk had taken up residence in the Ocaña jail since the death of the old woman with whom he had disagreed.

Manuel went to visit him, as much to satisfy a nagging curiosity as to encourage the prisoner. He came to his point without undue delay.

"Tell me something, Compadre,"[5] he said. "Among the people here in jail, what religion do they profess?"

"Why, Manuel, they're all Catholics—like us."

[5]Close friend.

"All of them?"

"Sure. All of them."

"What are they in for?"

"Well, that señor, yonder, is in for murder. The woman that just passed by in the corridor killed her own son—a baby. That man over there is a Cúcuta man. He's in for stealing cattle. And he burned a house." And so he went on, telling of the crimes of the other inmates.

"And they're all from the church?"

"What makes you keep asking that?"

"Well, I've read something I got from one of these people all of us despise—these *evangélicos*. Are you sure there are no *evangélicos* here in jail? Not even one?"

"No, Manuel, of these people—" his brother-in-law thoughtfully rubbed his stubbly chin, then shook his head, "there's not a one of them in this jail."

"Now isn't that queer! They say these people are so evil, don't they? I wonder just what we do have against them."

"Well, for one thing, they don't believe in the virgin."

"Now that's a rare thought. The people who do believe in the virgin seem to be doing more crimes than the ones who don't. Doesn't that strike you as odd?"

His brother-in-law shrugged. "I don't quite get the point of your questions."

Manuel told him then about the book he had read in which Jesus challenged a person to test the right way of life by its products—a tree by its fruits.

"By that standard, Compadre, it is the tree of the *evangélicos* that is bearing the good fruit—not ours."

"That's all wrong. Somebody's got you all mixed up."

Manuel shook his head. "I wish I were sure. It was the words of Jesus—His own words—in the book."

"Well, you'd better quit reading it. Don't get mixed up with that heresy. You're likely to be excommunicated."

Though Manuel professed to be an atheist, the mere thought of being cut off from the church made his blood run cold. Still, when Luis invited him to another meeting, he turned his back on his qualms.

"I've committed every sin a man can do except murder," thought Manuel, "and I've come pretty near that. I might as well commit the ultimate crime of my life." So with this daring resolve, he went to his first evangelical meeting.

Repeated warnings against the pernicious machinations of the evangelicals had prepared Manuel to anticipate weird and mysterious ceremonies, and he had steeled his heart against succumbing to demonic fascination. He would observe but he would not be drawn in, though they made him the focus of their wicked incantations.

The free informality of expression of even the lay people, in terms and ideas that seemed to have no double meaning, amazed Manuel. The directness and simplicity of the prayers, however, completely shattered his defenses. He knew that he was being persuaded into the evangelical faith without argument or threat or evil enchantment. God was a Reality to these people. Manuel sensed the divine Presence pervading the very atmosphere. The heaviness of his unbelief lifted even as he toyed with the idea that here was hope and release.

Still, he had a new reservation. In that little book that had made such an impression on him, in spite of his indifference, he recalled now that the Lord Jesus had made one other statement. Jesus had warned that those who were truly His followers would suffer persecution.

"If there's persecution, I'll believe. If there isn't—"

He did not conclude his thought. By now he wanted to believe. He even hoped that he had found truth. In his soul, however, he had become convinced that the little book that he had read and thrown away held the ultimate truth. He must put this evangelical faith to the test of that little book. He had been deceived once—

Not long after his marriage, in late June or early July, he moved with his wife back to La Playa, determined to settle to something he could depend on for a livelihood, since they antici-

pated a growing family. In the mountain village everybody knew
Manuel, and quite naturally he was invited to the home of one
of his old friends.

"It's a party," said his friend. "Bring your wife, but don't
forget your guitar."

"At the party Manuel refused to drink, since this was a mark
of an evangelical as he understood it. He joined otherwise with
the hilarity and was aware of no open criticism, though he sensed
that a few conversations were abruptly shifted when he came
within earshot. It was only as they prepared to leave that he
overheard his host discussing him with the same priest who had
earlier shattered his faith in God.

"You know what?" he heard his friend say. "I think Velásquez
has turned Protestant."

"What makes you say that?"

"He doesn't seem to enjoy our *parranda*. And did you notice?
He doesn't drink."

After a short discussion, the padre made a suggestion.

"Let's experiment and find out. Next Sunday, you know, is the
opening of the boys' school. We'll invite him to the fiesta and
watch him."

Duly invited, Manuel made his appearance at the fiesta together with another friend of old times, Eduardo Palonel. The
mayor and the local notary, as well as the priest, were among the
town's notables who had already preceded him to this important
fiesta. As was expected of him, Manuel had brought his guitar.

Entering the room where the members of the orchestra were
strumming discordantly at tuning their instruments, Manuel saw
immediately that drinks were being served to everyone. He kept
shifting his position, pretending to find bits of chatter of greater
interest in a part of the room where liquor was not being offered.
At last his old friend, Noel Variga, caught up with him.

"Here's yours, Velásquez."

"Later, Noel, later," said Manuel, evading the issue.

"But this is champagne!"

Manuel shrugged with studied indifference. "I'm just not drinking. Thank you for offering it."

"Well, that's a strange thing, Velásquez. A man who enjoys a drink like you do!'

"Look," said Velásquez. "I just don't have the inclination to drink. I'm perfectly content. Why aren't you?"

"But hombre, *se hace raro!*"[6] Noel was standing his ground, insisting that Manuel take his champagne. Manuel refused, just as firmly, and as he did so, the padre appeared at his elbow.

"Well, Manuelito," said the curate. "This is rather odd, isn't it?"

"What's so odd, Padre?"

"Don't you want to take a drink? It's champagne, man!"

Because of his stout refusal of any form of liquor throughout the day's festivities, Manuel's friends considered their suspicion of his infidelity had been confirmed. The word went around— Velásquez has turned *evangélico*.

The following Sunday Manuel went to Ocaña to attend another service. The attitude of his own friends had already provided some confirmation to his own test of the validity of the evangelical faith. Both he and his friends had so vague a concept of what constituted an evangelical that the only test either could provide was the matter of liquor. Enough of that was constantly around, however, to provide Manuel, as well as his friends, further confirmation to their dual experiments.

Coming back from Ocaña, Manuel could hear from afar that some of his old cronies were well on the way to a rowdy evening. As he drew nearer, he recognized some of them swaggering about on the cobblestone street in front of the house where they seemed to be obtaining their liquid refreshments. His own route led right by this door, and his taking any alternate street would mark him as a coward, to himself, if not to his friends. So he proceeded toward them with as much nonchalance as he could muster.

"Hey, look, guys!" he heard someone shout. "Here comes

[6]That's strange!

Velásquez—Manuel Velásquez. This is our chance to get him stewed."

Manuel heard a roar of approval, and a few more of the merry-makers sauntered out to take a position on the doorstep or on the street by which Manuel would pass. He recognized the man who had proposed his downfall. It was Lalo Guallerbo, an old and trusted friend. Why were these friends of his so intent on making him drunk? They had never worked at it so hard before.

"Manuelito," said his friend, using the affectionate diminutive, "why don't you stop a bit?"

"Why not, Lalo?" retorted Manuel. "What's new?"

"You've been to Ocaña?" questioned another.

"Why, yes, Emilio."

"So you've already come away from that *guaraparía*[7] they have there."

"No, Emilio, not from a *guaraparía*. I'd be more disposed to think you had one here."

"Well, tell me something," grated another of the group. "Tell me, what is a centurion?"

Manuel shrugged. "Wasn't that a Roman soldier that had charge of a hundred men?"

"Well, then," growled the man whom Manuel did not know, "if you know so much, you probably know what a *cinturón*[8] is too?" He did not wait for Manuel to wonder what was the point of this play on words, for the man pulled his own heavy leather belt from his waist. "This is a *cinturón*, Manuelito. And we use it to flay the guy that needs driving out of a town. That's what a *cinturón* is."

So abruptly had the atmosphere changed from friendliness to rude hostility that Manuel could hardly believe his ears. And not having been adequately indoctrinated to the meekness of evangelicals, Manuel did not proceed on his way before he had said a last searingly sarcastic word.

Having now thoroughly satisfied himself of the truth of the

---

[7] A still, used contemptuously—a place where persons become stupefied.
[8] A belt.

gospel, even by his own criterion that persecution must follow it, Manuel would have been entirely content to allow the matter to rest. Still, he felt obligated to live up to a saying that he associated in his mind with the Scriptures: *Is there a dog that doesn't bark?* Then he must bark. And bark he did, though unfortunately, like the yapping of a terrier, his knowledge of the gospel did not have enough force behind the fervor to do more than aggravate his troubles.

He did begin to talk systematically with his friends about the evangelical faith, and as he did so the words of the little book were increasingly fulfilled. He soon had more persecution than he had bargained for. Still, since he was living by the principle that there is no dog that does not bark, he continued to talk, augmenting his own limited but enthusiastic witness with some tracts he had procured at the church in Ocaña, which he had begun attending regularly and openly.

In his zeal he made mistakes he might not have made had he had an older believer to counsel him. Instead of dodging trouble, he ran into it head on. Over the simple matter of a rope barrier across the road—a common means of extorting money from the traveling public for almost any fete of the church or of church-associated projects—he made a vocal protest. The fact that he ridiculed the girls' picture of the virgin for whose fiesta they were collecting did not diminish the affront of his refusal to contribute. The priest heard of his impious lack of cooperation, and Manuel found himself facing a court charge that had been trumped up against him.

Since the girl who had brought the charges fled abruptly when she was asked to repeat her story before Manuel, the sergeant concluded that Manuel was correct to say he had been falsely accused. However, he forbade Manuel from continuing his proselytizing. The latter opened the Bible he carried, and showed the sergeant a passage he had marked.

"Jesus says the sacred Scriptures testify of Him. These are not my words, *Sargento;* they're words of the divine Master. And so I use the Scriptures to testify of Him. I don't belong to any proselytizing society."

"Well, Velásquez, I can't keep you from studying this Book. Just stay off the streets with it. Take it home and keep it there."

"But this same Book says there isn't a dog that doesn't bark. So I'm doing it."

For the last Sunday in August, Manuel invited Daniel Díaz and Luis Durán to have a service in his home in La Playa. They came, and Manuel prepared to receive the people he had invited during the week, hoping that they would come directly from mass at about ten or ten-thirty. This would save some of them a long trip made especially to attend his *culto*.

They came directly from the church—three hundred strong. Unfortunately, they were not coming to listen to what the brethren had to say. Sensing the fearsome mob temper of the swelling crowd sweeping toward their house, Manuel tried to get the two evangelicals away before they could be harmed, but he found himself and his friends surrounded by a mob raging with the lust to kill slowly, by torture. National police, stationed there to prevent political riots, rode to their rescue, but the mob nearly tore the men from the custody of the police, throwing stones, calling them Communists and insulting terms.

The police forced the mob back along the road toward La Playa. Realizing that the already badly battered evangelicals were escaping the horrifying fate of their declared sadistic intentions, they shouted at Velásquez, "We'll get you! We'll burn your house down!"

The latter threat was an unexpected blow. Since Isabel was not an evangelical, Manuel had never dreamed that his wife might be in danger after he had taken the evangelicals from the house. Now, though police made it possible for him to barricade himself and his friends in a house belonging to an aunt, Manuel became increasingly concerned about what was taking place in La Playa. The mob, thwarted in its lust for his own blood, would console itself with alternate victims. His flesh crawled with horror at what they might do to his wife who was alone in the house with their infant daughter.

Though torn apart with anxiety and grief, Manuel could not return to defend his family. The two evangelicals whom he had invited were still in mortal danger of torture and death. Only he was familiar enough with the wooded areas of his aunt's plantation to be able to lead the men from the house by a seldom-used path through the woods that conveyed them farther from the road and toward the course of a mountain stream. From there he told them how to reach another mountain town without getting back on the road.

Then he was alone—frantic to get back to Isabel and terrified of going back to La Playa. It was now eight weeks or more since he had cast in his lot with the evangelicals to prove whether their teachings were true. Circumstances now conspired to make him also prove the reality and faithfulness of their God. He stopped to pray before entering the outskirts of La Playa.

"Look, God, I got myself into this because of You. You are mighty enough to create earth and heaven. Get me out of this, will You? I ask only one thing. Don't let me weaken and be untrue to this faith."

He slipped into the house about midafternoon to find Isabel tearful and frightened. She served him something to eat, but he found it impossible to swallow anything; he was positive that the day's trouble was not over. Some of his old friends, still attached to Manuel and sharing his own disquietude, came over to stay with him.

"We'll stay with you overnight, Manuel," they offered. "We'd better stand guard over the house."

Manuel would have eagerly grasped the comfort of their presence with him, but the guns swinging from their holsters made him refuse their help.

"I don't want to get you into trouble because of my faith, fellows. God will protect us."

The night passed without any further violence. The week

passed. But after the following Sunday's mass, Isabel hovered nervously near the window.

"I see some men coming this way, Manuel. From town."

He stepped to the window and put a comforting arm about her waist.

"One is Juan Pérez Velásquez, Manuel," she said. "Isn't the next one Angel Lobo?"

"Yes, and the other is Pedro Ruedas."

Angel and Pedro were mounted on horses, so they arrived first, each one holding a loaded revolver. Manuel stepped out to the patio to greet them with his casual, "*Qué tal,*[9] Don Angel? And you, Don Pedro, how are you? Dismount. Come on in."

"We have a few things to discuss with you today," said Angel. "We've come to say something to you."

"Why not, Don Angel? I'll be glad to listen. Go ahead."

"Now here's the thing. You know that I'm Angel María Lobo. My companion is Pedro Ruedas. We are Catholics. You were one of us. You played for us in all our fiestas. You were one of the foremost persons here in La Playa—and you can't say you weren't. If there was a fiesta, we always invited you; we appreciated you. And today we've come to mend this matter."

"Mend this matter?" Manuel repeated the man's last phrase. "What matter is it you have come to mend? Hombre, you sound very strange."

"Just what I said before. We are Catholics. You were a Catholic. Will you come back with us to mass?"

Manuel was silent for a moment, already aware of their deadly purpose, though Pedro Ruedas clarified it still further.

"We won't stop at killing, if that's what it takes."

Face to face with his former friend, and having had a few minutes to think, Angel's zeal had cooled. He seemed now to regret their drastic purpose. He took an almost pleading tack.

"Take a look at your farm, Manuel," he said. "Look at those pretty rows of onions. Here is what you'll need for the future. Tomorrow we'll pull them all up."

[9]How are you?

By this time Manuel had read enough of the Bible to know that even Christ had been tempted by Satan about "things." Satan had shown Jesus kingdoms. Now these men were showing him his own small kingdom—the farm from which he hoped to live—the sweat of his brow. He saw his yuca. His plantains. He could understand the thrust of Satan's proposal.

"Don Angel," said Manuel, "the Apostle Paul—"

"I don't want to hear about that. Tell us if you are going to recant. If you don't, we've already told you we'll kill you. You are going to come back with us. Now look. You go get your guitar and get on my horse. You're going to take this bottle of brandy and take a swig right now. And we'll go back to the plaza of La Playa and circulate the good news that today you've returned to Catholicism."

"Look, Don Angel. I want to tell you something. St. Paul said—"

"Don't talk of that!"

"No? But the Apostle Paul did say, 'I can do all things through Christ which strengtheneth me.' I'm not going to retreat one step into what I used to believe. If you want to kill me, kill me. Go ahead. The Bible says in another place, 'Don't fear those who can kill the body; fear those who can kill the soul, and put it into hell.' "

Pedro snapped, "Stop preaching. We mean what we said. You retreat or—"

"And I mean what I said. I shall not retreat an inch."

Angel said to Pedro, "We're not such brave guys."

"What do you mean, 'we're not so brave'?"

"Why, this Manuel here is the only Protestant in La Playa. If he starts running toward the river, we've got him surrounded. If he runs into town, he knows we'll get him there. We've offered him a horse, and he refuses to take it. He's not going to go back on anything. If anyone around here is brave, it's Manuel. I think it's a shame to kill this kind of person. Let's go. I don't want to do it."

Pedro fingered his gun. Angel turned to Manuel. Rather than

carrying a renewed threat, his tone seemed to suggest that he had been trying to communicate a warning of exactly where the opposition had developed its forces. So serious, in fact, did Angel consider the danger that he had tried to get him onto his own horse.

"We're going, Manuel," he said, "but we're not responsible for what is going to happen."

Fifteen minutes later, the ominous mutter of a mob in the direction of the church reached into the frozen stillness of their anxiety.

"Manuel," said Isabel, "there are others coming."

"Can you see who they are?"

They were near enough already for her to recognize four of the men.

"Chabel," said Manuel, using the endearing form of her name, "these men are evil. It's me they're after this time, not Luis and Daniel. And they're in a mood to kill. God will protect you, if I'm—"

"Go!" cried Isabel. "They won't hurt me. I'm not an evangelical. Quickly—before they get here! Go!"

There was no time even for a last caress. Manuel slipped out by the back way. The cane fence that shielded him from observation also retarded his flight, and Manuel broke out in a cold sweat of panic as he chopped madly at the barrier that he himself had pridefully bound for neat durability. Even as he slid through the opening, the yelling mob reached the front of the house. He ducked behind the fence, crouching, then scrambled on all fours toward the next house. In terror for his life, he barged in without stopping to knock, then paused, trembling, in the kitchen. Would his neighbors betray him? He had no time to get away by any route, and if Angel's statements had been meant as warning, any route he tried would be cut off.

Fortunately for him, his neighbors had fled in terror, so Manuel was alone in the house. He found a room that had a view of the road and was horrified at the size of the mob—all friends and neighbors—now frenzied with the lust to kill. Someone had his Bible out on the street, and his heart wrenched as he watched it being stamped on and ruined. Other evangelical literature was scattered about. That meant they had broken into his house.

Then above the fury of the mob he heard sounds that made his blood turn to ice. He would recognize the cries of his little daughter anywhere, and he now heard her screaming. He thought he also heard the lament of Isabel. What should he do? If he ran to her, the hatred that was really aimed at him might augment her danger.

"Celestial Father," he prayed. "Save us! Preserve us! I don't know what they're doing to my baby!"

He fought an impulse to run out so that they would kill him and perhaps leave his family alone. Still, with years of national violence behind him, he knew that blood lust is only augmented with the perpetration of one crime. Even his neighbors had known that much and had fled for fear, though not at all involved in Manuel's faith.

"Lord, help us in this terrible nightmare!" Manuel groaned, without much hope. "If it is Your will to be gracious, grant a moment of opportunity so that I can get back to my family before the mob finds me!"

Even as he prayed, he opened the door a crack. His home was completely surrounded. What was Isabel doing? Was she holding them out to give him more time to get away? The crowd was milling about the house, old people and children among the clamorous mob. Some had rocks. Some carried leather horsewhips. Others grasped stalks of fique, the thick serrated blades of sisal cactus. Manuel shuddered when he considered these horrible instruments of brutality, visualizing the scores of sharp spikes tearing his flesh at just one blow. Many, of course, flourished guns and machetes.

Whether Isabel was holding the crowds off or not, he knew they would soon break in and search the house. Then they would fan out, as if they were hunting a fox or a rat. He crept from the house, keeping it between himself and the rabble, praying that the very numbers of people in the streets would provide him the security of being disregarded. Reaching the road, he plunged across it into a coffee plantation which gave him cover while he ran up the side of the mountain to a place where he could make more time along a road. About six o'clock he reached Labranza, where a friend loaned him a bicycle. With this help, he reached Ocaña by seven-thirty. He appealed to the police for help to rescue his wife. The captain consented to go. He would take twenty men with him.

"Twenty men?"

"Sure. A drunk mob fights anybody when it gets started. You know that!"

By this time the pacifistic indoctrination of the local evangelicals had penetrated Manuel's thinking, and it suddenly struck him that men would have to spill blood because he had committed himself to Christ.

"Captain," he said, "I've changed my mind. I'll go alone. God will see me through."

Clinging desperately to his new-found convictions, he retraced his steps, though his terror kept mounting as he drew nearer the scene of his flight. When he reached La Playa, the early morning sun revealed the devastation of his home. The doors were off the hinges, and some of his furniture, chopped to kindling, was lying, together with the doors, in the yard. His wife was there with the baby. She had escaped, she told him, about the time he had heard the baby crying. They had spent the night in the woods about two kilometers from the town.

"They were hunting in the woods with flashlights, Manuel. All night."

"Well, Chabel," said Manuel, "there's no use staying here. We'll have to go to Ocaña at least until this blows over."

"There's no point in staying here," she sobbed. "They've ruined our furniture."

"Not only that, Chabel. They've robbed us of everything else. I only have seven pesos in my pocket."

By Sunday they had been settled in Ocaña, with prospects of a small shop to eke out whatever they might be able to rescue from their fields. By this time too the senseless rage that provided the stimulus for mob action had been replaced by more sober reflection on the part of some of Manuel's persecutors. Manuel ran across an old friend, Martín Ruedas, who—unknown to Manuel—had chopped up the chairs, beds and the clothing in the Velásquez home the previous Sunday.

"Martin," said Manuel, going up to him, *"qué tal?"*

The man quickly averted his face and Manuel guessed the reason. By this time, after prayer and discussion with the other believers in Ocaña, Manuel had come to know that in such a crisis a Christian needs to claim Christ's love for his enemies even more than he needs courage to face his difficulties. Here was his opportunity to demonstrate that forgiving spirit.

"Is anything wrong, Martín?"

"I can't talk to you, Manuel," said Martín, his voice betraying his remorse.

"Has something happened, Martín? Are you in trouble?"

"Nothing's happened—to me. It's the things we did to you."

"Well, Martín, don't let that bother you. God has made me completely happy in spite of the loss of what is just 'things.' So you must not feel bad."

"I don't see how you can feel like that."

"You will, Martín, when you understand my new and wonderful faith. I know that I have a living Redeemer, and He has told us to lay up treasures in heaven, where neither moth nor rust corrupt, and where thieves cannot break in to steal."

And so, on his first contact with one of those who would have killed him, Manuel was able to bear a radiant witness of his faith.

Seven years later a church in La Playa had an attendance of thirty persons, with fifteen baptized believers.

11

What Price – Total Commitment?

Vicente Gomez paused on the trail leading into the mountains from Santa Inés toward Palmira. While he wiped streaming perspiration from his face, his eyes rested on the fertile canyon below him. Its splendor and richness of vegetation had inspired some to speak of it as La Esmeralda—the emerald. Sixto Machado and Armenio Pabón came puffing up the trail a moment later.

"After all these years," exclaimed Armenio in mild rebuke, "it seems that you would know how to climb a mountain. Look at you! You even wear us old mountaineers out."

Vicente smiled. This was not the first time he had been chided for his furious pace.

"Here's a good spot to catch our breath," he said. "I always stop here—even when I don't have a couple of winded rancheros with me." He gestured down across the heavily settled gorge below. "I never go by here without praying for the people of Honduras."

"You'll never stop, will you? Tell me, were there as many individual believers when you came to this area, Don Vicente, as you now have congregations—established congregations?"

Vicente's grin widened. He knew these men shared his own vision. "And you are suggesting that we call a halt? That we have reached all the people who need the Saviour?"

"What we are suggesting, Don Vicente, is discretion," said

Sixto. "You can't possibly take on any more than you have. You are ill far too much as it is."

"Oh, that! I think it's going down to the hot valley, and then coming up here to the mountains. It's those sudden changes."

"And the irregular meals. And malaria. And overwork. And responsibility that keeps you awake nights."

"Soon now, José Pinzón and Santos Millán will be through school. They help me a great deal during their vacations. And I will never cease to praise God for you and all the others. When I begin to thank the Lord for those whose testimony has created this work, I am completely overwhelmed."

It was characteristic of Vicente not to take any credit for the phenomenal spread of the gospel in the mountains. It was true, of course, that these plantation owners had aided him unstintingly in the evangelization of the region, and because of their experience in public administration and education, they had been able to give him priceless advice. It was Sixto who now unburdened his own mind.

"Too many of our people are illiterate, Don Vicente. As long as a man can't read the Bible, he can't be an effective leader."

"Not only that," said Armenio, "he can't be an effective Christian. And if no one in the family reads, they all remain immature in the faith. They sing in their family *cultos,* and they may repeat some verses. But they become stagnant. Some are even sliding back into the vices of their old life."

Vicente scratched his head thoughtfully. "It's not only a lack of education. We've been so eager to see souls added to our number that we keep preaching at the few unsaved in the congregation, ignoring the believers' need for spiritual growth and victory."

"I agree, Vicente. But even the best preaching can't take the place of the growth that comes through personally studying God's Word. Our people have to know how to read. We need a teachers' training school so that all our children will be able to read."

"I have definite word, Don Sixto, that the mission will open a school for teachers in El Carmen."

"Then my daughters will be of the first to attend!"

The evangelicals' problem of education was tragic. In Ocaña or Aguachica, children of evangelicals would not be accepted in the schools. Those who could get into schools in other parts of Colombia were abused and ridiculed, the instructor often taking the initiative in the persecution.

In his own community Sixto had not waited for mission-trained teachers. He and his wife, Carmen Rosa, had not only taught their own children to read but had taken in anyone in the community that desired help. The Machados had taught twenty-three illiterate adults to read. Some, unsaved when they began their instruction, had committed their lives to Jesus Christ during the time they were learning.

"How is the congregation at Caracolí?" inquired Armenio, when they resumed their climb along the slender thread of trail that followed the contours of the mountain. Vicente shrugged.

"What you would expect of a new area. It's like La Osa and Yegüera—like La Esperanza. A stranger enters at his own risk. There are killings and stabbings about every week. Weekends and fiesta days are worse, of course. I still pick my schedule with care."

"Well, see to it, then, that you don't go in alone."

"They'll soon be won by the grace and love of the Lord," said Vicente casually.

"Sometimes it takes a while," said Armenio. "I've been wanting to tell you about a man who made a commitment in Santa Inés not long ago. Do you remember Marco Franco's story about a *jira* of evangelicals coming along the trail toward Aspasica?"

"You mean back in 1946—at Christmas?"

"Let's hear it," urged Sixto. "That was before my time."

Armenio nodded. "Another fanatical town up in the mountains—Aspasica. Well, being fiesta time the whole countryside was waiting for some excitement. The brethren were still some distance from Marco's when they thought their number was up. One of the evangelicals was beaten, and they were stoned. One man pulled his gun and fired point blank at one of the believers.

It failed to go off. Then he shot in the air, and it went off all right. That shook him up. I think he recognized the hand of the Lord."

"Did that stop them?"

"No, the mob followed the evangelicals who, by that time, were running back down the trail. They kept stoning them and brandishing knives. They kept on down the mountain like that until they ran into another of these mountain canteens, and here was another bunch of men making whoopee. So they were between two fires. They could not leave the trail; that trail's one of the steepest. So they just stood still and prayed. Francisco Velásquez and Israel Navarro were in that group. Anyway, there they stood. They were waiting for death."

"And then?"

"An older man came out of a house and asked the evangelicals to get behind him. He stood between them and the rowdies. 'You've done enough to these people,' he said. I guess they looked a bit bruised and bloodied up by that time. 'They have a right to live even if they have a different religion from ours.' Then he took out his machete. 'Anyone who touches one of these *evangélicos,* I personally will kill.' He commanded respect. The evangelicals went on their way rejoicing for the way the Lord had raised up a stranger to protect them."

"That doesn't often happen."

"Don't forget that the gun didn't go off either. It was the Lord."

"And now—ten years later—one of those men who was in that mob has committed himself to Christ. And he did it at Santa Inés, the place Marco fled to after they ran him out of Aspasica!"

"That's the way it goes. The gospel wins out in the end. I've been visiting a man who tells me he gave the two of you a pretty rough time a few years back. David Sarabia of Lucaical."

Vicente stopped walking and turned to Sixto. "You've been visiting *him?* And is he listening?"

"I've had a couple of services there, Don Vicente."

"Well, he's certainly had a change of heart then, since Vicente and I visited him," said Armenio. "He told us he never wanted us to step on any of his property again."

"That's putting his message a bit mildly," chuckled Vicente.

"Well, he's open now, Don Armenio. And he's several hours nearer you than he is to San José. You'd better take advantage of the opening now that it's there. There's another home open: that of Félix Herrera. He's not exactly a sympathizer, but he permits services. And another Herrera—José—a relative. That's a toehold. We may have a church in Lucaical!"

The talk then drifted to ways and means of meeting all these new contacts and of instructing them in practical Christian living. One way they had been able to accomplish this was by means of short-term Bible courses such as they had been holding in centrally located churches like El Salvador, Betel and La Cruz, as well as in the new congregation of Ebenezer in the distant Magdalena Valley.

"The brethren of El Salvador are joining with those from La Osa and Jerusalén to build a trail. That will make it possible for more of the believers in that direction to attend."

"They had to pay five hundred pesos for permission to build the trail," said Armenio. "And for the men who are behind this project, that's a lot of money."

However, the financial investment was negligible compared to the investment of time and labor that went into cutting a trail along the rugged Andean range from the precipitous summit of La Quiebra to the higher but gentler ascent of La Osa, then downward to Jerusalén in the foothills.

The trail would necessarily dip down into the vast gorge of La Quebrada Honda,[1] the depth of the pass providing the district with its name. Naturally they made use of the existing trail that led just above the Sumalave plantation to which Pedro Márquez, an evangelical of Sión, had continued patiently to make long and tiring journeys to visit a rebellious daughter, Ana Matilde, and her husband, Arcenio, in the hope of breaking down

---

[1]Deep gorge.

their antagonism and winning them at last to faith in Christ. Other evangelicals had also begun to call on the family.

Arcenio Sumalave, a stocky man with the heavy cheekbones that indicated his Indian heritage and gray eyes that belied it, lived the depraved life of a mountain outlaw. Rearing a family with a common-law wife demonstrated his lack of concern for convention. He had less respect for law. His family had been feuding with a Montaña family for years, and he carried a gun at his belt and murder in his heart every time he rode out onto the trails. Nor was this an empty gesture. Each faction boasted that its feud was one to the death of the last member of the other side.

Arcenio's homelife was not much more peaceable. Ana used her freedom from marital ties to threaten Arcenio with desertion whenever he crossed or irritated her. It seemed to amuse her to make his life miserable. They quarreled frequently and with growing rancor.

Then Arcenio's father, always a diligent adherent of the accepted faith, aroused Arcenio to a dangerous level by permitting the evangelicals to have a *culto* in his home.

"How can a man of your experience be trapped with this false sect?" he raged, after a bitter diatribe against the evangelical heresy. "If you let them come back here, I'll see to it they don't ever leave. Do you understand me?"

The elder Sumalave understood, and sent a warning to the evangelicals. He knew his son too well to trifle with his threat.

Then Ana's brother was caught up in the new faith and, like all the others, he felt that he must pass it on. When he visited them, Arcenio used Ana's favorite tactic of placing on the phonograph a recorded message of the Virgin Fatima, who warned the faithful of dire results to come on any who listened to a Protestant. He replayed the record repeatedly and with deafening volume.

In spite of their outspoken rudeness, Pedro Márquez, Ana's father, continued to visit, though he no longer antagonized her by urging her to share his religion or to listen to how much his faith meant to him. Still, he always managed to wedge into the conversation some word from the Bible he always carried with him.

One day, Arcenio picked up the Bible that Ana's father had left. Thumbing through it carelessly, his eye was captured by a statement that led him to read on. So unsettling was this Book that he mentioned it to his priest.

"Does our religion follow the sacred Scriptures?"

"Of course," said the priest. "They are the source of our faith."

"Why are there two Bibles?" asked Arcenio.

The priest eyed Arcenio sharply. "Let me sell you the only authentic translation. It is the one you must follow."

On comparing the two Bibles, Arcenio found, to his amazement, that there were only slight differences in translation. He spent hours poring over the two volumes, pondering the implications of each statement that, in the process of comparison, he was scrutinizing so carefully. The Old Testament convicted him of idolatry; the New Testament convinced him that he was lost.

During this upheaval of spirit, a member of the feuding Montaño family entered his front patio. Such brazen audacity could mean only one thing. Arcenio whipped a wide-bladed machete from his belt and edged toward where his gun hung from a spike in the wall. But Manuel Montaño, he noticed, carried neither gun nor machete. As Arcenio approached, Manuel held out both of his hands to prove that he was not preparing to pull a concealed weapon.

"I have not come to fight you, Don Arcenio," said Manuel, "but to make peace."

"A yellow-bellied coward," Arcenio sputtered fiercely, and began to blast Manuel with a scathing tirade of abuse.

"I have been given the peace of Jesus," Manuel replied calmly. "He has shown me that the way to live is by love and not by hate. Can't we drop this feud? What do we gain by it?"

"What *we* gain is that we'll rid the world of the whole rotten tribe of Montaños, that's what we'll gain!"

"And then? Will you have peace then, Don Arcenio? Will that bring you peace of heart, and peace with God?"

Arcenio swallowed. Peace of heart. Had not the quest for peace drawn him to spend more and more time with the sacred Scriptures?

"Have you turned *evangélico?*" asked Arcenio, his high umbrage somehow suddenly deflated.

"Yes," said Manuel. "They have brought the gospel to the Magdalena Valley. We are hearing it in Mahoma now, though only occasionally. That is why I have come all this way, and have still several hours to ride."

"To La Quiebra?"

Manuel nodded, then spoke with enthusiasm. "Yes. They have invited me to a *cursillo*—a four-day course on the important teachings of the Bible. If you would only come, my friend, you would at least know what the evangelicals believe. Doesn't it arouse your curiosity, my brother?"

Friend and *brother* a Montaño had said to Arcenio, a Sumalave! A strangely suffocating constriction formed in Arcenio's throat, and his heart beat with a new excitement at the thought of having someone explain the Scriptures that had had such an unsettling impact on his mind during the past weeks. Here was his opportunity!

With that painful strangling sensation still gripping his throat, Arcenio wordlessly held out his calloused hand. Manuel grasped it and pressed it warmly between both of his. Tears coursed down his windburned cheeks.

"Do you forgive me then?"

Still unable to speak, Arcenio nodded. Then he mumbled, "Wait a minute, while I catch a mule. I want to know what can change a man like this!"

When he returned that day, Ana made him smart with her oblique remarks regarding infidelity and the dire consequences to those who allowed themselves to be entangled in heresy. Arcenio accepted her ridicule without an urge to retaliate.

"You might as well get it all said today, Ana," he said mildly.

"Then you won't have anything left to say tomorrow. This *cursillo* lasts several days, and I'm going again."

"You're not serious!"

"Quite."

Arcenio was not as bold at the *cursillo,* for he still felt definitely outside of the warm fellowship of the believers. He would hang back to enter the services late, and would slip out during the last hymn. He accepted the meals that were served, but always managed to straggle in when the leaders of the *cursillo* were safely seated at the farther end of the long plank tables. On the third day, when Manuel insisted that he meet Vicente, he hung back with embarrassment.

He had addressed this same intense, earnest evangelist with abusive language more than once on the trail. Would the man gloat that his enemy had come to terms at last? He watched Vicente closely for any sign of vindictiveness or sarcasm. He sensed only Vicente's warm, undisguised concern that Arcenio would listen with open mind to something that would enrich him personally. But of course, he concluded, the roving evangelist saw thousands of men in his travels. He did not recognize him. A flash of relief dispelled his embarrassed guilt.

"These meetings," he said, "have cleared up a lot of things for me."

"Why don't you bring your wife to tomorrow's *cursillo?*" urged Vicente. "She may change her attitude toward us too."

"She's down with malaria, Señor Gómez," said Arcenio evasively, but glad for a valid excuse. Ana would not even consider coming, of course. "She's been down with it for three or four days."

"Oh, I have an injection for that!" said Vicente.

"That wouldn't help much. I could never use one of those needles. And Ana would never let—"

"Oh, I'll come with you and give it to her."

"Why man—my hacienda is hours away. It's in Quebrada Honda!"

"I know where you live."

Arcenio gasped, and the dismay on his face was almost ludicrous. The sly twinkle that transformed Vicente's serious face to a winning radiance now crept into his eyes, and Arcenio knew, with stunning certainty, that Vicente remembered their encounters as well as he himself did. Still, he could not detect the slightest rancor in Vicente's attitude.

"If you will accept our hospitality for the night," Arcenio found himself stammering. It would be quite impossible for the evangelist to return to La Quiebra, unless he were to spend most of the night on the trail.

As they approached the house, Arcenio became more and more worried about their reception. What would Ana say when she saw he had brought home this evangelical preacher? He would tell her quickly, he concluded, that it was his concern for her that had prompted him to let Vicente come.

When they arrived, Vicente did not immediately come into the house, for he was fumbling in his saddlebag for his box of medicines. And, to Arcenio's relief, Ana was too sleepy to raise her shrewish voice before he could present his carefully prepared explanations.

After some rattling about with the kettles and blowing at the fire in the brick stove, he managed to boil the syringe that Vicente gave him, and to contrive a cup of *tinto* for his guest. Ana listened without comment when he deluged Vicente with a flood of questions that had come to him during his own reading of the sacred Scriptures.

Arcenio was not quite brave enough to suggest to Ana that Vicente had offered to give her an injection so that she would be well enough to go to the next day's meeting. Next morning, however, when she got out of bed to get breakfast for them all, he did ask her eagerly if she were better.

"A good deal," she said. "I'm grateful for that medicine."

"You might make him feel he had not come out here for nothing, if you went to a meeting, Ana," he said hesitantly.

Though she snapped a negative retort, Arcenio sensed that she was tempted to go. When Vicente mentioned the meeting, she appeared to be persuaded. In fact, they waited for her so long that they had to hurry away so that Vicente would not be late.

The older children went with them, and Ana watched them all climbing the serpentine trail that would lead them up to El Salvador. Why had she ignored Arcenio's invitation to go with them when deep down in her heart she was dying to go? She could have pretended she did it only to show courtesy to their guest. She did not stop to analyze the perversity that made her unwilling to appear docile or compliant to Arcenio's wishes. She was also ashamed to reverse her attitude toward this new faith that had so transformed the people who had embraced it, yet she admitted to herself that they all had a peace of heart that she desperately needed.

Acting on impulse, Ana scurried around to get herself and her youngest child ready for a day away from the plantation, and started up the trail alone. Then, when she had gone too far to turn back, a sudden darkening of the sky warned of a shower approaching.

"Well!" she exclaimed aloud. "I just hope I'll not be sick again, just for coming." And then from sheer habit of perversity, she added through her clenched teeth, "I'll make Arcenio pay if I do! He talked me into this."

Ana was panting from the exertion of hurrying up the steep mountain trail carrying her child when she came within earshot of the Church of El Salvador. She could tell that the meeting was well attended—and enjoyed—by the volume of lusty singing. She could make out the words as she drew near.

When the roll is called up yonder, I'll be there.

Would she be there? The question harassed her as she trudged the last few yards of the trail. Would she be too late to be admitted even to heaven because she was always hanging back, nursing her pride or some ill humor? Was Arcenio going to be involved in the *evangélico* way? Was not this the right way— the way her father had chosen two years before? And her brother?

Hadn't it changed them? When the roll was called up yonder—what right had she to expect of being there?

The mental picture that had been created by the hymn stirred her so deeply that she was not able to concentrate on the message that began immediately. When it was finished, she watched with a strange sense of personal loss when her own daughter, her oldest child, rushed to the altar with tears streaming down her cheeks. She was weeping unashamedly in front of this entire congregation. In a moment she saw Arcenio kneel beside the child and put his arm about her. Others whom Ana knew went forward.

When the roll is called up yonder, they'll be there, thought Ana. Her heart hovered at the altar in intense longing; her rebellious will held her to her seat. She sat there, twisting her fingers nervously in a long tress of her beautiful dark hair.

Two months later, however, when another short-term Bible course was being offered the new church affiliates, Arcenio induced her to accompany him to a service. When Manuel Jaimes challenged the audience to be committed to the loving Saviour of whom he had been speaking, Ana raised her hand tremulously for prayer. The moment she committed herself in that small act of surrender, peace and joy flowed into her soul, washing away her rebellion and hostility.

In the days to come, she herself was amazed at her love for her family and for Arcenio, and the joy of their relationship together as they earnestly applied all that they were reading from the Bible at their family *cultos.*

"It's like a new life together," she exclaimed happily.

"It is a new life," said Arcenio.

Ana had grown to care about Arcenio's moods, to watch for them. Now in his eyes, in his demeanor, she saw that he was not sharing her exuberant joy and that, as the days went by, he became more silent and thoughtful as though he were mulling over a secret sorrow. What was this problem from which he excluded her? He seemed to be walking in a loneliness that was of his own choosing. He was leaving her out even though, if anything, his attention to her had become more tender. He was unbelievably patient with those flurries of temper that she was trying so hard to control.

One day when she had labored up the hard slope with a large kettle of water fresh from the clear mountain stream, he took the kettle from her after he had taken the drink she offered him.

"This is heavy," he growled.

"Try carrying it up the side of a mountain then," she retorted without rancor. Mountain women accept as a fact of life that homes are built on elevations, and streams invariably flow in depressions. Arcenio let one of his huge hands rest on her slender arm in a gesture of tenderness.

It would be easier to tell him now, thought Ana, than when that sad mood of withdrawal came upon him.

"It takes a lot of water for a family of five," she said lightly. "It takes even more for a family of six."

"Six?" Arcenio said absently, then added, "but Manuel is here only to help me get out this new setting of coffee. After that—"

Ana half turned from him, but Arcenio glimpsed her expression.

"Ana Matilde!" he cried. Then joyously he caught her shoulders to look into her eyes.

"Yes, Stupid," she murmured delightedly. "I was afraid I was going to have to draw you a picture of a marimba[2]—with six notes."

Even as she spoke banteringly, the strong hands on her arms began to tremble under a sudden conflict of emotions; and though Arcenio's lips were still drawn in a wide smile, the life went out of it as the joy in his eyes turned into an agony of anxiety.

Arcenio's arms dropped like weights to his sides. "I have almost prayed for another child."

"Then what is the matter?"

"Will God forgive us if we have another child?" Arcenio

[2]*Marimba* is the Latin way of expressing *stairsteps* in height.

choked over the bitter words. "I am a married man. You are not my wife."

Arcenio sat down on a boulder. Nothing is quite so heart-rending as the sobs of a strong man, but Ana was hardly aware of Arcenio's grief as the impact of his words wrenched at her own conscience and dragged heavily through her heart like chains of ice. Dry-eyed, motionless as a statue of stone, her mind showed her the years she had had with this man. A spiteful shrew, she had made his life miserable, as indeed hers had been. Underneath the current of jealousy and rebellion, however, she had loved Arcenio. And since they had become Christians, their life together had become harmonious. Now—now that they had discovered how dear they were to each other—was it to end?

"You can't leave me now!" she cried in strangled horror. "You can't desert me and let me bear your child alone!"

Shamefaced relief stole into Arcenio's eyes. "We'll have that much time then."

"And then you are going to leave me—to go back to—to *her?* You can't do this to me, Arcenio."

"God is my witness that I can't," Arcenio said brokenly. He rarely spoke of his feelings, but now he blurted them out almost savagely. "I can't do it, Ana. I love you!"

With this knowledge, Ana began to battle for her happiness and for the happiness of their children.

"Arcenio, she is living with another man. She has borne you no children. Not one. I have given you three and, if God wills, we are going to have another. Are you going to desert your own flesh and blood to live with her—and *his* family? How will you get them apart without killing him first? Arcenio, this is madness!"

"She has already done this—this thing that I cannot do," Arcenio said humbly. "She is an evangelical. She has left him."

"And now she is waiting for you to come and support his children?" cried Ana, forgetting for the moment that she was a Christian and that she was supposed to love another believer.

"As far as I know, Ana, she is content as she is. I would be more than glad to support her—and the children. That is nothing."

"Then—"

The torment was back in Arcenio's face again. "I have read the Bible. I have sought advice of the brethren. Ana, *we are living in sin.*"

In the week that followed, Arcenio did not again refer to the sadness that weighted even their lightest moments together. By muleback he brought home long lengths of slender pipe and, to Ana's amazement, led water from a distant spring to their yard. Then he built a roof over the *pila*[3] where she had begun washing their clothes instead of carrying them all down the mountain slope to the distant stream. He built a shower, an unheard-of luxury in the mountains. Then, on muleback, he brought a porcelain toilet, something beyond a mountain woman's most extravagant dreams.

Arcenio, never able to express himself volubly, was demonstrating to Ana that she was very dear to him. She was grateful for this thoughtfulness, but she knew she was watching the loving labors of one who is weighing each trembling moment against the dreadful knowledge that it soon may end. She found herself keeping house with a similar desperate solicitude—as though each day had to be savored to the full, and cherished. Each hour had to become a sacred memory.

The mere fact that Arcenio and Ana were struggling against a secret grief did not prevent their neighbors from persecuting them. Some of his acquaintances demonstrated that they would rather make a detour than pass his home, and they refused to speak to Arcenio on the trail. Later they began to molest the home so much that he built a heavy fence around the building except on the side where the patio fell steeply down into the gorge from which the district was named.

If Arcenio and Ana were even tempted to forfeit their new faith, they ground the temptation under their heels without hesitation. Neither of them wanted to return to the wretchedness of

[3]Sloping cement slab used for laundering.

their former life outside of Christ. They soon had canvassed the community for those who would listen to Sunday readings from the Bible, or to preaching, whenever Arcenio could manage to get someone to preach. José Pinzón, when he was free from school, made La Quebrada Honda a regular stop, and soon the congregation was so large that Arcenio built a church. Samaria was chosen as the name for the chapel just above the Sumalave home.[4]

Visiting his relatives at Mahoma, Arcenio led his brothers Manuel and Modesto to faith in Christ, and was pleased that the feuding Montaño family was now worshiping with the Sumalaves. However, to Arcenio's deep distress, his father, whom he had warned so furiously against becoming an *evangélico*, now insisted that he had lost his chance and was too old to change his faith.

"I can't go to the meetings now. I'm too old."

This movement of God, however, did not depend on people going to church meetings. In the Magdalena Valley, as on the mountains, the evangelical faith was spreading rapidly from home to home, from community to community. Soon the old man was caught in the contagion of reckless faith that risked life itself to win one more soul to eternal hope, and Arcenio knew with joy that his anguished prayers had not been in vain.

On La Esperanza the same rash exuberance was spreading like a brush fire that sweeps up even those who battle its flame. In this most violent area, house-to-house visits were feats of courage. When Eulogio Quintero opened his home to Sixto Machado for a *culto,* he had shared the same danger. Since then, Eulogio had repeatedly been on the very brink of death for his own testimony of faith. Nicanor Plata was one of the men who perpetually menaced Eulogio's life, but the compelling power of his patience and love in the face of constant harassment won

[4]Many South American missions have boards of elders who deal with numerous marital complexities, of which the Sumalaves are but one example. For many converts, their decision would undoubtedly permit the believer with a family to remain in the relationship that was his at the time of his conversion (cf. I Corinthians 7:18-24).

Nicanor to share the same faith and, in turn, to share in its sufferings.

At first Manuel Contreras or Armenio Pabón took many services, or they came with Vicente Gómez on these hazardous expeditions to visit this new district. Eulogio, who was illiterate, as were his neighbors, learned to read by a miracle no less wonderful to him than his escapes from his enemies. Not long afterward he was able to take charge of meetings for himself, and soon the congregation could not be contained in his home.

The men of La Esperanza were not wealthy. When they decided that they needed a church, each one brought his own board up the perilous mountain trail; and they worked together to build the church which needed no other name more inspiring than La Esperanza,[5] the name of the community.

The ministerial students, who shared with Vicente the vision of the mountain parish, began dividing the responsibility between them during their Bible school vacations. Gradually the localities that would later be assigned as their own responsibility became defined, though there was overlapping of service, not because the workers were too many, but because they were always taking over when the other went to meet a new demand for a meeting.

José Pinzón, who had claimed La Quiebra for the Lord, found himself taking meetings in congregations that he could reach from that center—Palestina, Jerusalén, Samaria, all to the west of the range, El Salto to the north, Sión to the east, and La Cruz, where he had found faith in Christ.

Inocencio Trillos, now also in training for the ministry, remained in the foothill area about Betania, sharing with Armenio the preaching in Betel, Lucaical and Redentor, though he also began excursions with Vicente to Mahoma and Gamarra in the Magdalena Valley.

Santos Millán had been assigned to the responsibility of ministering to the congregations of La Cruz, Sión, La Esperanza and Honduras. In La Quebradita, the small canyon or gorge an hour

[5]Hope.

or two to the north of Sión, Santos had difficulty finding a home sympathetic enough to give a hearing to the gospel. A request to hold a *culto* was repulsed with insults and threats. But on the domelike summit called Cerro Redondo, they were allowed to hold a meeting in the Lobo home.

Santos recalled that Lucaical had been opened with youth meetings. Armenio's attractive daughter was now holding regular services in the Félix Herrera home with a growing congregation. They had used the same method of opening Guayabos, a district between Belén and Santa Inés where Aurelio Durán had urged the young people to bring their musical instruments and meet in his home. Later, Pólito Cárdenas had also opened his larger home to Guayabos listeners. Armenio's son Eliécer often took those meetings.

At one of the conferences Santos talked with the young people about his hope that Cerro Redondo could be taken over in the same way. They liked the idea. They would bring special music and testimonies. Many of them came together for this frontal attack on the new area. Perhaps they could stir up enough interest in this way to gain the nucleus of a group who would meet regularly.

Lalo's daughter, Alcira, and his son were of the party. Sixto's daughters from San José, as well as a daughter of Eulogio's from La Esperanza, also came. Young men brought trumpets, which seemed to be the favorite instrument of the mountains. Older evangelicals from the various congregations also went to the meeting which was scheduled for a Saturday night.

Santos was highly pleased that so many believers had come for the service, for a local audience had drifted in, evidently for various motives. Being in charge of the service, he was unaware that a rumor had also filtered in of a plan afoot to kill these outsiders as they descended from Cerro Redondo.

Such threats were almost routine in the mountains. The casual attitude of the young people toward another threat can be assumed from the fact that they even failed to mention possible danger to Santos after the meeting. Since he was familiar with

interwinding trails, he took the lead on his mule. He saw flashlights ahead at a point where the trail wound along the edge of a
steep slope, but he simply concluded that people were on their
way home from the service.

"Here they are!" yelled someone.

To Santos, still unaware of any peril, even this shout had no
particular significance, and he let his mule take him right to the
center of the ambush. Someone lashed at him with the buckle
end of a belt. Then a stone struck him. He yelled a warning to
the others following him, but Manuel Contreras, right behind
Santos, also received several lashes with whips, and the hail of
stones found several marks in the group behind them on the
trail, as Santos knew from the young women's screams of fear
and pain.

In the yelling, scuffling melee, Manuel lost his footing on the
dark trail and rolled down the incline. That left Santos alone,
surrounded by the shouting, ruthless men who were brandishing
machetes, whips, poles and stones. The trail was too narrow to
turn his mule about. Santos leaped from the mule, still dodging
blows. But the attention of the attacking men had focused on
the young women, and they pushed past Santos to dash down
the trail.

However, Santos' mule had effectively blocked the trail long
enough for the girls to scatter and scramble up the face of the
mountain. Santos could hear the men's angry shouts of frustration farther below; so before they came back, he also took to the
wooded slope above the trail.

After it became safe to take the trail once more, it took Santos
some time to find the other members of the party, who were
crouching silently behind low undergrowth. Manuel, who had
not been seriously injured by his fall, had joined him in his
search. They found their animals, but all of them had been
stripped of reins and saddles. They had lost their hymnals and
Bibles as well.

The consensus of opinion was that they would not be going
back to Cerro Redondo again for a long time—if ever. Santos,

however, felt that it was part of his parish. He had made arrangements for another service the following Saturday.

Santos dreaded going back to that vicious area, and he would have to face it alone. The national violence which still raged had made life cheap. Crimes of brutality and bloodshed were commonplace.

"Lord," he prayed during the sleepless Friday night, "if You've given me this field, I can't abandon it. If it's Your will that they take my life, they can do it; if not, they can't."

During the day, as Santos continued to pray, he received divine reassurance that he must go back to Cerro Redondo for his meeting. Santos' battle was over. He had faced death, and he had committed his life to God's hands. He was neither surprised nor overly fearful when he met five of the same young men who had attacked him the previous week. Again they shouted insults and threats.

Santos told them simply, with his disarming smile, why he risked death to tell them his good news. All five of them were soon also suffering persecutions for their own stand for Jesus Christ on that mountain. In less than two years almost everyone in the community had been won to faith in Christ.

As early as 1958, Trinidad Pérez de Pabón, a widow of some means, permitted Francisco Avilez to have meetings in her hacienda on La Osa. The first to accept the gospel were her daughter and a niece. Avilez also contacted Mauricio Rangel, who became the first adult believer. Vicente Gómez, Gratiniano Pino, Manuel Contreras and other roving evangelicals came to this mountain to have services, and often the new believers went to services at El Salvador.

Together with Sindulfo Pabón, one of Trina's sons, José Pinzón made some trips throughout the area. At one home they had been given permission to hold a meeting when two mountaineers threatened to burn their host's hacienda if he permitted a service.

Knowing that the plantation owner was not even truly sympathetic to the gospel and not wishing to subject him to embarrassment or danger, José assured him that they would not have the service.

"Look," said their host brusquely, "I said you could have a *culto*. Nobody is coming here to tell me what I can do in my own house. Go ahead."

The family gathered, but their host remained outside to argue with the troublemakers. "If anything happens to any of my children," the man warned sternly, "you're not up against *evangélicos*, who won't touch you." He fingered the machete at his belt. "I'm not an *evangélico. I'll* touch you!"

Finally the argument degenerated into a request for permission to come in for the service. José preached to an attentive audience.

On La Osa lived one man whom even the boldest of the evangelicals had not dared to visit, though he went by the deceptively mild name of Angel. Angel Bustos' vicious disposition had won him a certain prestige in the entire countryside. In one brawl someone had dared to disagree with him. Angel, who settled most of his arguments with a knife, had been almost disemboweled, but Angel's opponent died from his wounds. It was safer not to irritate this notorious ruffian.

A woman penetrated this harsh facade by giving him a tract. Though Angel was illiterate, he got someone to read it to him. In those mountains, Angel probably was unique in that he actually had to seek for someone to explain the way of salvation to him. Mauricio Rangel came, and the two spent all night speaking of the claims and the power of the gospel. So fantastic was the change in this man that the very fact of his conversion caused many to investigate his powerful personal relationship with a living God.

During the same year, after a Sunday morning service at El Salvador Church, José had returned with Manuel García to his home nearby. As the men waited for lunch to be served, they heard a shot not far away from the house.

"Let's pray," said Manuel. "They could be coming this way."

Three men carrying shotguns left the trail that ran right by the house and approached the two evangelicals. Bottles protruded from bulging coat pockets, and by the men's stumbling gait and heavy articulation, José and his host knew they had already imbibed a good deal of the contents. They had also passed the stage where they were harmlessly merry.

The sobriety of evangelicals seemed a constant challenge to those who fought private battles against the vicious chains of their habit. As often happened, these men offered Manuel a drink, which he politely refused.

"No man refuses a drink!" roared one of the men. "That means you're not a friend of ours."

"I'm your friend," said Manuel, "but I'm also an evangelical. You know we don't drink."

"Well, you will now," said the tallest of the three, flicking back the lock of his gun. "We'll see how much of an *evangélico* you are after you look into the barrel of this shotgun for awhile."

"You can kill me, Friend, but you can't make me drink," said Manuel firmly.

José, who had remained seated on the veranda, was not allowed to be a mere spectator. One of the men ambled over and crowded his burly hulk into José's chair with him. He leaned heavily against José and leered at him from hostile bloodshot eyes.

"Here, take a swig," he offered, pushing his bottle into Jose's face, his own breath guaranteeing the potency of his offering.

"Thank you," said José, striving to keep from his voice the repugnance the man's offensive manner aroused. "Like Manuel, I don't drink."

José moved slightly to relieve his chest of the heavy man's weight. Immediately the ruffian took offense.

"Maybe you don't like *me,* either, no? Maybe you don't like to sit with me?" The man was itching to start an argument, and Pinzón knew far too well how mountain men settle quarrels.

"I wanted to reach into my pocket." José had pulled a tract from his pocket, hoping for an opportunity to present it. "May I read this to you?"

The man snatched the tract from José and leaned roughly over him with the coarse insolence of a bully who knows that the man he is harassing will not fight back. In fact, all three seemed to take a childish pleasure in keeping their guns turned on the two evangelicals, threatening them and jostling them rudely. They continued their deadly game until midafternoon.

Manuel's wife came to the door at about three o'clock to say that lunch had been ready a long time and was getting cold. If she hoped that natural courtesy would cause the intruders to leave, she was disappointed.

"Don José," said his hostess, "maybe you could come to eat."

It would give him a pretext for getting out from under this drunken blackguard's weight, thought José. He stood up and walked into the house. His tormentor followed him. He stood by, watching, when José bowed his head in thanksgiving and began to eat. José knew that they were all in grave danger from any sudden whim of any of the men, and he was having some difficulty in swallowing the food for which he felt no desire. It was more appetizing to his persecutor.

"I'm hungry," he growled.

"I'll be happy to share my lunch with you," said José.

"It's not necessary for me to eat with any *evangélico!*"

In a moment he seemed to have changed his mind. He stumbled to the kitchen and asked Manuel's wife to serve him some food. Perhaps he was hoping for a tart refusal from her, knowing he richly deserved it. True to her convictions, she simply said, "I'll be glad to give you lunch."

"I don't need lunch!"

José had followed, with his plate, reluctant to allow the man to be alone with Manuel's wife.

"Well—"

The stocky man hesitated. His avowed purpose for coming had probably been to incite some act of resentment so that he could shoot in anger. To a man who was reluctant to kill in cold blood, to accept a meal from his intended victim possibly outraged even his dulled sensibilities.

His hunger seemed, at last, to spur him to action. He discharged his shotgun, aiming at José's feet. Then he struck

Manuel's wife across the ankles with the gun barrel so that she cried out in pain and sank to a kitchen chair.

The man gritted a foul epithet through clinched teeth and, drawing his lips back in an evil snarl, he swung back toward José. Having lacked the courage to shoot José, he now drew out his knife and crouched for a leap. Frozen with the knowledge of impending death, José was only half aware of the woman's strangled prayer that God would still save them. At this point, the taller of the man's companions appeared in the kitchen door, possibly to investigate the sound of the gunshot.

"That's no way to kill—you coward!" he snapped. "Why this fellow isn't even trying to stop you!"

José's assailant whirled with an oath of rage. He had been frustrated for lack of a quarrel. Here was one, ready-made.

"Who calls me a coward?" he roared.

"I do."

With another snarl of inarticulate fury, the stocky man lunged at the other with his knife. The larger man stepped lightly to one side and into the doorway leading to the back patio. Again the furious inebriate charged forward like a maddened bull, carrying his opponent into the patio by the sheer weight of his attack. There the two locked in a scuffle punctuated by grunts and shouted curses.

Manuel, who had followed the tall man to the back of the house, now strode forward to slam the door.

"Man," he said, sliding the bolt into place, "those guys have made me sweat today. I thought a couple of times it was all over for me."

Now that it was all over, Manuel's wife began to cry. "I've never been so scared in my life," she sobbed. "The next second he'd have run that knife through José!"

"Anybody as shaky as these fellows ought to keep their claws off their gun triggers. Was this shot in here an accident?"

"God restrained him from aiming his gun. It was when he came at me with his knife—"

"Or was it God who *made* him shoot it off! If it hadn't been

for that distraction—" Manuel shook his head. "I sure was getting edgy out there. The shot drew him back here to take a look."

"That shot saved both of us then," said José. "I believe it was
God's intervention for us. Your wife was praying, you know."

They slipped to the front of the house where the third man of
the trio, left to himself, had gone to sleep on the chair José had
vacated. They quickly bolted doors and windows, then prayed for
the men who continued to wrangle noisily near their back door.

In the same year, 1958, Manuel García, as well as scores of
mountain evangelicals, put aside their work to attend a very important short-term workers' conference which was held in Aguachica in the large house that Armenio had built. By some unfortunate chance, or because the Colombian calendar is a series
of fiesta dates, the conference took place at the time of the very
fiesta that had nearly brought tragedy to the Franco family six
years earlier.

The evangelicals, of course, were very careful not to arouse adverse notice and walked quietly through the streets that were
crowded with people amusing themselves by flinging handfuls of
cornstarch at unwary passersby.

The valley town steamed under the tropical sun. The municipal beauty queen had been chosen and conveyed through streets
festooned with bright crepe paper streamers. Costumes had become smudged and damp, and flinging cornstarch had lost its
allure. With time hanging heavily, the loitering celebrants began to look for new diversions.

The influx of four hundred evangelical leaders from many
miles around had not passed unnoticed and so, when the evening
service had begun, the town's queen, with a cortege consisting
of most of the residents of Aguachica area, arrived at the door of
the meeting place. The queen minced up the aisle to the front
of the audience with the intention of saying her rosary before
the evangelicals.

But before she had time to say her beads, the crowd became
impatient and began throwing the stones they had hauled to the
scene in trucks. The noise was thunderous and frightening, for

the roof was made of noninflammable corrugated metal. Stones and bullets crashed through the glass windows. When evangelicals closed and barred the doors against the rabble, they were broken down.

Fortunately for the terrified evangelicals praying in the house, national police heard the commotion and dispelled the mob. For the ensuing two nights of the convention they had police protection.

To most of the villagers, the disorder had merely formed a part of their fiesta. For Armenio it meant a great loss and several days of hard work. So, though he spent little time in Aguachica ordinarily, he was still in his house when a couple of men loafed near the building a few days later.

"We haven't done anything yet," said one of the men. "We're going to put a bomb under this house tonight—now that he's gone and the police are leaving it alone."

Armenio stepped to the door and said mildly, "You may bomb the house—but only if God permits it."

The men started in guilty consternation. Armenio had been a public official of acknowledged influence, and the fact carried weight. He had recognized the men, and they knew it. The bomb threat was never carried out.

The believers only intended to use Armenio's house temporarily. For some time the country churches had been taking up an offering to help the struggling Aguachica congregation build a proper church. When the fund drive languished, Sixto Machado made a large personal contribution toward the Aguachica chapel.

Eulogio Quintero, who still remained the most energetic witness of the brutal mountain district of La Esperanza, lived under continual threat. One of his neighbors kept coming to his meetings, heckling or demonstrating his antagonism with sudden outbursts of abuse. He always carried his knife and was quick to use it. Often in the service he would brandish his machete or strike it sharply against the back of the seat in front of him. By common consent, he always had ample seating space.

Evangelicals had to give this dangerous man plenty of room on the trails as well, for he clearly itched to start a fight. He would rant at them for their heresy, or humiliate and terrify them by forcing them to dodge his slashing machete which he would swing viciously at any one of them he might pass.

One day Eulogio found him asleep near the trail. Recalling the action of David in another generation, he took the man's knife from him. Later, when he passed the Quintero home, Eulogio called to him. Handing him his knife, Eulogio reminded him that the weapon of an evangelical is love.

Even this demonstration—that Eulogio could have done away with him if he had been so inclined—did not deter the cowardly ruffian from continuing his threats and annoyances. Though the evangelicals refused to fight back, a sympathizer became so annoyed with the man's senseless savagery that he reported him to the El Carmen mayor, who took steps to curtail the danger of further attacks.

On Palmira, Manuel Contreras had been so harassed and had suffered so much from thievery of his livestock and damage to his farm produce that neighbors and fellow believers were bringing this formerly prosperous family the food that they needed for survival.

Once when his wife Edilia was in bed with a newborn child the hate-filled ruffians entered the house, shot out the gasoline lamp and then hacked at everything in sight with machetes. The family, including the new mother, her infant and four other sleeping children, were routed from bed and had to flee to the mountain. When some time later they tried to return with the children, they were once more attacked and forced to spend the cold night out-of-doors, while their home and stable were again pilfered.

Even more revolting was the attack made on the family when they were grieving the death of Manuel's father, who had died an evangelical and had been buried by the evangelicals in their own cemetery. On the night of the funeral their home was attacked with guns and machetes. So serious were these attacks that Manuel finally moved his family into the comparative safety of El Carmen. More than once after that he was attacked and beaten on the trail when he went the long distance to work on his farm.

In Los Cerros the attempt to quell the evangelical advance took an entirely different form. As the gospel penetrated the conscience of the mountain people, many of those who had been living in concubinage for years and who had no previous marital tie were now being married, though many had families of older children. Often such marriages—illegal in Colombia unless performed by the church or in a civil ceremony—would be sought for months or years. Municipal authorities, influenced by local clergy, made civil marriages discouragingly difficult to obtain through deliberate obstructive or delaying tactics.

A group of priests made a tour of the Los Cerros homes of known sympathizers of the evangelical movement. In several instances the wife had already made a commitment to the evangelical faith but the husband was still more or less faithful to the church. Pressure was brought to bear on the husband to end his concubinage. Then, after the church marriage, the priests reminded the men that the ceremony obliged them to vow that the entire family would be loyal to the church.

The wives of both Velo Márquez and Manuel Sánchez discovered that they were being carefully watched so that they had no opportunity to attend further meetings. These women, thus driven to more robust personal faith and prayer, soon won their families to share their faith. Both husbands were soon attending the services openly as evangelicals, so the fact that they had previously received a state-approved marriage turned out to their advantage.

Sión, the church at Los Cerros, had been built in March, 1957, just where Lalo had visualized it, in sight of El Salvador and La Cruz. The La Cruz Church of Palmira, rebuilt twice, stood a shining white monument to the enduring faith and faithfulness of Manuel Contreras and others of that oft-molested congregation. In Sión the disturbances were more of the character suffered by the congregation of La Esperanza.

Lalo was personally assaulted several times, and Antonio Hernández, an older man who worked for him, suffered several severe knife wounds at different times. One young man tried to run his machete into Antonio's throat when the latter witnessed to him.

This young scoundrel often brought his companions to help him cause distractions during the services, maligning and threatening those who came. Several times he had also followed Lalo's family home after the meetings and chopped at his doors with a machete, keeping the family in a state of siege.

On one occasion the young man brought five allies with him. As soon as the singing began, they marched into the church, moving about menacingly, distracting attention and making themselves generally objectionable.

"Come on out here," he shouted to one of his companions over the sound of the trumpets and singing voices. "I have something to say to you."

No one knew what evil project he was about to propose, for they went outside to the rear of the building where the mountain falls away into the vast valley facing La Cruz. Suddenly the bully himself came running back into the church, covered with blood. Evidently his proposal had been objectionable even to his confederate, for this ringleader of the disorders had been fatally stabbed in his altercation with his comrade.

He sank to a bench, bleeding profusely, then slid to the floor. He seemed too intoxicated and weak to comprehend the evangelicals' anxiety for his soul. Though they did everything they could to help him, he died in the arms of Antonio Hernández, the man whom he had once nearly killed and one who had often borne the younger man's taunts and insults. So, temporarily at least, the open molestations at Sión lessened.

By the time José Pinzón had finished his schooling in 1960 and

was officially pastor of El Salvador, most of those who had ter-
rorized the evangelical population of La Quiebra by their mob
action had already come as whole-heartedly—if somewhat less
boisterously—to the evangelical side. Many of the people who
had once abused Vicente Gómez rode in to the service to which
he brought a young and attractive bride, Carmen, during that
year.

Vicente, who was still constantly in and out of all these communities, shared the dangers of each one. He had been first to
dare to enter the Canyon of Caracolí, though he had often been
joined later by Santos Millán and Manuel Contreras.

Luis Real became one of the first believers of that valley, and
through his witness many homes received the good news of salvation for the first time. His simple straightforward approach,
coupled with real commitment to his Lord, made him soon seek
full-time work as a lay preacher. He roved the area, speaking to
all who would listen of "this glorious way," and the light in his
face reflected the glory of the way that he had found. Their
church, named after the Thessalonian church of the New Testament which had also sprung up in the midst of great difficulties,
soon exceeded some of the older churches in membership, while
Honduras—the valley very near Caracolí over which Vicente
had shed so many prayers—soon became almost solidly evangelical
and built its own chapel, the Church of Galilea.

Mauricio Rangel, who had held services in his home until the
La Osa congregation built Palestina Church, moved to El Cuaré,
where he started another congregation with José Ortega. Soon
forty believers had built a chapel seating one hundred and
twenty people.

The valley work spread from Ebenezer in Puerto Oculto, to
Mahoma, Gamarra and finally to Ayacucho. In each of these
places a church was built by the local constituency.

In late 1962 the leaders from all the areas were invited to
another workers' conference, to be held that time near Cúcuta, a
distance that made the trip prohibitive for some of the mountain
and valley people. However, Armenio and Sixto never missed

the opportunity of accompanying Vicente to these leadership conferences. Afterward these men laboriously made the rounds of the multiplying evangelical communities to share their inspiration with those who had not been fortunate enough to attend the conference.

Sixto had made the trip to Cúcuta; but because of the isolation of San José, he had not been able to get anyone to take responsibility for the Sunday services at Nazaret Chapel. So he returned from the conference a day early. He spent Saturday evening in prayer and preparation for the Sunday Bible study, but the rest of the family, having worked in the coffee plantation since the first gray of dawn, retired early.

About ten o'clock they heard the dog barking savagely, and one of Sixto's daughters heard him leave the house to investigate. Later Carmen Rosa was roused from sleep by the sound of gunshots. Noting that her husband was not in bed, she ran to the yard.

So great a man of prayer was Sixto that she was not too surprised to see him on his knees near the gate of their patio; but as she approached him, she knew that he was mortally wounded. Their older son, who had run out when Carmen screamed, tried to help his father to his feet. Sixto shook his head, then turned his face heavenward and gasped out a prayer for forgiveness for the villain who had at last been able to consummate his dastardly purpose. Sixto had been shot at point-blank range, and so he had recognized his neighbor and longtime enemy in the dark. Even while he prayed for his assassin, he slumped, lifeless, into the arms of his grief-stricken wife.

Sixto was buried in a tiny cemetery near the church he had built. A brother who had been antagonistic until that time succumbed to the claims of the love of Jesus Christ and dedicated himself to the gospel for which his brother Sixto had given his life.

Little did it matter that the murderer was arrested, or that, because of intervention on his behalf by a politically powerful influence, he was soon released. It was too late to bring back this man who had labored tirelessly for the cause of Christ. But neither Satan nor his emissaries had been able to cut off the witness in San José. Marcelino and Amelia de Cárdenas, who had long been faithful in Sunday school and church, now assumed the responsibility as well as the danger of the leadership of Nazaret Church.

During the following year, the harassing of the Sión congregation was resumed. Three Thursdays in succession, a relative of the man who had died in the church led ambushes against the evangelicals on the way to their midweek prayer service. They threw stones in through the windows during the services.

For a few weeks the worshipers enjoyed a lull in these demonstrations of bigotry and hatred and then, in late June, 1963, during the night of the fiesta of Santa Rosa, the Sión Church was burned to the ground.

Undaunted, the believers returned to having their meetings on the veranda of the house where they had held meetings previously. There, too, though it was much nearer Lalo's own home, the persecution continued. Still, less than a year after the burning of the church, work was begun on a new and larger chapel to replace the one that had been destroyed. Inocencio Trillos, finished with his schooling, became the pastor of this hardy congregation, as well as receiving the charge of La Cruz, Galilea, La Esperanza and the new group in the savagely hostile ravine called La Quebradita.

Vicente, though now married, kept roving the dangerous valley parishes and mountain trails. Though his wife and children remained in Aguachica, which was centrally located, Vicente held regular services in the comparatively new congregation in Mahoma, but took one service a month in Betania.

His health continued to deteriorate with these constant changes of climate, and his relentless pioneering. Once, on the isolated peak of La Osa, he became desperately sick and had to be carried to Aguachica for help. Finally, thinking as much of his family as of himself, Vicente asked to be released from the responsibility of Mahoma. The mission offered him a parish where he would not need to do so much rough traveling. He could, at last, live with his wife and sons, whom now he saw briefly only once a week or every two weeks. But he had a question for the mission representative.

"Who will replace me in Mahoma?"

"We have no one to send."

Vicente stood staring for a moment at the far horizon while he pondered his own needs and the needs of the congregation that had to have spiritual leadership if it were to grow up into sturdy faith. The tired lines on his haggard face deepened, but the fire in his intense eyes had never gone out. He turned to the missionary with his answer.

"Then I stay in Mahoma."